How to be
WILD:

How to be WILD:

SIMON BARNES

with illustrations by Joseph Barnes

✳ SHORT BOOKS

First published in 2007 by
Short Books
3A Exmouth House
Pine Street
London EC1R 0JH

10 9 8 7 6 5 4 3 2 1

A CIP catalogue record for this book
is available from the British Library.

978-1-904977-97-1
Printed in England by Clays,
Jacket design: Jon Gray
Illustrations: Joseph Barnes

Joe —
wild companion

1 I had seventeen hours in Eden. Then, of course, the angel came to cast me out, but what do you expect? Lucky to get that much. But let us, at least, start there: for all the best books begin in Eden, even if they end in apocalypse. And Eden was all the better for being unexpected. Shuffling into a plane for a business trip, the phone: the voice of my old friend Chris Breen: "Fixed. You're going to the Valley. You'll be met off the plane." And not many hours later, I was present at the first morning of the world.

Luangwa mornings often, and for no very good reason, have a recurring theme. This was an elephant morning: to be more precise, an elephant-and-calf morning. The first tentative rains had greened the savannah after the long, hard, hot dry season, but had done so without filling the rivers and the dry lagoons. Still, there was at least a lessening of the ferocity of the sun and with it, a re-kindling of life. And as we drove at an easy pace, we saw elephants and we saw elephants and then again, we saw elephants, and always with calves. I know this place well, I am deeply at home here: these were not elephants as revelation, but elephants as old friends: elephants as reassurance. No, the world is not yet mad: for there are still elephants, and their calves. And elephants bring a very special joy. How can something so big still exist in a world that has got so small? How can something so slow exist in a world that has got so fast? Other places, other paces: the elephant mostly moves at the speed of her appetite: slow, unurgent, unending.

I sat at my ease, then, with Levy Banda, funny and knowledgeable, as we motored through this just-born land, admiring an elephant small enough to run beneath its mother and knowing that this meant it had yet to complete its first year: the mother feeding with quiet concentration, mild-eyed, with great breasts behind her forelegs – elephants really don't have teats, but grey and wrinkled, oddly disturbing breasts. In this long-familiar place, I was naturally showing off to Levy by telling him all the birdcalls he knew perfectly well already: the woodland kingfisher, which is Luangwa's rainbird; a pearl-spotted owlet still awake; a red-eyed dove saying "three cheers for the BBC" – and that's a cuckoo, it's a Klaas's, surely – and then, absurdly sweet, a willow warbler.

A willow warbler: like me, flown down from the far north. A little scrap of feathers and a scant mouthful of flesh: and he did all the flying himself, and now, from a patch of combretum scrub, he was singing the same song he sang in the hawthorn trees of northern Europe: a bird simultaneously homely and exotic.

The Luangwa Valley lies in Zambia, a southern extension of the Great Rift. It was here I first saw lion and elephant and zebra: it was here I spent two months on a mad, all-but-ruinous unilateral sabbatical: it was here I set my first novel. There was a time when I could recognise every Luangwa birdcall and I was on first-name terms with a pride of lion. I have seen leopard kill on three occasions here, in wild, lamp-lit expeditions, bucketing about the bush in a doorless Land cruiser. I have added grass owl to the Zambian Ornithological Society's list of Luangwa birds (resoundingly misidentifying it as barn owl, but my friend Bob Stjernstedt at least knew what we were about). I have seen crocodile strike from the water. I have seen the air turn cerise as a carmine bee-eater colony took fright. I have been charged by an elephant. I have stared down a furious male lion from twenty yards, learning in the process that the paralysis of fear is a survival instinct. I have known, then, what it is to be prey. I have seen wonders: better, I have lived with wonders, eaten with wonders, slept with wonders, woken with wonders, sometimes long before dawn and in a sudden funk: not at the lion's roar but at the sound of the lion's breath.

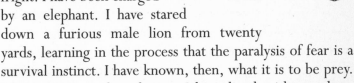

I was returning, then, to an idealised past as well as a beautiful present. A double Eden: one that exists in my mind: and which also, unlike most Edens, exists in the flesh. Unspoiled.

Let's dwell on that word for just a moment. These days, we use "unspoiled" to mean "pretty". It is an admission that a pretty place is exceptional. It is a recognition of the fact that in the normal run of things, most of the stuff we look at is spoiled. As a result, we need the mental Edens: but even more, we need the solid ones, the flesh-and-blood ones, the wood-and-sap ones. An old family story: an old family friend, in his cups, telling the French au pair: "You remember, Domi? When the garden was beautiful?" We can all remember those times, even if we have never lived them, for they come from deep in our human natures.

The lost garden is part of us. Eden is something we have lost: Eden is something we long for: Eden is something we hope for: but most important of all, Eden is something we need to touch. We need time in Eden, when the garden was beautiful, and Domi perhaps there too, as lovely and as naked as you would expect on this first of all mornings.

We need Eden in our minds; we need Eden in the special places; but more even that that, we need Eden everywhere. Little touches of Eden, little hints at Eden, brief vistas of Eden: in a rose, in the patting of a dog, the stroking of a cat, in the sound of a bird.

And there in Luangwa, there was for me, for anyone, an extreme sense of Eden: a near-total exclusion of the man-made, a place where a straight line comes as a visual shock. A place where almost nothing has been spoiled. A place where you can go and, in this unending abundance of the non-human, know what it is like to be properly human. Not a species alone and ever lonely: but one among many.

2 For three strange weeks that winter, I had felt like the human race. I'd become nature-deprived. It had happened a couple of months after I got back from Africa. Nature-deprivation is a hard thing to achieve when you live on the edge of a village in Suffolk. I have seen kingfisher, barn owl, marsh harrier, and whooper swan at my place; my wife has seen little egret. But I became cut off from all that. I woke, turned over in bed, and the world performed a triple sal-chow. Oh God, I thought at once, I know what that is. I was right, too: a problem with the inner ear; the balancing mechanism, the semi-circular canals, affected by a virus. The result is to make you seasick on dry land. I walked clutching walls: I sat with a Zenlike stillness. I ceased to turn my head to acknowledge my family. I learned to move

like an adept of tai-chi. But mostly, I stayed in bed, re-reading favourite thrillers, my head carefully arranged on a pagoda of pillows; or I watched the Winter Olympics with my head jammed into the corner of a wingchair. I did not go out: did not dare. Car journeys filled me with nausea; walking required me to sink to my knees every twenty yards.

Absurd. I didn't feel too bad: unless I moved. So I accepted stillness as my lot. Housebound. Barred from Eden. The odd thing was that I didn't feel nature-deprived unless things broke through my imposed stillness. A sharp drum-roll from the little copse behind the house, and I was startled: good God, great spotted woodpecker. Something must be happening out there. It seemed that spring was starting without me. I was watching the Nordic skiing on television, still mired in winter, reading about Modesty Blaise. Then through the curtain, the sound of great tit: that strong, defiant call: teacher, teacher, teacher. Great tits are brave birds, and like to see the winter off good and early. And I remember the sudden wild skirl of mistle thrush, perhaps my favourite song of them all, whistling the winter away with a witch's spell of spiralling defiance. But me, I had lost my balance.

And the earth was stirring and the year was turning, and it was doing so while I watched the televised triple salchows in perfect stillness: but I was a person for whom the seasons had stopped. Like the human race, I was too much taken up with my own small problems, my own small consolations. The wild world was something separate from me: not a place where I lived, but a place I hoped vaguely to visit sometime soon. I lost track of the daily comings and goings: lost my feeling for the larger patterns, and I was scarcely aware that I was doing so, save when some sharp reminder came through the windows: a rare bit of sun, and with it, the flat merry burble of dunnock. Little by little, without

11

my noticing, almost with my consent, I was losing touch with nature.

It was a deeply disquieting experience. And it's why I am writing this book. To keep my mind on the job. To make sure that it doesn't happen to me again. To make sure that it doesn't happen to you again. To remind us all to keep things open: eyes, ears, hearts, minds. And souls, I suppose.

3 Unlike the human race, I got better.

4 Klaas's cuckoo was named by the great French explorer and ornithologist, François Le Vaillant. Klaas was his Khoi Khoi manservant. Le Vaillant also named the Narina trogon. This is a particularly lovely forest bird, found in south-eastern Africa, green above and red below – and Le Vaillant named it for his lovely Khoi Khoi mistress. Narina was in fact a nickname, a lovename that he bestowed on her. It means, in her language, flower. It seems then that Le Vaillant also had his time in Eden: in the company of a bird of shimmering green feathers and a Narina that might shed her outer petals when in the right mood.

After my seventeen hours in Luangwa, I returned to Lusaka and spent a week researching stories for the *Times*. The Christmas charity of that year involved the sending of wind-up radios to African villages, and I wrote about why. I visited schools whose main building was a tree, whose equipment was a blackboard the colour of dirty milk, whose teacher had no formal qualifications. But the radio beamed in lessons and never needed new batteries. The

radio beamed in education: the pathway to paid employment: the way out of life on the edge, which is the life of
the subsistence farmer. The radio beamed in hope.

It could be argued that by promoting education, by
promoting hope, I was contributing to the destruction of
Eden: that I was siding with development, and against a
harmonious living with nature, if subsistence farming can
be so described. Certainly, these fine people believed that
education would bring their community a better material
life. All lives are the richer for hope.

So there was contradiction in what I did: loving
Luangwa's peace, and wanting my fellow-humans to have
hope. But human life is full of contradictions: each one of
us lives with thousands of them. Most of us want to be
faithful to one true love and to have a thousand affairs: most
of us want to travel and most of us want to stay at home:
most of us want to have children and most of us wish to live
a life free of responsibilities. It is the way we live with our
contradictions that determines who we are, as individuals,
as nations, as a species. We have destroyed so many of our
Edens in the search for progress; in the search for hope: and
in doing so, we have discovered that hope lies elsewhere.
Now increasingly, we seek hope in the wilder places, in the
greener places. We must readjust our understanding of this
contradiction. We need, above all, to rediscover our sense
of balance.

5 Lapwing. And it was is if the entire nature of the day
had changed. Lapwing, I was sure of it, for all that the
sound, faint and intermittent, was almost hidden under the
wahs and jacks and caws. Lapwing: now promoted to the
status of Special Bird. Once a bird you mostly ignored, for,

like the 49 bus, you knew there'd be another one along in a minute. Now a bird that lifts the heart. That's one of the triumphs of human life: to take an everyday bird and turn it into a living national treasure. As if love can only ever be too late.

Shut up, I told myself. The cold was making me gloomy, and it was cold all right. It hadn't been above zero in a week, and around the drum from which the horses drink I had collected seven unbroken discs of ice. Spring had stopped in its tracks: it felt as if all the processes of life had been put on hold. Every time I went outside, I looked for spring: and mostly looked in vain.

The lapwing, then, were doubly welcome. Along the skyline – in Suffolk, most things are along the skyline – a tractor, ploughing a big field that had been stubble all winter, and as a result, full of life. Mostly fieldfare: I could still hear them in the treetops, looking down at their field, quacking in dismay at the changes. Quack-ack-ack. But they'd had a damn good winter of it and soon they would fly north to nest in Scandinavia. But not soon enough, not for my money. They were hanging on here, insisting that it was still winter. Making sure that it was still winter; yes, I was rather inclined to blame them for this extrusion of winter into spring. Behind the tractor, a great pheasant-tail of white: gulls, all black-headed, arcing around and screaming cheerily to each other. On the ground, a black line of rooks and jackdaws. The damp upturned surface of the newly bared clay shone in the horizontal winter sun, as if maniacally polished, gleaming dull gold like the horse brasses on the wall of a pub.

The sound was clearer now, and I was right, which is always cheering. Unmistakably lapwing. That double-reed sound: oboe, plaintive, pleading, almost beseeching: a sweet version of the sound you can make when you blow across a taut blade of grass. Peewit: the old name has it right. As I walked closer, I raised the binoculars: yes, standing on the shining earth, a couple suddenly up and wheeling briefly on black-and-white strobing wings, and then returning to earth again to stand on their long legs with a preoccupied air, little whippy crests giving them a slightly daft look. But this was serious business: a good feed like this doesn't come every day, especially not when the ground is too hard to penetrate with a beak. No hint of the wild cries and crazed flight that they will perform when the blood flows hot and strong and their minds are all taken up with sex rather than food. That would be soon enough, at least I hoped so very much. But it was too cold for sex, too cold for the butterfly flight and the wig-wag flight, too cold for frivolity of any kind. This was a serious day, and so far as the lapwings were concerned, it was still winter. I counted: eighteen. Good.

I was walking on an intersecting course with the tractor, a natty and powerful Claas, a machine not named for a Khoi Khoi manservant. I raised a hand to acknowledge the driver as he made his headland turn, and I saw that it wasn't Tompkins, the landowner whom I know slightly, but Aubrey, whom I know well. He stopped and opened the door of the cab. Small in stature, stocky, immensely strong, neat grey beard. Loves to work. Always the air that he knows he's one of the last of his kind. Maybe 70. Endangered species.

"Nice of you to bring some lapwings along."

"There's a few out there." (Pronounced "foo", this being Suffolk.)

"I counted eighteen."

"There's plenty more than that. Nice to see 'em."

"Don't you wish you were out in the fresh air, instead of frowsting in that stuffy old cab? Bet you miss driving the old Fergie."

Eyes looking past me at endless acres and more than half

a century of ploughing them.

"Been times I've got off a tractor so cold I couldn't stand." A brief laugh at the absurdity of it. "Couldn't bloody stand."

He completed his turn, and drove back over the field, looking as if he were towing a half a dozen dazzling ridges across the stubble. I looked back at the distant line of lapwing, heard a brief oboeing. Nodded approvingly. Endangered, yes. I made a headland turn myself and walked back. Too damn cold.

6 We have changed the way we look at nature. Lapwings were once common birds, but life and farming practices have changed. Our efficiency has troubled the lapwings very greatly. Rank, wet fields are no longer a major part of British farming, and this is the lapwing's heartland. The move away from mixed farming, the switch to winter-sown cereals – a way of farming that does away with the winter stubble fields that my local fieldfares loved so much – led to a halving of the breeding population of lapwing in eleven years. We are much better than we used to be at running the countryside as an open-air food factory: we are much worse at keeping birds, at keeping all forms of wildlife. A field full of lapwings was nothing to get excited about when I was a boy birder: now it is a sight that brings a sharp delight. This new delight comes in two forms. First, delight in the undeniable beauty of the birds, a beauty made much more apparent by their scarcity. Second, delight in the fact that they are still around, still sometimes found in decent numbers. There is a strange, deep and consoling thrill in a meeting with any declining bird: a grateful almost prayerful feeling that we haven't fucked it up. Not completely. Not

yet. At the sight of a group of lapwing, hope and despair meet in a brief moment of delight: and hope wins. Always: but sometimes narrowly.

It's still working. Ted Hughes's response to the annual return of the swifts: they've made it again, which means the globe's still working. This kind of joy has its basis in relief: relief that the great complex mechanism of the earth is still somehow functioning.

Still somehow unfucked.

This feeling of relief is a new emotion: an unprecedented way of looking at wildlife, a completely new way in which humans interact with nature. The idea that nature is vulnerable has only been part of the human experience for the past few decades. The idea that humans are responsible for damaging nature: and the idea that only humans can undamage it: these make for a different way of seeing. Gilbert White didn't know about that kind of seeing, nor did Charles Darwin.

We cannot help but see the natural world in a manner that the great observers never dreamed of. It's a disturbing thought. Neither Darwin nor White was ever overwhelmed at the fragility of it all. We 21st-century people see nature beneath a sword of Damocles: the more precious, perhaps even the more beautiful for that. We have a new way of looking: we must work towards a new way of understanding.

So let us return to that throwback moment of the tractor, its anachronistic driver, the anachronistic lapwings. Should we bask in nostalgia? Should we long for what's past, regret what's lost, weep in the face of progress, oh my lapwings and my Fergie long ago? I think not. Time has passed: and you can't unpass time, any more than you can put toothpaste back into the tube. Vain regrets about the lost beauties of the past are not helpful. Not if you want to save the world, anyway. And if you like lapwings, you are rather committed to the idea of saving the world. It's a matter of disgusting, basic, bracing practicality: and it is an important part of the new way we look at the world. A sweet, sad whimsy doesn't do the job any more.

When Aubrey was driving his Fergie and failing to stand up, there were plenty more lapwings. Aubrey has no wish to return to the days of *plein air* tractor-driving. No more does he wish to return to the days of the working horse. Days of the working horse: it sounds great, doesn't it? How wonderful if the oil should run out and we return to those days. Me, I once drove a working heavy horse: a Suffolk, what else? It was great, marvellous, of course it was. But I don't suggest a return to the bitter toil and hunger and injustice of the past. That's whimsy.

And even if I did suggest such a thing, what's the point? I can't bring back the days of poverty and overworked horses with low life expectancy, and ploughmen ditto. It's the future that we can affect, not the past. A love of wildlife these days is a complex business: and it has to involve an opinion about the future. If we love wildlife, we want wildlife to survive. That colours our view of what we see; changes our way of looking at the world. We see a place of infinite fragility, peopled by infinitely vulnerable beings. Any great natural sighting gains an added element of wonder from the fact it may not be with us much longer. A group of lapwing: and a feeling of privilege is mingled with an odd sense of sweetness: like the last tender lovemaking in a doomed love affair.

But behind all that, there is also a fierce sense of joy: a joy that is bellicose, confrontational, determined. This is too good. Too good to lose. No, they shan't bloody ruin it. Not this.

And this too is part of the new way of seeing.

So all right. If you have good feelings about wildlife, then you consider the present and the future, not the past. You accentuate joy rather than gloom, hope rather than despair, solutions rather than problems. That is to say, life rather than death.

7 The following day, the furrows had ceased to shine. The moisture of the newly upturned earth had burned off; for all that the chill was still brutal. Aubrey had finished: the long furrows all done, and then the cross-woven furrows of the headland. The birds had gone: such invertebrate life as they had missed in the first rapturous turning of the soil had reburied itself, to escape the cold as much as to escape the killing beaks. Oh yes, the sweet lapwings are killers all right.

And then a moment of drama. A high-speed run at zero feet, the downbeat of the wings just a fraction above the bare earth, so that the slightest miscalculation would make it stumble out of the air and crash ignominiously onto the furrows. But sparrowhawks don't do miscalculation. Same tonal range as the earth itself: a matt, sneaky, stealth-aircraft grey. Only in sight for a second or so, and not a bird you see often out in the open like this, but for all that, unmistakable. The directness, the purpose, the intensity, the flap-flap glide of its flight. A female from the size of her, females being bigger than males, looking to ambush a bird that might be feeding on a furrow-bottom, unable to see death approaching. No luck today, but you had to admire the punt, and the aplomb. Such a thing improves a dog-walk no end.

There are two ways of enjoying nature. One is to go out and look for it: nature as a special treat, nature as something to be found in special places. The other is to take note of what is all around: nature as an aspect of ordinary life.

Nature is an occasional pilgrimage, and nature is also part of daily devotions. Many of us, perhaps most of us do both on a regular basis. In fact, I am convinced that many of us, perhaps most of us do so without even being aware of the fact. The trouble with modern life is that there are fewer opportunities to rub up against wildlife on a daily basis. We get less of a chance to savour the quotidian, the, as it were, ambient nature of nature. This is not just because there is less nature than there was, it is also because our lives take us away from nature. For most people, work and education take us to places where wild things are hard to find. Many people make a journey, away from green suburbs and towards the leafless city centre. Nature has become a treat rather than a daily experience. Some, a few, seek nature by means of dedicated birdwatching expeditions, but more seek nature in less obvious ways. Going for a nice walk is the most popular leisure activity in Britain. People play golf, go fishing, do the gardening, go to the seaside, sit outside with a pint, choose to live in a greener place than the inner city, and look forward to every weekend.

It's another of those contradictions. We love the treat, we love the ordinary. I love to make expeditions to wild places: I also love the daily wildness that I find around me. And there, on my favourite dog-walk, a passing, vanishing hawk. She, too, was finding it bloody cold but she also knew that a freeze makes birds vulnerable. She missed out on the plough, but I didn't think she'd be hungry that night.

Endless small dramas: endless small, stirring moments. Marvellous, but let's get home now. Too cold. Whistle for the dog, who was a distance off, savouring nature through her nose. More for us both to savour tomorrow. Though not, I think, spring.

8

I stumbled across a parable told by the Jain sages of India. The way through the forest "is dangerous and arduous. For as soon as one enters the straight path, there lie in wait for him terrifying creatures, lions and tigers, that obstruct the way to the city he seeks. They pursue him until he reaches the city that is the object of desires... the city that is the object of the traveller's desires is the city of peace". It is clear, then, that the forest is the symbol of all that is wrong: the city of all that is right. "The tigers and lions are destructive passions such as lust, pride, greed, delusion and anger, all of which are obstructions to the attainment of liberation." Parables are meant to be understood with your gut. The Jain master wanted to give his hearers an antithesis: the safe and cosy, the dangerous and frightening. And it was the city that comforted, nature that alarmed.

Nature is bad, not to be trusted, full of dangers, an implacable, almost a personal foe. Human civilisation is good, safe, to be cherished. Civilisation is, in short, the answer. Civilisation is a series of small, perpetually threatened islands in a sea of wilderness. This was the situation for all humankind from the time of the invention of agriculture 10,000 years ago, and it held good until the last two centuries. Now the situation is the exact opposite. It is hardly surprising that human nature is struggling to cope with this extraordinary reversal.

These days, the wild places are small, beleaguered islands in a sea of civilisation. These days, it is nature, not civilisation that is under siege. These days, we seek peace in nature and destructive passions in the city.

We are finding this adjustment a bewildering process. We are confused about how to look at nature, how to react to it, and what to do with it. At the same time, the

European Union is funding the conservation of the Iberian lynx, and funding a road straight through lynx habitat that will quite probably wipe them out. This reflects not just the muddle in the EU, but the muddle in the human spirit. Like many, I have left the city for a break, and gone to seek lions and tigers. And like many more, I have sought relief from the stresses of the city by walking, visiting beaches, playing games in the outdoors, sitting outside pubs, or even by watching lions and tigers on television.

Mostly, though, I seek relief in the countryside all around me. I am not looking for birds out there. I am looking for the city of peace. And you don't find such a place in the city any more. We humans have changed the world: but we have failed to change with it. Making this change is the great challenge for our species.

9

A day later, and just as cold. But utterly different. An exaltation: nothing less. That is the collective noun: an exaltation of larks. And I learned that one skylark can be an exaltation all by himself. High above the beak-proof fields – on the pasture side of the big, dense hedgerow, not the plough side – a skylark sang his song. The skylark's theme is endlessness: a song that continues, flows, gushes, without cessation, without pause: you'd think the bird could sing for ever. But when does he possibly breathe in?

Invisible. Sometimes they sing at a stationary point far above the ground, sometimes they sing in a wide circle, sometimes as if they were being wound up on a piece of string, singing with every inch of their ascent. And it's strange to think that skylarks are, in truth, ground birds. They keep low, live low, nest low, feed low. Only when the cock bird wishes to celebrate spring, and to claim and keep a territory and a mate, does he take to the skies. It is a kind of defiance.

He defies not only the departing winter, but the sparrowhawk. Only a bird of much mettle could dare do such a thing: that is the message of his flight and his song, and it shows the world that he is truly mate-worthy. He flies wildly high, shouting at the top of his voice, daring the sparrowhawk to take him on. It's about breeding, yes, about passing on his immortal and no doubt selfish genes, yes. He has strictly biological reasons for singing, but is that *all* a song is to him? Is he just a feathered clock, a device set to ring at the beginning of spring, in answer to the promptings of those genes? Or does he sing because his heart is full? Does the song itself matter to him? For there really is no special need for the song to be that long, that loud, that lovely. It could just as well have been a peevish squeak, uttered from the ground.

And another mystery almost as great: why do we humans respond to the song? Why does the song also put humans in good heart, better able to face the troubles of the day? Why does the skylark's challenge to the other cocks, his come-on to all the hens, stir not just skylarks but humans? For certainly, we respond to the singing lark: and the lark is able, in some way, to share his own sense of elation. And don't tell me the skylark is not elated. I have responded to the promptings of my own genes more than once, and I have felt elation at doing so. It is hardly possible that the skylark doesn't feel at least something of the same thing. At the most basic possible view, it's good policy for a gene to reward the host body for doing right by the gene.

On and on and on: endless, and endlessly complex, one of the hardest songs of all to analyse, yet one of the easiest to recognise, especially as it is the one song that comes down from the open sky. The best way to understand the complexity of a bird's song is to record it and slow it down.

There are, especially with the skylark, so many more notes than you expected. Birds are better at separating tiny fragments of sound than we are: it is a matter of the structure of the avian ear. And so the skylark's song is, to a skylark, even more complex than it is for us. Nor does every skylark sing the same song. I once heard a skylark song transposed for piano: not impressionistically, like the fabulous work of Olivier Messiaen, but note for note. The skylark was the composer, and he gave us a piece of startling and befuddling complexity.

But it sounds better on the instrument for which it was composed: the syrinx of the skylark. This is spring, he said to me, and this is me. Deal with it.

This was not the first skylark I had heard that year. A couple of weeks earlier, I had heard three of them: a freak warm day of February giving rise to an unseasonal and unseemly optimism, and with it, an exaltation. They soon shut up again, and stayed shut up, too. The one over the stubble had now gone, of course, since the ploughing. That same day, two weeks back, I had also been startled to see a primrose in a sheltered bank: *prima rosa*, first flower. It was still there, I noted, and looking a bit rueful. I had already spoken to it, in the tones of Sergeant Wilson addressing Captain Mainwaring: "Do you think that's quite wise?" It stood there, grimly trying to face down the frost.

So yes, of course I am beginning with spring. Spring is the only place to start. But I intend also to end with spring: where else to do find nature's climax? So this is both a straight-line journey and a circular one, time being both unswervingly straight and unendingly cyclical. Fifteen months on from now, the world will have moved on and so will I: but March will come again, along with April, May, primroses and skylarks. Always changing, always the same. Time's arrow flies endlessly straight, and endlessly comes back to the archer. This is the rhythm of life: the rhythm that is part of the temperate nature of those of us who move among the seasons. We thrive on the constant change: we thrive on the fact that everything stays the same. We learned this from nature, and it is a truth that still governs our lives even when we have lost touch with the rhythms of natural life.

10

I spent a couple of weeks in India, covering the cricket for the *Times*. I love the place, but was not at my best, after my three-week struggle with the labyrinthitis virus. I was no longer reeling about, and could turn my head without throwing up, but I was in poor spirits and more than usually inclined to self-pity. I had one free morning, so I hired a car and driver and left my hotel at six to visit the Sanjay Gandhi National Park outside Bombay. It was at best a qualified success. I sought peace and solitude and a place where things were a good shade of not-spoiled green: I found noise and people and litter.

At length, driven slightly demented, I turned and actually ran at random into the forest, at last shaking off the people and the abysmal trail of rubbish. And heard the sound of koel, a bird long familiar from the years I lived in Asia, piercing the canopy with its far-carrying double-whistle: un*real*! Un*real*! After a while, I felt a little – only a little – less unreal myself. I took a long and pleasant sit before returning, to find my driver eaten up with anxiety: "You must not go into the forest! Many cruel animals there!" He drove me back inexorably to the cruelties of city life.

11

But there was one wildlife moment that delighted me in India. It came on the telephone, in my hotel room in Bombay or Mumbai as I was researching a piece for my wildlife column in the *Times*. I heard about the kunkies, you see: and the idea seized me with delight. Kunkies are trained elephants whose job is to chase away the wild elephants when they come crop-raiding. I was inspired. I wanted to be a mahout: I wanted to ride a kunkie, I wanted to go out into the dark in the terror and danger, the clicking tusks, the furious squeals, the snaking trunks, and put my elephant against the biggest crop-raider of them all and see him off, the rest following him, defeated, back into the forest: simultaneously performing great work for conservation and enjoying what is surely the most thrilling sport ever devised.

Once I rode an elephant in Nepal. I don't mean I sat on one: I rode her, like a mahout. She knelt down, at her real mahout's instruction: I seized an ear in each hand, placed a foot in the middle of her forehead and stepped onto her head, turning round and taking a precarious seat on her neck. She stood up; I, arms spread not like a cool mahout but like an amateur tightrope walker, stayed on: the ground looking both hard and impossibly distant to my horseman's eyes. I placed a foot in each of the hollows behind her ears: I can put a finger my own equivalent hollows, a size nine in hers. I asked her to move forward with a gentle foot-nudge: she did nothing whatsoever, clearly understanding that I was not a mahout but a dude; that is to say, a greenhorn. So I imitated the rapid earpoking bumshuffle I had seen the mahouts performing over the previous few days of elephant-backed wildlife chasing: a manoeuvre that said: listen, I'm serious about this. It was a rum thing, feeling instantly so confident: but I have been there a million times before with horses. I knew exactly where I was: I was being tested by a large herbivore: and the elephant, to my inexpressible delight, responded: and we walked this way and that, and she turned to the left or the right as my feet and my mind requested. After I had dismounted in an inelegant slither, I thought for a moment that I might throw my life away: never return home, dedicate the rest of my existence to these wonderful and lethal creatures: never wanting anything but the monumental silences of elephantkind.

I was quite all right the next day.

But kunkies are not the answer. Kunkies are a holding measure. If we want to have wild elephants in our increasingly tame world, we must do something about it. The kunkies reduce the people/elephant clashes, cut down on the hostility, and with it the human deaths and the revenge killings. But elephant don't want war: they want food. They want food and shelter and peace, just like people. The way to bring it to them is not by chasing them but by establishing safe areas so that elephants can cross from one bit of fragmented forest to another without getting in people's faces: a series of safe journeys between one wild food source and another. Conservationists are working hard trying to establish these: the work goes on and meanwhile, the kunkies help the wild elephants to mark time. First the holding measure: then the long-term measures. First you attack the proximate problem: then the ultimate cause. That is not just one specific situation: it is the pattern by which we humans can reclaim our planet. It is only by human will that the wild world can continue to exist. This is not a contradiction we can resolve. Rather, it is a contradiction we must accept.

12

Have you ever tried to do the shopping after a heavy meal? You come out with a packet of chocolate biscuits and a jar of mustard. You simply can't imagine what it is like to be hungry. I came home from India to the bitterest of bitter winters: and I was shocked to the core. I had been given enough warnings about it in telephone conversations with my wife, Cindy: but humans never take warnings seriously. Trouble was, I simply couldn't imagine what it was like to be cold. (That, incidentally, is one of the central truths of conservation. Everybody sneers and calls us disaster-mongers. Then they say: oh look, there's a disaster, where on earth did that come from?)

Oh look, it's cold. The owl for all his feathers was a-cold: and so was I, beneath seven or eight layers instead of a linen suit – jacket worn on the thumb – and cotton shirt. I walked in a fussy, busy sort of way, hoping not to see a bird, for stopping was rather too much of an adventure, fingers cleaving to the twin barrels of the binoculars, expecting the flesh to be stripped off them by the east wind – the Suffolk wind that doesn't blow but sucks.

Fieldfares, of course, Fieldfares were still everywhere. On the sunken path, the ground-feeding birds were at eye-level, moving away from me in a gentle wave-motion: up above the stubble stalks – for Aubrey had ploughed only one of the stubble fields – and down again, talking to each other in their mellow triple quack. Spring was on hold: time was on hold: it was as if the earth had stopped going round the sun, marking time in the solar system, so that we were stuck for ever in a time of bitter chill, earth hard as iron, water like a stone, and all for the conveniences of these dapper little thrushes, undulating through the stubble: grey heads showing on the up-curve, up: black tails on the down. Quack-ack-ack. My mind accepted the fact that spring would come but my heart and soul and essential guts refused to believe it.

And so I imagined myself riding into battle on my kunkie, my war-elephant: taking up arms against the winter, bringing about the annual conquest of the spring, the fieldfares fleeing before us in quack-ack-acking dismay. Me and my kunkie, making a berserker run through human folly, scattering the forces of destruction before us.

13

A voice, strident and joyful, calling the world to order. Summoning the forces of righteousness for their annual conquest of the dark and the chill. I heard it from my bed, and knew at once a powerful surge of delight. Yes, in my essential guts. Taking a phrase, trying it out two, three, four times, and then moving on to another. Endless repetition, endless variation: always different, always the same. All the rhythms of the natural year were in the song: the song of the song thrush.

I see now that learning birdsong was one of the profound changes of my life. But it was not an advance in my bird identification skills: it was an adventure into the essential guts of the natural world. Gradually, I got in tune. Me, not the birds. The patterns of the year, the movements, the comings and goings: I began to understand all this by means of my ears. And now that I could hear the soloists, I was also able to hear the bass: and that was nothing less than the rhythm of the earth. I was in touch with Mr Bass Man.

Seasons shift one into the next almost imperceptibly, as a rule: but not this time. With the sudden summoning call of the song thrush, the kunkies of spring took out the winter in a single mad charge. I knew this the instant I stepped out of the house to do the morning chores – still well layered up, but relishing the unexpected warm lick of the sun. And then the entry of the flute: the first blackbird. It was the turning of the year: but this time the year had turned on a dime, a sixpence if you prefer. It was a virtuoso display from nature: a glorious melodramatic suddenness. And another sound of spring: a mad boinging. It was my older boy, Joe, making his first trip of the year to the trampoline: rising bird-high above the bushes, his long hair standing from his head in a mad hoopoe crest at each leap. He was feeling the rhythm of the earth in his own essential guts.

14

And I was filled with a mad anxiety: something that always counterpoints the soul-filling joy of the arrival of spring. There is, for me, the faintest note of sadness in the exuberance of the song thrush's repetitions, in the gentle beauty of the blackbird's flutings. As the chorus rises and swells, and bird after bird joins in the long, great, sustained crescendo of spring, there is an additional voice, and I'm not the only one that can hear it. There is something sad about the loveliness itself.

What if it all went wrong?

Do I sound too much of a misery-guts for hearing this voice? But in some sense, the anxiety actually adds to the beauty of it all: bringing with it a sense of fragility, of impermanence, of the need for quick delight in the now, rather than the relaxed, assured feeling that we need not pay attention today because it will all be the same tomorrow.

Spring is not something we can take for granted any more. *Silent Spring*: title of Rachel Carson's apocalyptic book of 1962, the book that first told about the processes of destruction. Every post-Carson murmur of birdsong is a bonus: a fighting back against the conspiracy of silence.

Mine is not going to be a gloomy book. Some great advances have been made since Carson first spelt out the problems for us. Other things – rainforest destruction, climate change – have got worse, so this is not going to be an entirely cosy book either: but listen, for the growing cacophony of spring defies the silence. Spring is for us all – nature-blind and nature-deaf included – a time of hope. Even the most town-bound people feel the change, feel the new optimism, feel the need for a fresh start, walking from the house with the heavy coat abandoned, the scarf still on its peg. The spring singing filled me with wonder and delight: and also with a belief that we will get it right, that we will get the hang of living on this planet, that the silence-mongers are, indeed, destined to lose. The spring singing is not only a symbol of hope: it *is* hope.

And so I took a short walk along Southwold grazing marsh, a few miles away from home, to see two seasons sitting side by side. A winter gathering of teal: exquisite little ducks that always make me want to preach an endless sermon on the beauty of the commonplace: the chestnut head of the drake with his green eye-patch: all delicately picked out with white. But alongside this group, things were stirring. Meadow pipit is a bird that specialises in drabness: but in the spring the males become as gaudy as a little brown bird with a feeble little voice can possibly get. They shoot into the air then parachute down, shouting excitedly all the while. It's called making the best of what you've got, and there's a lesson for us all. Birdwatchers refer to such birds as LBJs, Little Brown Jobs. This was an LBJ's Technicolor moment. Above, a skylark, performing his endless solo, telling the meadow pipit than anything you can do I can do better.

There was also a winter gathering of lapwing with the

teal, feet in the cold puddles of the marsh. Occasionally, one bird or another was seized by the unstoppable forces of spring, leaping to the air to dance a little, all the time accompanying himself in his wild double-reeded voice. It was the time for the dances they had not performed behind Aubrey's plough: a ballet on their floppy, round wings, strobing in the bright spring sunlight. First, a flight low to the ground with deep, exaggerated wing-beat; bird behaviour books, overcome with sudden poetry, call it the butterfly flight. After that, a side-to-side wig-wag flight, yawing violently on a crazy zigzagging curve; then suddenly, melodramatically, up into the air, only to dive down again, sometimes to bomb a rival male, sometimes pointedly avoiding him (but remember I could get you if I wanted to).

And the air was filled with the wild oboe-shrieks to accompany the wildness of the dance: and it was as if thoughts of silence and fragility had never entered my mind.

15
When I was eighteen I was, for a few weeks, beautiful. Irresistible. Unfortunately, the people unable to resist me were all male, and this was not to my taste. I was in Paris at the time, seeking both adventure and employment, and I had numerous offers of both – all dependent on my sexual availability. The most persistent of my admirers was a harpsichord player. He played wonderfully well and sought to befuddle me with a combination of red wine and music. It was a stylish assault on such virtue as I had, but I was forced to explain to him that my preference was for girls. Kindly, tolerantly, generously, he explained to me that I was completely wrong about this. I was homosexual. It was just that I didn't know it yet. We discussed this subject

at length, and his world view by degrees became clear. Everybody was either homosexual and knew it, or was homosexual without knowing it. "He's gay, but he doesn't know it yet," he said. And later: "Of course, he's gay, but he tries to cover it up by sleeping with women." Now my harpsichord player was obsessive on the subject of sex – Scarlatti came a distant second – and any conversation about books or music or religion invariably came back to the subject of men doing it with men. Of course, he said, I was homosexual. Neither the wine nor the music nor the argument convinced me.

Now, as I set out on the adventure of writing this book, I find myself in the same position as the harpsichord player. A missionary position, needless to say. I divide the whole world into lovers: you are either (a) a lover of nature or (b) a lover of nature who doesn't know it yet. The word "gay" – meaning homosexual rather than cheerful – was only just beginning to be heard outside specialist circles when the harpsichord player invited me, hectoringly, to his bed. And now I find that I have – we have – a need for a similarly useful change-of-use word here. To say that you are green or not green doesn't work: being green has come to mean that you take your bottles to the bottle-bank and drive a car of non-megalomaniac dimensions. So let's go for wild. Either you are wild: or you are wild without knowing it.

It is my belief that we are all wild: but frequently, we seek to express our wildness in strange ways. This is no doubt a result of repression, a result of an unwillingness to incur the censure of society and the strange looks of our neighbours. I have already talked about the seeking of wildness by means of walking, with or without dogs, feeding birds, fishing, playing golf, swimming, sunbathing. (Have you noticed the way that joggers always run through the park, or along the river, or round the reservoir in Central Park? They don't normally run round the city block.) But this list doesn't go far enough. These activities are excuses to get away from the concreted-over: not reasons: and it occurs to me that birdwatching itself is an excuse. The missionary position of this book is not to get people studying micromoths or buying bat-detectors but to encourage and explain and explore wildness. We don't need wildness because it is important to tell one species from another. We need wildness because it is essential to answer the needs of the wild thing within ourselves.

I write on sport as well as nature, and sport needs no missionising, being oversubscribed already. But I suspect that following sport is also a seeking after wildness. Most of it takes place out of doors: and that brings us into a direct relationship with the weather. At Wimbledon and Lord's, the weather decides whether or not we get any sport to watch: football and rugby union require a willingness to defy the prevailing climate. And whether you wear a tee-shirt or a Barbour to express your defiance, you are forced into a relationship with stuff that is beyond human control. Without an element of the non-human in our lives, we are not properly human.

16

If you are thinking about entering a thicket and you hear a sort of hissing cackle, reminiscent of mistle thrush alarm calls, then I advise you strongly to alter your plans. Otherwise you might die. You are listening to yellow-billed oxpeckers, maybe half a dozen of them. They are not very dangerous birds unless you happen to be a tick: but they frequently search for their ticks on the backs of hippopotamus, rhinoceros and buffalo. You don't really want to intrude on the personal space of any of these.

If you see a vulture descend to the ground, then it might be an idea to pay him a visit: he might have found fresh meat, a protein bonanza. If you see green pigeon making a beeline for a distant tree, then it might be worthwhile to investigate the tree's possibilities: chances are it is in the middle of a superabundance of fruit. When humans first walked on the savannahs of Africa, such bits of nature-spotting were life and death matters. But nowadays, we humans tend to an awful condition: nature-blindness, nature-deafness.

Humans – perhaps all mammals, perhaps all creatures – have an ability to block out the inessential. If you have a meal in a restaurant in good company, you probably won't be able to say what music was playing from the speakers while you were there. You might not have noticed the music at all, any more than you can describe the restaurant's wall-paper. Such blindness, such deafness, is a useful talent at times. In my day job as a sportswriter, I have frequently written long pieces for the newspaper in a football stadium while the match is going on, scarcely hearing the hooting crowd. I could hardly get the job done if I listened to every inflection of their din, after all. In the same way, I expect early humans tuned out the sound of the Cape turtle dove from their minds. The great ambient sound of the African bush is the Cape turtle dove's incessant triple note – work *har*-der, work *har*-der. It gives you no clues about anything except the prevalence of Cape turtle doves.

And so we modern humans have developed and refined the technique. These days we are able to edit out all bird-song. Birdsong is just the soundtrack, the elevator music for a country walk, the aural wallpaper for an evening drink. It's not that most people can't tell one bird from another: it's more that most people don't even notice that there is any singing going on.

Nature-deaf. I was like that myself for all but 40 years. I was not even properly aware that birds sing more in spring than they do in winter. I was aware, I think, of that fact intellectually: but it was not part of my experience: not something I lived.

I am incomparably the richer for having found my hearing, and for having developed my sight. Not in terms of expertise, but in terms of noticing. It's not that I am a better scientist or a more useful recorder. It is rather that I am that little bit wilder. As a result, that little bit richer, that little bit happier. Joe found frogspawn in his own small pond, and a goldcrest sang, high and thin from the top of the pines. I looked, listened, wildly.

17

A garden tick! Such excitement! And it came about in a very ordinary way, for it's a regular thing, in its irregular way: groups of black-headed gulls fly over the place, generally going to or from the sea; that is to say east–west or west–east. They travel in elegant straggles: not the tightly disciplined vee of geese, but in something more free-form and more prone to rapid shifts of formation. They make an elegant calligraphy across the sky: swashes and arabesques: one bird tucked in behind the other like cyclists on the Tour de France, and for the same reason. Let the leader do the work, let him shift the unyielding air, and you can slipstream agreeably behind him. I glanced approvingly at a smallish group, no more than a dozen birds, flying over (east–west) as I was doing the morning feeds, and one of the birds said, in the voice of a pantomime dame: "Eoh!" And another replied: "Eoh!"

Now as everybody who has read *Finnegans Wake* knows, black-headed gulls don't say "eoh!" They say "quark!"; as in "three quarks for Muster Mark". These were two Mediterranean gulls, and since they were the first Mediterranean gulls I had seen from my place, this made them a garden tick. I must say, I was inordinately proud of them: not for the birds themselves, but for my own bird-watching skills.

There is something particularly pleasing about a garden tick. The birds come to you: they are not part of a special journey to a nice place, to a nature reserve, to a well-known place where birdwatchers gather, to a hotspot, a honeypot. The birds give a welcome touch of wildness to the place where you live, telling you that your life is not wholly enclosed by central heating and doubleglazing and bills.

Your place, you own place, where you lay your head at night, is also part of the wild: part of the world. It may be a solid place with a mortgage millstone: but for a second, as you recall a particularly pleasing garden tick, it is as if it were the camp of nomads.

You probably have no wish to live that life for real: to move on as the pasture grows sparse, to sleep on the ground, to endure the heat of the summer and the winter's brutal cold on the unforgiving earth. But that touch of you that remains wild is reawakened by a visit from a cheering bird: it might be a flight of Canada geese honking past in a better vee than the black-headed gulls ever managed; it might be a sparrowhawk high above, a tiny silhouette that would be unrecognisable, even invisible, if the silhouette wasn't so distinctive. The seeing, the knowing, the understanding of the sparrowhawk means that you have the wild credentials to appreciate it: you have your wild soul touched, restored, reinvigorated by the soaring distant sight.

A garden tick brings home to you the truth about your own wildness. Bringing it all back home: yes.

18

But I haven't been anywhere special yet. Not since Luangwa, anyway. I have only mentioned the chance-encountered, the ambient: the wildlife seen around my Suffolk garden. On dog-walks, the casually met, routine sort of wildlife. Most wildlife books and most wildlife television programmes stress the extraordinary, the brilliant, the exceptionally beautiful, the scary, the dramatic. So far, at least, this book has been the wildlife equivalent of *Diary of a Nobody*. Charles Pooter, the diary's fictional author, writes at the beginning: "Why should I not publish my diary? I have often seen reminiscences of people I have never even heard of, and I fail to see – because I do not happen to be a 'somebody' – why my diary should not be interesting. My only regret is that I did not commence it when I was a youth."

And so Mr Pooter tells us of his dear wife Carrie, his son Lupin, his friends Cumming and Gowing, about painting the bath, planting mustard and cress, parlour games and days at the bank. Well, I suppose my intention is something of the kind: and in this way, to point out that you don't need to be David Attenborough to enrich your life by means of wildlife. A seagull passing over my house, a sparrow chirping in the roofspace, stands not only for itself, but also for all the vast wildness and diversity of nature: for the endless forms most beautiful that have been and are being evolved.

Luangwa is my special place, my Eden. Most of this book is, then, by definition, about Unspecial Places: about places of glorious ordinariness, places that have a kind of beauty because they are places in which life goes on. In other words, all Unspecial Places have their specialness.

19 It is a rare and elusive thing: when a creature ceases to be a member of a species, and starts to be an individual. Yet the process is something we long for. Gardeners talk about "my robin"; a robin whose intimacy, whose confiding nature, implies a special trans-specific relationship. The bird recognises you for yourself: trusts you: sits on your spade handle, and does so every time you are out there gardening.

My robin, my blackbird (the one who really sings for me), my hedgehog, who comes to the garden for his saucer of Kit-E-Kat, my fox who drops by and raids the bins: people who love nature with a forgivable touch of sentimentality often tell you of such things. Well, here's a boast, a bit of a beast-drop. At one stage of my life, I was able to say with pride – note the *mot juste* – my lions. When I made my long stay in Luangwa, there was a pride of lions to the north of our camp, and another to the south. In fact, I was inclined to think that they used the camp as a boundary marker.

The pride to the north were mine. We watched them – me and Bob and Manny – followed them, entered into the drama of their lives. They were our joy, they were also our bread and butter. The clients wanted to see lions. So we got to know where the lions hung out, and where they were likely to move to next. We listened to the roaring in the night, to see if they had moved. When they had killed, we had them pinned down for a day or two, for they would stay by the corpse, binge-eating, sleeping it off, quarrelling. Mostly, they killed buffalo: in Luangwa, the lions are buffalo specialists: they have established a culture of hunting and killing the strongest and most aggressive animal of them all. Which makes them, in my totally biased view, the toughest lions of them all. My lions were the best.

There was a basic core of twelve: hard, canny females, with a few young males coming into their strength, just beginning to grow manes: bumfluff lions. There were also two females who had sloped off from the main pride and had three cubs between them. The cubs might have belonged to a single lioness, or not, of course. The females might have been mother and daughter, or sisters: a pride is held together by related females. The pride is an essentially female organisation, hippy and bosomy and, in the post-binge euphoria, a luxurious place to be.

There was also the pride male, the alpha male, who was so cool, he mostly kept himself to himself. But the minute the bumfluff males started taking too much interest in the females, they'd be out on their ear, have to make their own way in the world, just as he once did. He was the best male ever: huge, black-maned, unspeakably majestic. He thought quite hard about killing me that morning when I'd had the puncture and unwisely walked back to camp: but he had been shagging himself senseless for God knows how long; the ethologist George Schaller recorded one lion copulating 157 times with a female in 50 hours. (Manny, then a young lad working as a guide at the camp, used to share Boy's Jokes with me on this subject: "How d'you make out with that cute lioness?" "I'm getting old, man. I couldn't do the 158th time.")

And as a result of all that shagging he really wasn't in the mood for active chastisement, even of people who had interrupted his Afterglow. So he turned and ran, leaving me rooted to the spot with terror, muscles locked in a savage reaction to fright.

Survival mechanism: if I'd been less frightened, I'd have

run, and he'd have followed and whacked me.

See what I mean, about the survival of our ancient and wild selves? I'd never faced a lion like that in my life, but I knew exactly what to do. But oh, the intimacy with these creatures. I remember the blowtorch stare of the females, one female, presumably the boss female, in particular, when we came a little too close on foot. In a vehicle, they would all tolerate us, even to the point of driving right into the middle of their gatherings. And I learned about their social organisation, by reading and by observation, and saw how rough and ready it all was, how readily they would break their own rules. They love the social life: and yet every now and then, one or other would go off on her own for no very obvious reason. At a kill, there was no easy dominance hierarchy as there is with wild dogs and wolves. With lions, everything is messy and hotly contested and disorganised, unless the boss-man turned up. And then no one was allowed to eat except him: unless, of course, it was one of the cubs. The cubs could take untold liberties, almost snatching the food from his mouth.

Lions are social animals: but they never seem to be terribly good at it. That was the fascinating thing that emerged from this period of intimacy: they needed to be together, but they never found it easy to do so peacefully. Loving company: but feeling constant urges to be solitary. And always capable of breaking any rule or convention; a social life most imperfectly evolved. Not unlike the social primates who were observing them.

For two months, I lived in almost daily contact with these lions. I remember coming across another pride else-where: it felt like a betrayal. I remember seeing a female – one of our females – marching by herself across Lion Plain, their heartland. Where was she going? And why? I passion-ately wanted to know: I wanted to follow her all night: it was my business, after all. My pride. But we had clients in the vehicle, who wanted to see other wonders, not being, as we were, on first-name terms with every member of the pride. So we turned back: and I still wonder where she was going. My guess was that she was in oestrus and seeking out the black-maned fellow.

And most vividly, I remember the morning by the Luangwa River when we saw the buffalo coming up from a drink, a long black line that took five minutes to pass. Bloody hell, I said to Bob. (I have had too many adventures with Bob.) Bloody hell, that's where the lions were sleeping off their latest kill last night, wasn't it? So we drove onto the beach – and found a nightmare. The buffs must have walked straight onto the sleeping pride. They weren't even hungry, but what do you expect? Lions are only human. The twelve of them killed three buffalo: had done so just minutes earlier. Three black and mountainous corpses: a few lion eating, in a lackadaisical sort of fashion, stomach contents of one buff ripped out, still steaming. One of the bumfluff males had removed a foetus from one of the buffaloes and was just dancing about with it: playing with it, tossing it about like a cat with a catnip mouse, thinking it was all no end of a lark.

They were pretty awesome, my lions. Not always nice, but you love your relations for all their faults, don't you?

20

It was a couple of days after Christmas, a good few years back now, and I went out to check the horses, there being a good precedent for spending as much of Christmas as possible in a stable. It was after eleven, last check before bed. There was snow on the ground, and a hard frost made it crunch and crackle beneath my feet. Scarcely a star in sight: dreadful light-pollution, which came from one of the best full moons I have ever seen, a vast gold medal awarded to the night for its victory over day. It was ridiculously, newspaper-readingly bright, the sky more blue than black. And the ground hammering, thrumming. After a moment I realised that the horses in the back field, which was then owned by a neighbour, were charging wildly about in mad excitement. Why should they be doing that? I was at once concerned for my own animals: and it was then that the sound hit me: a wild bugling, answered, re-answered. It was this sound that had sent the horses crazy: and why wouldn't it? I looked about bewildered for a moment and then all at once, I had the wit to raise my eyes to the sky. And there, above me, hammering down the river valley at breakneck speed, a tight vee – not the loose gullish, calligraphic straggle – 24 birds. I counted them in awe and wonder. Whooper swans, for God's sake. Stirred into restlessness by the extraordinary nature of the night, feeling the urge of movement strong in them, unable to resist the demand to take to the floodlit skies and move in a strong, arrow-shaped, arrow-direct flight to the coast.

And they were gone, and it was the quintessential moment of wildness: that from my house, from my own place, such wild angels should pass by, sounding their wild angel trumpets, and stirring the wild heart of the tame horses beneath them: and my wild heart with it. It was a garden tick. It was a revelation of perfect beauty, perfect wildness. It was a moment that explained the truth of it all: that my home, my heart, is also wild. And so is every one else's.

21 I get lost. My occasional thoughts about giving it all up and becoming a game guide in the South Luangwa

National Park rather falter on the fact that where some people have a bump of location, I have a declivity. There are areas of the park I have travelled again and again: and still I couldn't tell where one place is in relation to another. I have even managed to get lost in New York. This takes a bit of doing, as a moment's thought will tell you. Here's how to do it: have a drink in a bar that is either on an avenue, or on one of those broad streets that *feels* like an avenue. Then you come out and think that the street is an avenue, or the avenue a street. After that, you set off at a bold 90 degrees to your intended direction and see how many blocks you can walk before you notice. An extravagant talent for getting lost is pretty inconvenient: but at least it ensures that you live in a world full of surprises.

So I walked one of my favourite walks, starting from Blythborough, along the estuary, then cutting across the heath to the marshes of Walberswick. But somehow, I missed my way at Hoist Covert and ended up – well, I ended up at Hoist Covert, which was not what I'd planned. So I set off again, taking different options and ended up at – now Hoist Covert is an exceptionally pretty place, but I cursed it roundly when I came on it again. The cloud cover was effective, and I couldn't see the sun, so I couldn't even make a guess about my direction. So I thought I'd turn the whole experience into a profit and walk into Walberswick for a quick drink. After that, I'd walk the full length of the marsh, rather than arrive halfway across. What a good decision that was.

I bumped into some serious birders at Hoist Covert car park. "Much about?" I asked, as custom dictates. They didn't take me for a serious birder, despite my decent bins, because I wasn't carrying a telescope and tripod, and my black Lab, Gabe, was walking with me. (To say she was "at my heel" gives overmuch impression of unthinking obedience.)

"Possible alpine swift."

"I saw a few swifts, very high up," I said. I had, too: first of the year, and very cheering it was.

"Yeah. We're going round to Dunwich to see if we can get a proper look."

"Good luck."

I walked on to Walberswick and had the quick one, fairly slowly, for I was in a mood for savouring. Nice birds, alpine swifts: last ones I saw were flying over the Olympic Village in Athens. Apparently there had been quite a few turning up in this country: well, good luck to them, and to the birders, too. Chasing rarities is just one more way of being wild; though not mine.

Reed-bed. Now being in a reed-bed is one of mine all right. Reed-bed is a place that sings to me. Literally as well: the wind in the seed-beds: soughing. Duck your head below the seed heads, and you are at once in another world: wet, mysterious, rich with life. It doesn't look even remotely tame.

This is a mad bit of coast: I was brought up with Cornish cliffs: the melodramatic transition from land to sea. But in Suffolk, there is land all right, and there is sea, too: but there are also the wet squashy bits that can't really make up their minds which they are. And that is the way that life once was around Suffolk: the sea advancing and retreating, the rivers flooding and unflooding: old reed-beds drying up, new ones springing up.

One of the things you have to understand about reed-beds, or, for that matter, about ponds and heathland and grassland, is that all these places are trying with all their might to become an oakwood. The process begins with the silting up, the dying back of vegetation; the consequent deposit of humus; the colonisation by new plants that prefer things slightly drier. And then to the next stage: as the scrub and the brambles take over the once wet, the pioneer trees, like birch, take a hold, and ultimately, the oaks march in: the climax vegetation of lowland Britain.

Landscape is not a fixed, for-all-time thing. Landscape – even oak wood – is shifty and volatile and responsive to change, as the hurricane of 1987 showed us. If you have a grass meadow and you want it to stay a grass meadow, you have to work quite hard to stop it being an oak wood. You can put grazing animals on it, and you can mow it: but the one thing you can't do is leave it to its own devices. Not if you want it to stay a meadow.

And here's the thing about reed-beds: they are not being spontaneously created anymore. There is a seawall. The rivers are canalised. The Minsmere River meets the sea not in an estuary but a sluice. The water levels are controlled by the Environment Agency. Volatility has been phased out. Humans have taken control of their environment: and having taken control, we are suffused with longings for the wildness we have destroyed. We are, indeed, contradictory beasts.

So why haven't these fine reed-beds turned into oak woods? Because humans want them to stay as reedbeds. Humans want them to be wild: and so we have taken on the job of rewilding. That is something we must increasingly understand: the process of rewilding. On one side, as I walked, I could see a vast tract of reed-bed that had been smashed to bits: dug out by a bulldozer. It looked like the most comprehensive act of vandalism and yet it was nothing of the kind. The smashing up halts and reverses the oak wood tendencies: stops the place drying out, scrubbing up, becoming something other than a reed-bed. As a result, the reed-bed is rewetted: and new reeds, young and green and eager, spring up, and in a vivid moist place, life will thrive.

There are now many miles of reed-bed along the Suffolk coast: all of it saved, managed, rewilded. And I walked through it, with a wild wind picking at the bones of my face and, along the very stretch that I would have missed, had I gone the way I meant to, I saw, in rapid succession, three great heroes of the rewilding.

22 Perhaps the most significant moment of rewilding in the history of Britain took place by accident. During the Second World War, a soft area just behind the seawall near the Minsmere River in Suffolk was allowed to flood, to make life harder for invading Germans, and a small brackish lagoon or two were created. As a result, a funky little bird came back to breed in Britain for the first time in 100 years. At Minsmere, and also at Havergate Island, the avocet returned. Avocets like brackish lagoons: and if you provide the lagoon, it seemed that the avocet would come and breed there. It was a classic accidental breakthrough: and it demonstrated the fundamental truth: that if humans can get the place right, then the wild things will come and thrive. The arrival of the avocets changed everything: it inspired pioneering conservation work and the creation of the Scrape at Minsmere: an avocet haven. This was cutting-edge conservation all right: it was living vivid proof that conservation worked. The Royal Society for the Protection of Birds adopted the avocet as its logo: as a great, and prophetic symbol of the way forward. That is to say, rewilding.

Minsmere is now the RSPB's flagship reserve, a great beacon for birds and birdwatchers. It provides the best and probably the easiest birdwatching in the country: the birds are, as it were, served up for you on a plate. It's a wonderful place. And I wasn't going there the day I got lost and kept finding Hoist Covert.

But as I walked through the reed-beds, I could see a

small lagoonette in the reeds, between me and the seawall. On it, six avocets. Three pairs. Each bird scything away with a daft turny-uppy beak: a perfect vignette of avian elegance. And there was something odd about this: because I valued them more highly than the avocets who would be at Minsmere now, more than a hundred of them, scything and mating and quarrelling with equal enthusiasm in one of the great sights of the birding world.

But though I love Minsmere and go there often, there was something special about these six. They were wilder, you see. Oh, Minsmere's birds are properly wild, they don't get fed, they come and go as they please. But there is a special joy about the avocets you see outside Minsmere. They are spreading out from the, as it were, city centre of Minsmere to the suburbs of Walberswick and elsewhere. They are no longer birds of fabulous rarity. When you see an avocet outside Minsmere, it is as if Imperial Minsmere has burst its boundaries, has annexed Walberswick and Dunwich and the Dingle. As if the wild is fighting back – and actually winning.

23

The more time you spend with wild things, the more you see things. You get better at seeing things in a very short space of time. You don't say, what the bloody hell was that? You start to know. Your mind is better at processing scanty information: and as a result, you become significantly better at seeing. That explains why I was able to revel in a single-second moment of perfection and wonder. A movement: movement always attracts the eye, so if you don't want to be seen, you stay still. But this was movement, and it dragged my eye in an instant. And an instant was all I had. Dark. White chin. Smooth, sinuous shape: splashless from bank to water. And gone.

Otter. Fucking *otter*. It was as if I had just drunk a large glass of champagne on an empty stomach. There are dedicated otter-trackers who never set eyes on the creature they love and serve: instead, they must concentrate on the joy of finding a nasty fish-stinky turd: spraint, infallible sign that otter are about. Otters are not visible beasts in England: but I saw one.

Years ago, I saw three others playing in the water and on the wet shore on the Island Mere at Minsmere: saw them every evening for a week. I was the one that saw them first and put the word out; by my last evening, the hide was full as for a theatrical first night. Last year, I saw a big dog-otter, dead by the roadside, hit by some hurrying fool as it made its way from water to water. Good news and bad news: the good news being that the sad and chunky corpse at least spelt out the truth that there are otters about.

Well, indeed there are: otters are increasing. This is because our waters are much less polluted than they once were. As a result they are full of fish: and so the otters have somewhere to go. So, for that matter, did I: the Ship at Dunwich, for a pint.

I walked on: and just behind the old wind-pump, a thermal column of warm rising air, and riding it, gaining height without effort, a few gulls, and with them, three marsh harriers. These birds never went extinct. They were just down to a single pair. They nested, you will be unsurprised to learn, at Minsmere. Direct persecution, habitat destruction, and DDT were the main problems: DDT affects the insects, and builds up in the bodies of those that eat the insects, and those that eat the insect-eaters get a hefty dose, which just happens to cause the thinning of the eggshells of birds of prey. You can't breed if your eggs keep breaking: and all birds of prey took a hammering until DDT was declared illegal in the 60s.

Now, in this rewilded chunk of England, marsh harriers are almost common. They are birds I see as a matter of routine. And among this three there was a male: silver, sable and copper, as handsome a bird as I have ever seen in the world.

Avocet, marsh harrier, otter. All creatures that have come back from the brink: that have come back because humans wanted them back, because humans have gone to the trouble of rewilding. And I wonder: who has done whom the favour?

24

There's something uncomfortable about flying south in spring. It's not that it's not pleasant: it just feels like cheating. I was in Turin, to cover a football match for the *Times*: the sudden sun warmed my bones and obscurely troubled my heart. It didn't seem right, to be seeing my first swallows of the year skimming over the river Po. I was pleased to see them, of course I was, but I didn't feel entirely at ease with them. The entire point of a swallow is that he comes to you, trailing spring in his wake. If you go to the swallow and find spring as a result, it is a profoundly different experience. It didn't have much to do with me. These were Other People's Swallows, this was Other People's Spring: and though I was perfectly capable of enjoying them and it, I did so with the underlying feeling that I was an outsider. I hadn't seen the swallows arrive. It was me that had done the arriving: and that was not right. There was not the personal link with the bird, the sort you get with a garden tick, or the first swallow of the year swooping (swallows being great swoopers) above your house.

I had a couple of hours before getting the plane home, so I took a stroll along the Po. It was warm enough to have a beer on a pontoon. As I walked, drank, looked, read, I was amazed, for the thousandth time, at the way birds sing in foreign accents. Italian accents here, obviously. I heard a wren: and for a moment, I took it to be a goldfinch, not a conventional confusion. There were great tits singing with new and explosive variations. Great tits are repertory singers, which means that they don't have just one song, they have several: bold, strident, laconic. The more variations a bird has, the sexier he is. Under Oddie's Law, a principle formulated by Bill Oddie, if you ever hear a bird you have never in your life heard before, it's a great tit. These Italian great tits were as sexy as the great Italian tenors, and, it seemed, as conceited. And there were blackcaps. This is a lovely song in England, but here in Italy, they sounded quite different: bravura, extravaganza, coloratura. It wasn't like being at home, no.

25

I remember a trip I made to former East Germany shortly after the wall had come down. We travelled from former West to former East: and it was as if someone had with a jerk switched on the volume. Suddenly, there was a cacophony of birdsong. The East was spared the horrors of the Common Agricultural Policy in its full rigours: as a result, the countryside was full of shaggy bits, hairy bits, untidy bits, rough bits, unkempt bits. Wild bits, in other words: bits where things grow and live and breed: and so the countryside resounded with wild songs, all, needless to say, in German accents. I was there on a press trip: a firm of chocolate-makers had put some serious money into the conservation of the European white stork, and wanted some publicity. So I and a couple of other nature-writers were whisked out to Germany for the day by a pretty PR girl who knew nothing of nature or conservation, but found herself filled with a delighted curiosity at what we were looking at.

I remember that we all had a picnic lunch at a table in a wood. The conversation was as you might expect.

"Nuthatch."

"Hm. Got it. Tree creeper."

"Redstart."

And so on. And the PR girl's face lit up, making it prettier than ever, and she said in a tone of incredulous delight: "You're recognising birds from just their songs, aren't you?"

It sounded as if she was saying: "You're turning the water into wine, aren't you?" In a way, we were: turning noise into sound, turning unison into the most complex form of polyphony, a music with a dizzying number of interlocking voices, each individual a crucial part of a single masterpiece.

Many nature-writers give the impression that they know the voices of birds, or the names of the trees and the flowers, by, as it were, nature. It creates the impression that there are two types of being: those that can interpret birdsong and otherwise understand nature, and those that can't. But that's a nonsense. Any skill can be acquired. It's wanting to that matters: it's the desire to listen, to see that you need: and we are all born with that. It's called being wild.

26

As I sat by the Po, sipped my Peroni and listened to the extravagant twitter of Italian swallows, I read my book: a biography of Durrell. Well, there are two Durrells I might have been reading about: the high, difficult, serious one, and the fluffy, cuddly, silly one. I was writing about the more important of the two. Gerry, of course.

Gerald Durrell was important to me as a child, because I loved all his books, especially *My Family and Other Animals*. I now love it all the more, because I've read it to Joe at least twice all the way through, and the favourite chapters many more times, along with many others of his books. There was an enjoyable dramatisation of *My Family* on television over Christmas, and we recorded it and watched it half a dozen times. And that prompted me to get the biography, an excellent piece of work by Douglas Botting.

Now at one stage I might have frowned on the idea that Gerry was more important than Larry. Lawrence Durrell wrote *The Alexandria Quartet*, a four-novel sequence, each volume representing one of the four dimensions. I have always taken literature seriously, and love many big and difficult books, to the extent of reading them when there's no one watching. I enjoyed the *Quartet*, and wanted to write Pursewarden poems, and better, to write a huge rambling masterwork in which time and place got confused into a great warm sexy spicy foreign melange full of gorgeous sexy enigmatic sundappled women.

But Gerry was the important one. Inclined to peppery anger and boozy gloom in his later life, he once said: "Many people think that conservation is just about saving fluffy animals – what they don't realise is that I'm trying to prevent the human race from committing suicide."

Durrell's chief weapon, as he sought to talk the human race down from its position on the ledge a hundred stories from the street, was humour. Don't jump: laugh. Humour is a great life-force: laughter is a celebration of being alive. When we have family parties, we spend most of our time drinking and laughing: we celebrate the family by means of hilarity: and Gerry celebrated the wild world by making us laugh at it. Laughter makes a person more, not less serious. It was by means of humour that Durrell opened people's eyes: showed them how much they loved the natural world, showed them that they loved it more than they knew, and also showed them its terrible fragility. Durrell then told us it was our job to put it right. The lesson went home to many: and it did so because The Magenpies made us laugh. The Magenpies trashed Larry's room on Corfu, and scattered ink and excrement over his work in progress. The Magenpies were doing a greater job than Larry ever managed: they were opening the eyes of the world to the importance of all that is wild.

27

I had a dismaying vision of the future. I went to cover a tennis match for the *Times*: as a result I spent three days in a shopping mall. The event was a Davis Cup Tie, and it took place at the Braehead Arena in Glasgow. This is a smallish sportshall that is part of the much larger shopping complex. Your taxi drops you off at Marks and Spencer. To get to the tennis you walk though food, past household, through gents outfitting and then into the main drag: Clinton cards, Vodafone, Waterstones: and on to the food hall, where you can eat various kinds of shit wrapped up in plastic. After that, a dash across the fearsome rain-lashed expanse of concrete before you got to the press tent. Spring? What's spring? Wasn't it something they had in the old days?

It was a dismal few days: cut off from that strange place called Outside. And yet inside, the caverns and catacombs of the shopping mall made a pathetic attempt to imitate Outside, knowing that this is what humans actually need: plants in tubs, fountains, lofty ceilings, skylights. Fake spring: fake hope. And of course, the place was packed with shoppers. Shopping is an act of desperation, and yet it is seen as one of life's great pleasures. Shopping for clothes is better than wearing them; shopping for lovely objects is better than using them or gazing on them; shopping for food is better than eating it. Shopping is a way of living in the future, of living in a neverland in which nothing can ever go wrong. The act of buying something protects you against the insupportable nature of the present: it gives you a talisman that will protect you, take you towards the future with higher and better hopes. Shopping is not living. It is just a way of putting things off. Perhaps that is why it is considered the highest pleasure of the 21st century. Sorry about all this: I get gloomy in shopping malls, gloomy when they won't let me see the sky. So do we all, but perhaps I'm a bit quicker to notice it than most.

People go to shopping malls as much for fear as for convenience. A shopping mall is policed, full of security staff. It is controlled. You are safe from evil. Loud drunken boys are asked to leave. Fear has changed our relationship with nature. There is, more than ever, a feeling that human control must extend even to open spaces. Open spaces get less and less wild: you must have a cycle track, approved sitting places, designated walks, interpretation boards and places to put the excrement of dogs. If you fell over and hurt yourself in a truly wild place, who would you sue?

I remember my boyhood on Streatham Common: lurking about the place with John Murtagh, my neighbour, playing football and cricket, and, better, climbing trees. This was against the regulations and occasionally the park-keepers – angry men in brown trilbies with badges on the front – would shout at you. Not, I think, for fear that we might injure ourselves, but that we might damage the trees.

We had a very close relationship with those trees. We knew them as individuals. Different trees presented different challenges. Some were pleasantly easy, and we climbed them for the playful rhythm of branches that grew like step ladders, or like spiral stairs. Some we cherished for the broadness of their branches, for the wobbling journey out towards their tips. Some we liked for the technical challenge: the big reach, the scrabbling of plimsoll against trunk, the hooking of the leading leg around the bough, the switch – the key move in tree-climbing – from an inverted sloth position to fully upright branch-straddling conquest. But height was the best thing, of course. There was one we called the Pigeon Tree; there was a pigeon nest when we first climbed it, just visible, a few feet above the highest climbable point. This tree was right on the edge of our nerve. It took you higher and higher, constantly seducing you into the next stage, and then the next, because the challenge of its branches was so enticing: just one more reach and scramble and heave, and you were six feet higher, surveying the next problem, which was also just on the edge of possibility, especially if you didn't look down.

There was one dodgy bit, about two-thirds of the way to the top, when you had to make a 360-degree spiral around the trunk and in doing so, gained about four feet on three different branches. One of these branches was slender and dead: we put our weight on it gingerly, as near the trunk as possible, and then swung around as quickly as we could to the next foothold.

And one day, when we climbed the Pigeon Tree, the dead branch had gone. We found no dead boy beneath the tree. Perhaps it had fallen of its own accord. After that, we could no longer reach the summit. Was I a little relieved?

This tree-climbing youth was nothing less than a deep and intense relationship with non-human life. Streatham Common was the centre of our lives. There were, of course, stories of nasty men in the lavs, but we climbed above such worries. Today, parents that gave their children such rough-and-ready freedoms would be regarded as criminally irresponsible. But a shopping mall: that's quite a different matter. There, it's only your soul that's in danger.

28

Taking a walk in Suffolk is all right, but taking a walk in Africa is better. It's not a question of the scenery or the birds or the butterflies being better, though. Rather, it's because there's always the chance you might be killed doing it. Not a very big chance: not if you are sensible and go with a guide, and the guide goes with a scout who carries a gun and whose duty it is to make sure that you don't get killed. But all the same, it's a possibility that you have to bear in mind.

I remember when Bob and I went to look for a gorgeous little bird called the Angola pitta. At least, I assume it's gorgeous, it looks lovely enough in all the pictures, but I have never seen one. On this occasion we were foiled because we walked straight into a herd of elephants. It was thick vegetation, not the sort of place you are supposed to go walking if you have any sense, and there was a lot of crackling and crashing and branch-breaking ahead of us. They seemed unaware of us. Because of this, Bob wanted to stay on and look for Angola pittas, but I overruled him, not an easy thing to do.

The perpetual presence of very large dangerous mammals is a wonderful thing. You might not see any that day; you might not see any the whole trip, though that's unlikely. But you know they're about. And it has a very strange effect on you. Everything you see is much more vivid. The place itself acquires a sense of perfect magic: as if there's nowhere like it on earth. And it's because you are not alone. It's not the proximity of death: if that was the way to get your fun, then birdwatching in the middle lane of the M25 would be one of the world's great experiences. Rather, it is because the means of death is so thrilling: that death might come from a large animal.

I have waded the Luangwa, a river notorious for crocodiles, and done so armpit deep. I have canoed on it, navigating from hippo to hippo. Elsewhere, I have tracked black rhino on foot, once walking to within a cricket pitch of the great bicorned slumbering giant. All these things I have done not to be brave, or for the dare. It's not like bungee jumping: a simple adrenaline hit. But I have to admit, it's not much like science, either. I haven't done much to advance the frontiers of human knowledge, but I have been out there with a good number of fairly alarming creatures. Why do it? Because it's wild, obviously. Because it is the best way of all of getting in touch with my ancient, wild self: to experience some of the same excitements and fears that humans felt when we first walked upright. This deep nostalgia for our lost selves: it is best found on the floor of Africa.

29

The signs of spring are also like the 49 bus. The 49 bus is an important part of my personal mythology. It goes past Streatham Common, and from the top deck, the Pigeon Tree was once (perhaps still is) clearly visible. Every Saturday, the 49 bus used to take me to the Natural History Museum in South Kensington. I was ten and went there unaccompanied, for this was back in those fine years for a child before paedophiliaphobia was invented. The 49 bus: wait and wait and wait and then three or four of them all come at once.

So it was with spring. What a day: chiffchaff, the first of the migrants, coming to the English spring by express delivery, just a short hop from southern Europe: chiffchaff, chiffchaff… a song that is monotonous and unstintingly joyful at the same time, a rare double. Then a blackcap: less fruity and exotic than the Italian blackcaps, but a powerful and beautiful song even in its milder English accent. This is another short-haul migrant: some of them even brave the English winters. The sight of a hare always fills me with delight: and then there was a fox, too, glimpsed in the same binocular circle. They were apparently quite uninterested in each other, the fox padding silently into the hedge on urgent business of his own, while the hare just sat there looking floppy and daft, instead of the majestic spring athlete you always expect. Then a baby bunny: ridiculously tiny, looking absolutely bereft of any kind of sense, the world's least likely survival machine. And still the day was not done: more and more blackthorn in flower, though this blackthorn winter was now distinctly warm; and then celandine, a little yellow sun crash-landed at my feet, and the sudden buzz of a bumblebee right by my ear, making me jump: now there's no escaping the advancing spring. And now more primroses: a bank of them, looking as if they had at last got the time-and-place thing right. After that, a clenched fist: a punch as I bruised the unoffending air as if a great goal had been scored: the year's first butterfly. It was a small tortoiseshell: an animal that represents a small gap in my otherwise vast ignorance of insect- kind.

How's that for a day? I rejoiced, of course I did: who would not? But it was not an uncomplicated form of rejoicing: it never is, these days. We have changed the way we rejoice.

The globe's still working, as Ted Hughes said, but the way it works is changing before our eyes. We can actually see it changing. The climate is different from one year to the next: measurable changes, which at first we had to take on trust, or deny by guesswork. But now there are changes we can feel through our senses, in our bones, in our hearts. The spring is coming earlier: and this is the cruellest thing of all, because spring itself has become a destroyer of joy. What we rejoice in is good: but it is also bad. We can still feel that primitive-man surge of joy at the sight of a celandine, the buzz of a bee, the first butterfly: but then we cannot help but wonder if it's not too early, if it's not all gone terribly wrong.

The mechanism of the globe is altering, like a watch that keeps gaining time and so becomes less proficient at the task it was designed for. One problem: the annual glut of awaking insects starts earlier and earlier: but most of the migrant birds arrive at the same time, and so they miss the spring glut at its peak. In this way, the life of the migrant gets harder and harder every year: and above all, it's the migrants that give meaning to the northern hemisphere spring.

I don't want to be a misery-guts: and I'm not one, not by any means. I don't look at the sun and see the rain to come: I don't look at the butterfly and see the chicks of migrant birds dying in their nests. But I am deeply aware that the simple joys of spring are now more complicated than they were. Joy in spring is one of the deepest and simplest emotions that a human being can feel: but now it must be complicated by the fact that, like everything else on earth, spring itself has felt the touch of human hands.

As a result, when we hear a chiffchaff or a blackcap, glimpse a hare and a fox and a baby bunny, catch sight of celandine, blackthorn blossom, the prima rosa, hear the buzzling (as my wife's mother always playfully put it) of a bee, or see the year's first butterfly (a small tortoiseshell in a mixture of marmalade and burnt toast shades with a speck or two of white), it is time for sorrowful rejoicing, for regretful delight, and for a thanksgiving that at least things are no worse than they are. And with all this, an irritated resentment that we are no longer permitted to wallow in the wild world's simplicities.

Instead, we must make some kind of accommodation with the new complexities: both in the way we live and move among the wild world: and the way we act and think on behalf of the wild world.

30

It has become an annual mistake. I do it every year, and perhaps it wouldn't be really right, perhaps it wouldn't be really spring, if I didn't. I was leaning on a stile, at the outer extremity of my usual out-and-back dog-walk, and I heard a merry twittering above. Oh-ah, I thought: goldfinch. I looked up, for a quick glance at the merry things, but it wasn't. The year's great double take: it was a swallow. It was the first swallow of the year, not counting those rogue Afro-Italians, and if it didn't make a summer, I didn't doubt that there would plenty more following on behind. I knew then the annual delight: the annual quickening of the year: now, at last, we can really get on.

The songs really aren't terribly similar – the goldfinch is much more tinkly. But the swallow takes me by surprise every year: oh yes, yes of course, *that's* what swallows sound like. I had forgotten: I had forgotten what it is like to live in a world of swallows and sunlight, just as when autumn comes, I can't believe that the cold and dark of winter will really happen.

That is, I think, the way our minds work in the north of the world, with its massive seasonal differences, its huge shifts in day length. We live in a world of constant flux: and yet we cannot believe that the changes will ever actually take place. In summer, we think: surely the world will never be so cruel as to send us those long, cold, dark nights again, and those short hardly-light days. And in winter, it is hard to believe that relief, that spring will ever come. It is as if we are trapped in the land of eternal darkness, like the crew of the Dawn Treader in *The Chronicles of Narnia*: "'We shall never get out, never get out,' moaned the rowers. 'He's steering us wrong. We're going round and round in circles. We shall never get out.'" And the stranger on board leaps to his feet with "a horrible screaming laugh. 'Never get out!' he yelled. 'That's it! Of course. We shall never get out. What a fool I was to have thought they would let me go as easily as that. No, no, we shall never get out.'"

But then, in a lovely passage, an albatross appears, and flies around the mast where Lucy, the book's heroine, is standing, and he leads them back towards the light. And as he does so, only Lucy hears his murmured words: "Courage, dear heart."

The swallow's ungoldfinchlike twittering gave me the same message: and I took courage, walking on toward the light, filled with the sudden hope that a solution to the world's ills was not only possible but imminent, while the dog made futile attempts to catch bunnies, feeling no complexities or ambiguities in her own heartfelt rejoicing at the new season, the remade world.

31

Hope is easier in the spring: but perhaps hope is irrelevant. Hope was certainly irrelevant to Beowulf, one of my all-time heroes. I was never much of a whiz at Anglo-Saxon when I wrestled with the poem as an undergraduate, and all the scholarship to do with the poem rather passed me by. But Beowulf himself did not. Beowulf has stayed with me ever since: the hopeless hero. He defeated Grendel as a good hero should: and then he defeated Grendel's far more fearsome mother, as a good superhero should. But he went beyond both heroism and superheroism when he took on the dragon. Because he lost. What's more, he knew he was going to lose. You might ask, then, what the point of fighting was. Wrong question: the point was not the winning: but the fighting. Or rather, the point was being on the right side. Winning or losing: these are small matters compared to the importance of being on the right side.

My neighbour buys up chunks of rainforest. He also buys bits of coral reef, elephant corridors, Patagonian steppes. His name is John Burton, he runs the World Land Trust and his aim is to buy the entire world. So far he's got 350,000 acres of wilderness. "Some have suggested that John is a megalomaniac," said the birdman John Gooders in his foreword to *The Big Bird Race*, "but everyone who meets him soon realises that under that innocent exterior lurks a power-crazy fanatic." People have suggested to John many times that his aim of saving the whole world is futile. He will then do the crazy laugh, something he does worryingly well, and say: "I know!"

There are two points to consider here. The first is that the World Land Trust has safeguarded some impressive chunks of endangered habitat. The organisation has helped to save 262,000 acres of tropical rainforest in Belize, the island of Danjugan in the Philippines, 15,000 acres of coastal steppe in Patagonia, 22,000 acres in the Paraguayan Pantanal, eight reserves in Ecuador, is working to save some of the last remnants of the Atlantic forest in Brazil, and as a bonus, is also seeking to buy elephant corridors in India, the stage that follows the holding operation of the kunkies. And if there's a fair bit of the world still to buy, it's still a great and glorious adventure. The second is that even if all conservation work is doomed to failure, and even if the world is in an irreversible process of destruction – well, so bloody what? If we are going to lose, at least we are fighting on the right side. It is better to fail triumphantly than win in shame.

My delight in futile heroism was reignited when I was in Japan for the 2002 World Cup. I was very taken with the classic tale of the 47 ronin. These warriors were determined to avenge their lord's death. So they bided their time for a year, acted as drunks and wasters, and were treated with utter contempt by everybody. And then, a year later, they rose up as a body and took a prolonged and bloody revenge: after which they were all required to disembowel themselves. They all did this with great good grace, their good fight having been fought and won. Naturally, they are all regarded as heroes. But some Japanese have argued that the approach adopted by the 47 ronin was insufficiently futile. They shouldn't have waited for a year. They should have hurled themselves intemperately on the enemy at once, with a hunger for revenge that brooked no waiting. They should have fought to lose, rather than waited and fought to win.

Either way, it's the fighting that counts. I'd sooner the forces of conservation actually won, myself: so I'd side with the 47 ronin who bided their time: quite apart from anything else, I have great aptitude for the part of the drunken waster. But all the same, victory and defeat are nothing. Winning, losing and drawing are nothing. What matters is fighting: what matters is fighting on the right side. What matters is that we never give up.

32

I grew up in a religious family. I always especially loved the midnight mass that started on Holy Saturday and took us over the top into Easter Day: the chanting of the Exultet – Rejoice, heavenly powers! Sing, choirs of angels! – the blessing of the waters in the font, the lighting of the paschal candle, the graceful passing from darkness into light: the darkened church lit by one candle, and then by many, each member of the congregation holding his own candle, occasional hot drips of wax warming my praying fingers. Life returned, hope rekindled, gloom, and blackness gone. The Gloria, not sung since Lent began six weeks – forty days and forty nights – back, is sung again. And after two days in which mass could not be heard, so deep and dark are the days of Good Friday and Holy Saturday, mass is at last said again on the holiest of holy nights: and the bread and wine are raised and consecrated.

All this happened at St Peter's Church, Streatham, a ten-minute walk from Streatham Common, a few minutes further to the Pigeon Tree. And when the priest raised the host and then the chalice, the church would erupt in an earbustingly glorious trumpet fanfare. Two musicians, hired for the night at vast expense, would mark the eternal significance of the moment by rending the heavens with their brazen voices. God is risen, the season of life is with us, rejoice: for that life is good.

And we would come out, and misquote Tolstoy's *Resurrection* at each other: "God is risen, Simon Barnesovich!" "He is risen indeed, Rachel Barnesova!" And then we would go back to our house in Hill House Road and drink what my mother called "troublesome whiskies" – hot toddies made with lemon and brown sugar, a teaspoon in each glass as I poured in the boiling water, to prevent the glass cracking and losing its troublesome contents.

Easter Day is still a great family celebration. I may have lost the faith myself, but the rest of the family more than makes up. My wife, my two sons and I go down to a hotel in Cambridge to meet my father: me, alas, the only Godless person there, the others all having done their Easter duties. And we drink champagne and eat a nice meal and then we go out on a punt. My father, this year, was 77, and still delighted to pole through the Cam. It is part of the ritual that, as he bows on the punting platform to pass beneath a bridge, he must test the echo with a Venetian "O-iiii!".

It was the turn for the Granchester way, rather than the college-backs way. Towards the wild, rather than towards civilisation. Le Côté de Granchester, as opposed to Le Côté des Collèges. Always my preferred route. And as my father poled adroitly – time has not reduced his delight in his skill at this delicate task – we heard the great trumpet call of spring, the Easter fanfare of joy, the confirmation that the season of new life was here and would continue.

From a thicket of watery willows, the liquid, lisping song of the willow warbler. As unstrident a song as has ever been sung: a sweet trickle down the scale. The tiny bird had flown here from southern Africa: last time I had heard this song had been in the Luangwa Valley, in the company of Levy Banda.

A miracle. Nothing less. Such a journey: and this modest song of infinite sweetness to celebrate this most impossible of journeys. The Easter celebrations were complete. Life was, indeed, rekindled. We went back to the hotel and had some tea and quite excellent cakes.

33 More butterflies. And my heart leapt, again, yes, because every sign of spring is the best sign of spring. I saw two, and from one of my favourite vantage points, the top deck of a horse. Riding past a nice line of hedge: a fluttering-by: the first a small tortoiseshell, the second, a peacock. How I relish the sight of a butterfly: I am so deliciously ignorant of butterflies that every small scrap of knowledge I possess seems to me like a major advance for science. But the beginning of recognising, of telling one from the other, is the beginning of understanding. These creatures seem almost absurdly well designed to please the eyes of human beings. Like the baby bunnies, these polychrome flutterers are unlikely survival machines. But survival machines they are: and highly effective ones. And in this country, they come with the warmth and the sun: not so much an emblem as an embodiment of the good-times months of the British year.

I have written about being a bad birdwatcher: but as I have already boasted in these pages, I count myself a good bad birdwatcher. Well, I am unquestionably a very bad bad butterfly-watcher. There are only about 40 species of butterfly you can see easily in Britain: the top twitchers will have British bird lists that go above 500. Me, well, when it comes to butterflies, I can get into double figures quite easily. And then, once again, as usual, as always, confront my ignorance. My ignorance seems sometimes as boundless as the wild world itself.

I am not a lister, so I can't tell you how many species of birds I have seen: I'd say maybe 1,000, all over the world. It would be more if I didn't keep going back to Luangwa and seeing the same birds all over again. And it means I have about 9,000 to go if I want to see every bird species on earth: a thing a few people have actually tried to do – the record stands at 8,400. But when it comes to butterflies, I have more than 100,000 to go. The great Edward Wilson – no lesser term will do – had a go at computing the number of species of animals alive on this planet in *The Diversity of Life*. Butterflies and moths, he lists at 112,000 species. There are only (only! How many can you name?) 4,000 mammals, including ourselves.

Are you a good fly-watcher? There are 98,500 species waiting for you to discover them. But all else pales when it comes to beetles. There are 290,000 known species of beetle. This prompted the famous remark of JBS Haldane, geneticist, evolutionary biologist and writer. He was asked by his theological colleagues at London University what he could deduce about the nature of the Creator from a lifetime's study of His creatures. After a moment's thought, Haldane replied: "An inordinate fondness for beetles."

The Creator also seems fairly partial to nematode worms: at any rate, there are 12,000 known species of them. I am a very bad nematode worm-watcher, myself. I am not much better at annelid worms: and there are another 12,000 of them. And there are 73,400 species of arachnids – I'm not sure that I would like to meet all of these at once – and 50,000 molluscs and – well, Wilson gives a list of 1,032,000 species of animals. Such a list is never a permanent thing: it is in constant flux as new species are discovered, others go extinct, and scientists change their minds about the status of still more. Of this million-plus, I can recognise a couple of thousand: sometimes with a pretty coarse guess that gets no deeper than genus or even family. I reckon I'm not bad – reasonably aware – and yet I've scarcely scratched the surface.

I find this a wonderful, headspinning thought. Because science itself is in exactly the same position. Yes, science itself has scarcely scratched the surface when it comes to unravelling the diversity of life on earth. The number of animal species that actually exists is far, far higher than Wilson's million-plus estimate of the creatures already known to humans, as Wilson himself well knows: the unknown vastly outnumbers the known. Some say that the true number is ten times as high. Others go farther, some much further. It has been suggested that there are as many as 30 million species of tropical insects still undescribed.

Some reckon that the true number of animal species is 50 million. These are fantastic, dizzying numbers.

And I love the feeling of there being more and more and more: more than you can ever know, more than anyone can ever know. Diversity isn't an awkward trick that nature plays on bad nature-watchers: diversity is the basic method by which life works. The natural world operates by making more and more and more different kinds of living things.

That is why being baffled by identification conundrums is such a joy. Learning a few names is a way of peering into the mysteries of life. It is like putting on a mask and sinking your face into the sea above a coral reef. At once you perceive a new world: one that was previously invisible, one from which you were, a moment ago, utterly cut off.

To learn the name of a few birds and a couple of butterflies is your entry into the wild world: to see that it operates by means of a great mass of different things. And sometimes, if we can look and listen, we can begin – just begin – to understand not just a butterfly but the way the whole wild world works. Our ignorance – my ignorance, your ignorance, the ignorance of the greatest scientist and field observer that ever drew breath – is the key to a vast and deeper understanding of life.

Haldane again: "Now, my own suspicion is that the universe is not only queerer than we suppose, but queerer than we can suppose... I suspect there are more things in heaven and earth than are dreamed of, or can be dreamed of, in any philosophy." So next time you see a butterfly and say: hmm, nice, I wonder what the hell that was? – you can dive straight into the greatest and deepest mystery of life, which is diversity: an inordinate fondness for nematode worms. And indeed, for lepidoptera. Peacock, small tortoiseshell: what next?

34

Once or twice I have come across the delightful theory that in the symbolism and legends of dark-skinned people, the colour black represents everything good, while white is the colour of evil. This is, of course, a nonsense. For a human, light is always good: dark is always bad. Dark is difficult, dangerous, frightening, threatening: dark is when nature renders you helpless. Light is safety: light, above all, is life.

For those who live in a temperate climate, the coming of spring is the most important thing in the world. It changes everything. It brings hope: it brings light: it brings life. It brings Easter: the great celebration of the renewal of life, the conquest of death: the conquest of dark: darkness chased out at midnight mass by the new fire. The light of spring seems to breathe life into me every year: I can almost envision a great Blakean figure, robed and bearded, or perhaps better, eternally nubile, breathing the stuff of life into my body: in-spiration. I get the blues in the winter, like many of us, a touch of seasonally affected disorder, or SAD. I have brightened my life and my spirit with a light-box, blasting synthetic sunlight into my eyes and my mind: to fool me that everything is all right, that hope is sustainable even in winter's murky depths. But it's in the wildness of spring that I find the real thing, the real answer. The longer days and warmer light bring a death-blow to depression.

A fizzing sparrowhawk along the hedgeline: the briefest of sightings and yet unmistakable. The time of plenty was already here for this bird: the young and helpless, the fully grown and preoccupied, were here in numbers to feed a new brood of hawks. I saw a kestrel, too: hanging in the sky as if air were something you could lean on, like the bar in the White Horse. Hawks are killers: but then no one ever said that nature is nice. That is not the deal.

The changing seasons put a spring into my step. What was there to be gloomy about, after all? It was easy to be hopeful: to believe that the tide of destruction had turned, that there was a real understanding in high places of the importance of safeguarding wild things and wild places, that there was, increasingly, a political will for change. That wasn't something I felt too often in January.

Spring, Easter. But wildness is not a substitute religion. Wildness doesn't give you an ethical structure. Wildness doesn't demand faith (hope is quite different from faith). Wildness doesn't give you a community. Wildness doesn't ask you to believe in anything. Wildness doesn't have an organised historical continuity over 2000 years. Wildness doesn't ask for an orthodoxy. Wildness lacks leaders. Wildness brings no miracles. Wildness requires no concept of prayer. Wildness has neither a universally recognised system of symbols nor an organised mythology. Wildness doesn't have canonical texts. Wildness doesn't have its prophets, saints and sages. Perhaps above all, wildness can't explain why we live, who we are, why we are and what happens when we die.

Wildness offers a cause, for conservation is an aspect of wildness. Wildness implies at least some moral questions. Wildness offers a continuing preoccupation with things greater than yourself: for wild eyes are always moving to flying things, to growing things, to living things. But if there is any link at all to be traced between wildness and religion, it is that both offer the most extraordinary and vivid moments of spiritual exaltation: in the sight of sparrowhawk, perhaps. Or a kestrel.

The best example is "The Windhover". In Gerard Manley Hopkins' poem, his heart in hiding stirred for a bird. The poem is unambiguously dedicated "To Christ Our Lord": and in the poem, the glorious sight of the kestrel is a manifestation of Christ: as if the poet had seen Christ's bird streaming in the firmament.

But I sometimes wonder if Christ doesn't make the poem a mite crowded. Hopkins' heart would have stirred for the bird, Christ or no Christ. It was a fabulous sighting of a fabulous bird and it came to a man with wildness is his eyes and his soul. And if thrilling to a great wild wonder is a religious experience, then I am still a fanatically religious person.

35

In most nature-books, the narrator is alone with his subject: alone but not lonely, isolated but in tune with the great wild world beyond humanity. But it is also true that the wild and lonely places are a wonderful way of enjoying human company. Love of the wild can be an intensely shared thing as well as an intensely personal thing. There are two marvellous ways of enjoying the wild world: on your own, and in the right company. On this day, the right company was Joe, my twelve-year-old son.

My day job is chief sportswriter for the *Times*; Joe has always hated sport with a passion. As soon as he could walk, give him a ball and he would kick it into the nearest bush and carry on with something more interesting. To this day, if I am watching sport on television he will leave the room: not rudely, but because he simply can't see the point of staying. He recoiled with horror from a rather hearty school we investigated, because they talked obsessively about sport when they showed us round. For him, a place dominated by spreading green-and-white playing fields was a place of unspeakable menace: a place that was trying to steal his soul.

People occasionally ask me if I am upset by this. Well, I

am, but not very. I'm sorry we don't and won't have sport to share, as my father and I do; I'm sorry I won't be taking him to the cricket and so forth; I'm sorry that sport won't be part of our system of jokes and conversations. We'll have to find other things. But the point is that your children are invariably the people they are, not the people you want them to be.

But if Joe hates sport, he loves to be wild. It is a deep and very personal thing with him. He is not obsessively knowledgeable and widely read – though he is pretty good – but it's rather that he feels very clearly indeed that the wild things matter, and matter to him. So naturally, when I suggested that he joined me in a hunt for badgers, he jumped at it.

We went to meet Margaret Grimwade, chief badger person with the Suffolk Wildlife Trust: and the first thing she gave us was a course in badger architecture. Because of this, I understood something very important, something I would otherwise have missed: and that is that badgers dig: not just for need but for love. Digging is the heart and mind and soul of the badger: *fodo ergo sum*, I dig therefore I am. As a horse runs, as a nightingale sings, as a swift flies, so a badger digs. Digging is the essential expression of badgerness. A badger sees the world as something to be dug: the surface of the earth is merely a place between hole and hole. Any given piece of land is, to a badger, something that hasn't been dug yet. Margaret showed us some setts, on the way, pointing out badger-sign: little conical pits into which they have probed for something juicy or crunchy, snuffle-holes, they are called; also paths, tunnels through grass, dung pits.

And then the sett itself: always extraordinarily theatrical. They like a short, steep slope of soft earth, and into these, they dig. They are not mere functional holes: the holes represent the compulsive virtuosity of the diggers. A sett is a monument to the culture of digging that has been passed on and elaborated by one generation after another: badger after badger that had used this place and dug and dunged and snuffled here.

Joe's response to these wonders was extraordinary, too. He flung himself into the holes with the same unstoppable compulsion with which the badgers did the digging. It seemed he had to be part of this: that his experience in learning badgers required some kind of participation, some kind of communion. Being a wise person, Margaret didn't stop him. I think she understood the impulse herself, even if she perhaps disapproved of Joe's wholehearted capitulation to it, leaving distressing bits of man-scent on the badger's own well-dug soil. But she certainly also thought that the more human beings the badgers have on their side, the better.

Woody Allen said he was "at two with nature". This is a sad thing. (The culture of the Jews of the Diaspora is vitally important to modern life: the fact that much of Jewish culture is at two with nature has placed a difficult and dangerous element into our thinking and understanding. This is precisely what you might expect if you confine an intellectually brilliant people to ghettoes: inner-city enclaves with not a green thing to be seen for one generation after another. Such people will not be prone to windhover moments.) The fact is that most people strive, from time to time and in different ways, to experience at least some kind of oneness, even if it is only by playing golf. At the badger setts, Joe went for oneness without an instant's self-consciousness. Most of us know very well the feeling that prompted this even if we don't express it quite as unrestrainedly as Joe did with the badger setts. Every time I see a pride of lions sleeping in a great furry huddle, I feel the impulse to join them: to fling myself from the vehicle and rub against the warm fur, and rest my head on those soft bodies, and feel the warmth of deep and intense feline companionship, just as Hopkins' heart in hiding soared and flew with his kestrel.

And so Margaret explained badgers to us, and in between, I taught her a little birdsong, for in wildness as in everything else, it is always at least as good to give as to receive. We startled a couple of roe deer, who sprinted away in a sudden flash of white bums, goat-sized and dapper, and then, as we came down through a dry ditch and up the other side of the hedgeline, they were waiting for us, in the classic deer-and-antelope position of alert: still, poised to run, staring hard, exactly on the cusp of their flight distance, the maximum distance at which they allow us to be before they have to run again. Something I have seen a thousand times in Luangwa. But the sky was darkening: it was time to talk to a few badgers.

36

People sometimes ask me what I like best, wildlife or sport, as if they were exchangeable things, like stamp collecting and Meccano. Well, I love writing about sport: the job of writing about humans in conflict, in triumph and in disaster is enthralling to me. I have done it for the past 25 years, and I am not even remotely bored with it. It is fabulous and vivid and thrilling, and I couldn't want anything better to write about.

I also love writing about wildlife. I find it more difficult, more elusive, more challenging than sportswriting. But hey: if sport was suddenly abolished all over the world overnight, I expect I'd find some other way of writing about people. If wildlife was abolished overnight – alas, a far more likely prospect – I'm not sure that I'd want to carry on living.

37

Joe now showed he was as good at stillness and quiet as he was at running about and diving down holes. We sat in a hide for an hour as it grew dark, occasionally talking in whispers. The hide was a wooden hut, with sealed glass windows: it was not just the sight of ourselves that we had to cover up: we also had to conceal our smell. We looked down over a classic badger bank: another great theatre of excavation. And finally, an hour gone, at last, amazingly and impossibly: from one of the many holes, a black and white nose. Tasting the air: committing head, then shoulders, and at last the wide and furry back end.

I have seen some marvellous wildlife sights all over the world, and this moved me as much as the bathawk over Luwi lagoon, the first night hunting Luangwa leopard, the impossible glimpse of jaguar in Belize. It was the same sudden soul-deep sense of privilege: to be alive on such a planet and seeing such a thing of wonder. Oh brave old world that has such creatures in it!

There is something deeply improbable about a badger. We know what they look like; they are one of the first things we see: Mr Brock, star of a thousand children's stories, with an outrageous stripy nose and a comic bumbling demeanour. So much so that this works a kind of trick on the brain: some part of you believes that something as improbable-looking as a badger can only be fictional: that like dragons and unicorns, badgers are mythical beasts that have been used as a convention by storytellers for hundreds of years. I always had a deep respect for Mr Badger, who rescued Ratty and Moley from the snow and then led the Four Friends in the retaking of Toad Hall. Badgers are not rare: but rarely seen, save as sad, round, roadside corpses. Badgers like deep cover and the dead of night. If you want to see a badger, you need to try pretty hard.

And so the gloriously improbable snout gave me a deep and complex delight, in which childhood joys and present fascinations were joined together in a single moment of wonder. Out he came, a battle-scarred one-eared veteran, bearing open sores, but plainly unconquered. Time to savour the classic badger shape: a pear, pointed and striped at the front, wide and powerful and silver-grey at the back.

He retreated underground after a few long minutes of snuffling; a brief glimpse of a second, and then a third, a young sow, lithe and slim by badger standards, hoovering up the peanuts we had put out for them. Joe had flung them out for us, doing so without invading the badger-ground and leaving his scent around the holes. Finally, one more, a young boar, perhaps destined to be the top male in the badger group, supplanting the as-yet-unconquered old boy who had started things off. And the light was still not entirely gone as we left. Something very special: not least because shared.

38

The hedges were not only full of blossom but full of noise: a full, rich, faintly dangerous buzzling. As the hedges found their voice, it seemed that the whole world was set fair for salvation. There is a little  spice in the sound of the humming: I was pleased to hear the bees but had no urge to fling myself in among them and stroke them. Few of us feel the urge to get cosy with insects. The most dangerous animals I have ever encountered are, of course, all insects: mosquitos kill more people than lions. I have twice been stung by the famous African killer bees: once in slightly exciting circumstances. I was looking at a monitor lizard inside a hollow baobab, and the other inmates quite rightly objected. I was stung twice. It was almost humorously painful. As more bees joined the attack, I and the rest of the party fled to a vehicle and roared off, leaving the bees to make rude signs at us and tell us not to come back. A little later, someone removed a stinger from my ear lobe with the tweezers from my Swiss Army knife.

39

I was leading out my old mare on a merry sunlit morning when I heard it. Or thought I heard it. We were walking across the gravel at the time, so the crunching of the little stones beneath her big, wide hooves was filling my ears. But when we stopped for a moment, I heard it again and I was right. The whitethroat were back. Another good thing in a good spring. Neat little warblers, who sing a cheery, scratchy – always the whitethroat *mot juste*, I have tried hard but I can't better it – song. They love the hedges and the brambles around the pasture: and they make one of the great lesser voices of the rural spring. I smiled an equally cheery blessing in their direction, and walked the old girl out to the grass. The song still in the background: pause, repeat, pause, repeat. Good moment. If you want to rate these things, it was blessed enough, but not quite the full windhover. Father Hopkins would not have reached for his pen, but would probably have murmured to himself that, yes, indeed, he was right when he said that the world was charged with the grandeur of God.

Religion began in nature, even if nature has been rather edited out of religion in the modern world. Early humans needed religion to understand the nature of the world and to establish the principles of communal living: to understand why we live and what happens when we die: why plants grow for us and sometimes fail to do so: why some hunts are lucky and others are not. We have evolved to live life by way of religion: religion is part of what makes us human. When we fail, some of us, to believe in the requisite gods and prophets, we still need a religion, or at least some kind of substitute, if we are to be fully human. Perhaps the point is that we need a religion that we don't believe in.

We humans are as much the product of the history of our species as we are the result of our individual upbringings. Humans lived for several million years as fully wild beings: only in the last 10,000 did we invent agriculture; only in the last couple of centuries did we invent industry. We are a species that has spent 99 per cent of its history as hunter-gatherers. We haven't had time for our unconscious minds and our unconscious needs to have changed. If you like, our souls have not changed, and this is true whether or not we believe that we have them. And our souls' need, or one of our souls' needs, is for wildness: for space, for green, for running water, for the fizz or even the faint buzzle of danger: and as a result, to feel some of the grandeur of God – even if we don't believe in Him.

And people frequently – daily – realise that what I say about our need for nature, for wildness, is true: but not because they have a windhover moment. Rather, they have the exact opposite. They feel a vacancy, a blank, a hole in the soul. Don't it always seem to go, you don't know what you've got till it's gone. Joni Mitchell sang a deep truth in a deceptively simple song: and it's a truth that people find with wives, landscapes, houses and rainforests. We don't really know how to live in the 21st century: it's not the sort of life we evolved for. By time we've found out how to do it, it may be too late to put the correct principles into action. Because there is not enough wild left to satisfy our non-existent souls.

40

We are clearer about what we want and what we need when we are children. And what we want and need and demand are animals. "Once upon a time and a very good time it was there was a moocow coming down along the road" – the beginning of *A Portrait of the Artist as a Young Man*, James Joyce's book (which is at least in part about the need to escape from religion in order to develop the soul that you don't necessarily believe you possess). All our first picture books have moocows in them and horses and doggies and sheep and bunnies. Before children can use speech with any certainty, they can tell you what noise a cow makes and what noise a pussycat makes. Moo! Meow! We acquire humanity's most precious and unique achievement, language, by identifying ourselves with our fellow animals.

I admired Mr Badger, I laughed at Toad, and I loved Moley, but I *was* Ratty: forever writing poetry and having picnics and messing about in boats, a good friend, a dangerous enemy, brave but never bellicose, an animal who knew how to live, a romantic soul, an animal who loved his river beyond measure but harboured a yen to roam the world, an animal who loved peace but was always prepared to take the adventures life threw at him.

We will take the adventure Aslan sends, as they say in *The Chronicles of Narnia*: the great series by CS Lewis in which you pass through a wardrobe into a land where animals speak and God's representative is the all-wise, all-knowing, ferocious, compassionate, vengeful, forgiving lion Aslan. The books were written as Christian fables, and some fools say that this disqualifies them from excellence. I loved them, not for their purpose but for the stories themselves, for the wildness, for the adventure, for the world, for the beavers, Trufflehunter the badger, Bree the horse, Fledge the father of all flying horses, and above all, for the indomitable heart of Reepicheep, the great mouse warrior who took the last adventure and sailed over the edge of the world in search of Aslan's country. I still read these books, when the mood is right, and my love for them has remained undimmed over the years.

Did I love *The Jungle Book* better? Do I love it better now? It begins when Chil the kite brings home the night that Mang the bat set free, and then Mother Wolf faces down a tiger to save a human child and adopts him as her own cub, and he continues as the wildest of all wild boys. They call him Mowgli – Mowgli the frog – and he lives and grows up in the jungle, gets abducted by the monkey people and is rescued, and then takes his final dreadful revenge on the tiger. And I too lived with wise old Baloo the bear, and with the coolest cat in the history of literature, Bagheera the black panther. To live in the jungle and be spoiled (and occasionally beaten) by a black panther who calls you Little Brother: what dreams can compare with that?

These people, these beasts who spoke *en clair*, sometimes in Kipling with biblical sonority, sometimes in Lewis with gnomic meaning – they shaped my mind – my soul – in boyhood, and I am in part their product. I read many other things then, of course I did, but *Just William* and John Buchan and Rider Haggard and the *Famous Five* and Sherlock Holmes have left a much fainter mark. It is the books that had some kind of wildness that always mattered most: and they still matter to me. Desert Island Discs: what book would I take? *Ulysses*, my endlessly reread favourite of grownup life? Or the Chronicles, boyhood favourite and in adult life, the comforter that always comes in times of need? It's not a dilemma I'd like to face, to be frank. I'd say *Ulysses*, but smuggle in the Chronicles, and *The Jungle Book* as well. No question about the luxury item: I have that on my desk as I write. A pair of Leica 10x42s: the better the optics, the more opportunities your heart has for stirring, the further you can reach out... stretch out and touch the wild.

41

Of course one swallow makes a summer. The idea that it doesn't is one of the most pissy and pusillanimous proverbs in the English language. The first swallow is a pretty good indicator: you know that once the first has been sighted, there will be a good few following close behind, towing the good weather after them. The first one I saw on home territory was in front of the stable block on the top field: skimming past with a buoyant, easy confidence in his flight: why not? His wings had just carried him 8,000 or so miles, and he didn't seem tired of flight, either, making his pattern of circles, flat spirals, loops and curlicues as he hawked for insects, underneath him steady air.

The first home swallow: and a summer made, damn the thing else. The day after, another joyful sight: bird-shit on one of the saddles. Ha! This didn't mean that the swallows were back: it meant that *my* swallows were back. Each year, a pair nest in the tackroom, flying in through the open stable doors and hanging a sharp right, to fly through the roof space as far as the end wall, where their nest had stood all winter, crisp and waiting for their return from Africa.

Learning to rejoice at the sight of a speck of shit: to feel a genuine stirring of the soul at a lump of excrement, is a good test of personal wildness. Otter-watchers know that better than most.

So I rejoiced at the splash of whitewash and carried on. Later that day, after mucking out, I decided to have a cup of tea at the top stables, my custom on fine days when not overstretched with work (a double demand seldom actually met, alas). I unfolded my folding chair and sat on it, drank tea – good rooibos tea without milk or sugar – and surveyed the spring: the meadow sloping down to the river, the little copse. It was good.

And then it got better. I heard it. Did I? Do it again. What? Did I imagine it? No, I bloody didn't, there it was clear as anything, a merry raspberry from about 30 feet up, and I looked and damn well saw it, too: the martins were back, the house martins, white underneath, navy on the top with a white bum.

House martins mean more to me than swallows: or perhaps I mean that my house martins mean more to me than my swallows. The swallows nest in the outbuildings – there's usually a second pair in the lower stables – which is wonderful. But the house martins build nests on the actual house, and they bless and sanctify and bring wildness to the place. It's even better than a garden tick. The martins stay here: they are part of the history of the house. They belong to the house, and the house to them. They come back, every year, to tell us that the globe's still working: and they leave stinky white trails on the pink Suffolk walls.

I finished my tea and went back down to pass on the great news. They weren't back over the garden yet, so this pioneer martin was probably just passing through. Not a resident. Cindy at once made a mud-pool, playing the hose on the ground in front of the house: for in the dryness of the current spring, the martins would find it hard to find the material they need for repairing their ancestral nests beneath the eaves. I remember, a few years ago, Aubrey came round for a cup of tea and remarked that for the first time in his life – not a small piece of time – no martins were nesting at his house. Cindy told him about the making of mud-pies: and the warring of rival elements in his nature was almost comical.

He was a farmer: farmers don't help nature. Nature helps itself: and sometimes you fight it. Sometimes you fight it very hard indeed. It couldn't possibly be appropriate to help it. Aubrey knows more about the outdoor life than I do, by about a million miles: he was born in the village, has always lived in the village, and has done much to shape the village. He has a feeling for the wild things, as we have seen. But the idea of going out of your way to help wild things goes against everything he has always done and known. He loves his martins: but they have gone. We still have ours (but for how much longer?) and that fact that we make mud-pies may even help them. But certainly, it helps us: and it does so by defining our attitude to the wild.

The wild world needs our wild selves in order to survive. A need, then, for wild farmers as well as wild householders.

42

A stink from the river. The river not actually flowing. It flows, or should flow, right in front of the house. There is a bridge between us and the world: not, alas, a drawbridge. I have known the river an inch or two below the bridge on my neighbour's drive, and going like the clappers. That house has flooded within living memory: ours, a couple of feet higher, has not. But save in times of spate, the river has dwindled. It ceases altogether to flow in the summer. Aubrey says it always did. It becomes shaggy with growth when the water isn't there to keep it down.

The stink was Tompkins' fault. He had allowed some slurry – dilute cattle-shit – to get into the water-system, and it had washed straight down to the river, where it stayed put. The place it stayed put was right in the middle of my place. He very decently came round and apologised and offered to bring a digger to get rid of the stuff, but we thought the solution would be worse than the problem. Good neighbourly relations were able to continue, but it certainly stank a bit. Rain: that's what we needed. It had been a very dry spring.

My attitude to rain has changed since I moved to Suffolk. Certainly, I used to understand rain as a good thing. I didn't have the townees' hatred of rain: a thing expressed time and again by the great Shane MacGowan of The Pogues, for whom rain is final proof of the indifference of God to his own suffering. MacGowan has written of Rain Street, that it's just another bloody rainy day, and that it was raining worse than anything that he had ever seen.

But me, I used to see the rain and say, well, I accept that this is a Good Thing. A pity it's doing it now, but I accept it. But I left all that behind when I reached Suffolk. My water is pumped up from a well; I have a bit of river on my few acres; I have pasture. I need the grass, I need the rain, or my horses will suffer. And so when it rains, I respond not with my mind but my guts: rain, how truly fabulous. It is an extraordinary adjustment, a new way of seeing the world. Water doesn't come from the tap: it comes from the sky. My water is wild.

43

From the bridge, above the still and stinky river, I heard lesser whitethroat. Another migrant: another nail in the coffin of winter, another brick in the edifice of spring:

the Babel tower that is annually built, only to fall annually each autumn. I am always secretly proud of being able to pick out lesser whitethroat from the rest of the singers. I remember, as I was learning the warblers, my horror at finding that once I had learned whitethroat, I was expected to learn lesser whitethroat as well. I felt like giving up: absurd, to think that one person could know all these birds. Biodiversity: all too much. Your reward for learning a bird is to be given a still harder bird. I felt like Shasta, in *The Horse and His Boy*, one of the *Narnia* books. Shasta has just faced down a lion after a long, hard chase: now he is told he must run, run and save the land from invasion. "Shasta's heart fainted at these words for he felt he had no strength left. And he writhed inside at what seemed the cruelty and unfairness of the demand. He had not yet learned that if you do one good deed your reward usually is to be set to do another and harder and better one."

So, Shasta-like, I did the still better thing and learned lesser whitethroat as well: another of those invisible birds whose voice adds to the spring cacophony. I could not reliably identify a lesser whitethroat on sight, but they are easy enough to pick out from the sound: a bit like a yellow-hammer, but harsher. The yellowhammer traditionally sings "A little bit of bread and no cheeeeese"; the lesser whitethroat never even raises the subject of cheese.

It was another voice: one by one the chorus swells, till it's a mighty noise, as The Incredible String Band sang in the haunts of my youth. These days, I can hear each new voice and actually recognise it as it joins the choir: the year unfolding before me. I couldn't do that back then, my head all filled with cosmic beauty and Blakean visions. I suspect that back in the hippy days, I would have regarded too much precision as a bad thing: would have believed that any kind of accuracy about the names of birds would spoil things somehow. I take the exact opposite view now. I remember the beautiful garden of the ghastly hall of residence where I lived in my first year. In a room overlooking it, we sat up so late and so often and smoked so much and discussed so many vast and heady things: beauty, the meaning of life and our – highly theoretical – love of nature and the wild. The answer was, of course, outside the room, not within it. Perhaps it always is. The other day, I recalled, with a friend from those days, how we each wrote a poem for the autumn. His own offering was:

Truth is
an autumn leaf.

I responded with:

Autumn
only five leaves left

This, I should explain, was a reference to the Rizla cigarette papers: when you were running out of "skins", you would come to a slim piece of card, a warning, bearing as it did the words "only five leaves left". I remember my sadness when this was changed to "time to buy another packet", an unacceptably mercenary approach.

But I remember, in the late spring of the year that followed, those nights when there were only five leaves left indoors but many beautiful green ones outside the walls, the way the night-long smoke-filled room would change with the coming of the dawn and the wild spring chorus would hammer through the window and force us to draw the curtains, telling us that a night of excess must be remorselessly brought to its close. I would stagger barefoot and bedwards through the garden wet with dew, rejoicing in the belief that everything that lived was holy, and that the pride of the peacock was the glory of God and the lust of the goat was the bounty of God. And certainly, that the road of excess led to the palace of wisdom.

These days, I understand all that rather better, I think. I sometimes wonder what birds sang in that lost and lovely garden (where I did briefly dally with a passing Eve), and whether there were nightingale. Certainly there would have been blackbird and song thrush and blackcap and garden warbler: but then, I listened to an awful lot of really bad music on the stereo, and birdsong was just a generalised if holy sort of din.

The lesser whitethroat sang to establish his territory in the hedge along my neighbour's drive, and another sang in the hedge along the back field, sang to seek a female lesser whitethroat, there to perch in lovely copulation bliss on bliss, to raise chicks, adding no doubt to the holiness of life as he did so, and then to fly back to Africa, another day, another season, another miracle. Another harsh rattling call: another: another. The lust of the lesser whitethroat is the bounty of God.

44

Now more swallows, and now more martins: the air was filling with hirundines, swept-back wings, forked tails, the pretty chatter of swallows and the cheery farting of the martins. The warm weather brought everything to life, my heart in hiding among them. Since that primal explosion, it seemed more of a slow-motion process than usual: the migrants trailing in ones and twos rather than in an instant invasion: but bit by bit, the place was filling up. Surely, I thought, it will now always be like this: always warm, always spring, always the sky filled with hirundines and the air fizzing and buzzling with hope. It was impossible to imagine a world full of bad things. In the warmth and joy of the spring, the wild world and the civilised world seemed truly at one. It would never be cold again, never be dark, life would always be around us in full vigour. The forces of conservation were winning: the fightback and the rewilding were unstoppable: the deserts would shrink, the rainforests cease to be attacked, the climate would stabilise, the way of the migrant would be safe for ever, because humans had come to terms with the wild world and found it good and necessary and important. And I thought: I should remember this mood: because it is no more true than the uprising of gloom that comes at other times of the year, those times when life seems to have no future and the entire world will be concreted over within five years.

45 May is a special month. *The* special month. The holy month, if you like. Personally, I reckon that being forced to work in May is a denial of basic human rights. I always take a fortnight off, and I wish it could be more. May is the culmination: the celebration of plenty. May is the sharp end: the horny time of year, when every holt and heath echoes to the sound of sex – sex rearing its comely head at every twist and turn. It is the time that birdsong reaches its height, when every last voice joins the chorus: the time of the spring's completed masterpiece.

And it opened with a day of glorious life-giving promise. That is to say it rained: a long, gentle day of soaking and soaking. It was as if the field behind the house had its tongue hanging out, and was lapping up life. You could almost see the grass growing; you could almost hear the trees slurping the rain up through their roots like a child with a straw.

I felt cheer in my heart almost as an African does. An

African does not celebrate the return of the warm weather: in Africa, the sun is always with you. Instead, it is the rains that bring hope and cheer. In this country we do things the other way round: the wet is always with us, but when the sun comes, it is something to sing about. The equation is the same in both places, in every place: sun plus rain equals life. But here, we are inclined to see the sun alone as the life-giver; the rain as a mean and destructive trick of hostile nature. The Africans, of course, have it the other way round. But it's the two together that does it: and so, as I prepared myself for my Maytime holiday, I rejoiced in the wild and the wet.

The May trees were, appropriately, in bloom. This included a spinney of twenty trees I had had planted a few years ago: some of the plants were in bloom for the first time, and were sending spindly branches up above my head. I took three buckets full from the rainbutt at the top stable; when I returned, an hour or so later, it was already full again. Droplets bounced off my boots. The horses every now and then shook themselves like dogs. And the river picked itself up and began to flow again, and Tompkins' slurry was no more than a memory.

In the evening, sitting upstairs with a nice drink, I could hear the chatter of house martins on the nest. My martins, our martins. My house, their house.

46
I had to spend three days of May away from Suffolk, a refined cruelty brought about by the sporting calendar.

Actually, I can't complain that much: the event I had to cover was the Badminton Horse Trials, an event that is never a trial for me. I left with the swallows belly-skimming the front pasture, and the sound of a garden warbler from the corner beyond my new spinney.

It really was a garden warbler. Not a blackcap. These two are species that are notoriously confused, but I get it right every time. My method is simple: I listen to the song, make my diagnosis and walk on. I never look for the bird. That simplifies things enormously.

Am I being frivolous here? So what if I am? There are many ways of enjoying nature, and expertise is by no means the only one, or even the most important one. The first skill is wildness itself. All other things are excuses or reasons to bring wildness into your life. I suspect that the most important skill is not knowing but noticing. The most important gift is not knowledge but curiosity. Knowledge is not a way of taming the wild: it is a way of finding out how much more there is to learn. That is true of me and it is true of you, and it is also true of the greatest natural historian that ever lived.

47

On the way, I stayed overnight with my old friends Mark and Lucy in London. We drank champagne and then cold beer, we ate takeaway curry, we talked. And they gave me news of a mutual friend, a man I always remember for his unrelenting good cheer and unstemmable flow of jokes; he shared a flat with them, he played rhythm guitar, and sang in a pub band the three of them were involved in. He was man you could rely on to cheer you up in any circumstances. But alas, no longer: his older daughter is a sad and troubled creature, prone to episodes of self-harming. The details you don't need: they are as terrible as you might imagine.

But Mark and Lucy told me some good news: that the

girl is now interested in photography. The one thing that brings her calm is to be in nature: to find something wild. She sits and waits and when she finds something nice, she clicks: as if she needed to keep what she found there. I was shown a picture she had taken, and had given to Mark and Lucy: a nice macro-lens close-up of a six-spot burnet: a day-flying moth, grass-green with spots of red, a very handsome thing altogether.

I confess, I sobbed when I saw this picture. That someone as desperate as this poor girl could find some sort of comfort in the wild makes such clear and vivid sense to me: the only place where you can find an easy, non-judging sanity; where life is harsh and beautiful and humans are just one more species; where humans matter that much less; where human concerns retreat. All troubled people need the wild: and which of us does not have our troubles?

48

I wondered what the sad girl would have made of my dog-walk. She might even have found a tiny moment of peace. There is a section of the walk that becomes a tunnel in May: a bank rising to three or four feet on one side, a rich and ancient hedgerow on the other. Branches extend outward beyond your head as you walk; the other side of the trees, a stream, tributary to the river that crosses my land, hence, of course, the slurry. You are almost completely enclosed. It's a still, warm, sheltered, moist-aired tube, and by the beginning of May, it is almost absurdly filled with life. It is like a private little stretch of rainforest: something special and set apart.

Criss-crossed by butterflies, flies and bees, it also held swarm after swarm of dancing midges, hanging in the air in a little cloud, performing a gavotte that was almost pedantic in its exactitude: every dancer in motion, but the cloud itself always motionless. What are they doing, these dancers? And why are they doing it? In John Steinbeck's novel *Cannery Row*, Hazel (named after an aunt in a moment of absent-mindedness by his overwrought mother), amiable, simple, almost Christ-like in his good nature, strong as a horse, wonders what a stink bug is doing when it raises its back-end into the air. Doc, the wise and flawed hero of the book, replies:

> "I don't know why. I looked them up recently they're very common animals and one of the commonest things they do is put their tails up in the air. And in all the books there isn't one mention of the fact that they put their tails up in the air or why."
>
> Hazel turned one of the stink bugs over with the toe of his wet tennis-shoe and the shining black beetle strove madly with floundering legs to get upright again.
>
> "Well, why do you think they do it?"
>
> "I think they're praying," said Doc.
>
> "What!" Hazel was shocked.
>
> "The remarkable thing," said Doc, "isn't that they put their tails up in the air — the really incredibly remarkable thing is that we find it remarkable. We can only use ourselves as yardsticks. If we did something as inexplicable and strange we'd probably be praying — so maybe they're praying."

Doc is a biologist, so you must make your own mind up as to how serious he (and Steinbeck) is being. In point of fact, the midges weren't praying. They were after sex. But perhaps that too involves — or even is — an act of prayer. You can decide for yourself how serious I am being here. But certainly, any walker through this vivid tunnel would be well advised to wear a face mask: not so much to protect himself as to protect the sexed-up midges from a sad little death in the eyes, nose and mouth of a human intruder. Jains, of course, wear a face-mask at times, and do so as a holy act: it is a crime for any Jain to destroy any living thing, even by accident. Jain monks will ceremonially sweep the ground before them, lest they tread on any small scrap of life and commit accidental slaughter. William Blake believed that everything that lives is holy. Jains believe that all forms of life are equal, and that the midge you inhale by carelessness is – like yourself – a soul on its long journey towards enlightenment.

The walk through the dog tunnel is for me in May a small but significant act of prayer. And perhaps, when my old friend's daughter took her picture of the six-spot burnet, she too was praying.

49

One image. One picture that says everything I want to say in this book, one picture that leaps into my mind when I think about wildlife, biodiversity, the tenaciousness of life, and its fragility. And when I try to seek it, I find it at once, and to my amazement, it's not Luangwa. Nor is it anything to do with Suffolk, nor with the rainforest. My mind leaps to the desert.

The desert has something special for some people: but I am not among them. All the same, it is a vision of the desert that has such power for me. It's Namibia, a place where I once spent a thrilling few days looking for the elusive desert rhinos. And though I was unlucky there – we passed some steaming fresh sign, but the beasts themselves, no doubt deliberately, eluded us (or lucky – some of the looking involved some adrenaline-fuelled creeping through the thick tunnels of tamarind trees that punctuate the vast wastes of cat-litter, a place where neither the rhinos nor the seekers of rhino get much warning of each other's presence) — I was utterly captivated by this trip all the same. And it was the oryx that did it: gemsbok, as the Afrikaners call them, with a good fishbone-clearing noise on the first consonant. These are dry-country antelopes: superb at coping with extreme conditions: no rich food resources, little if any drinking water. There are never very many of them together: a group of half-a-dozen is exceptional. Mostly you seem them alone.

And that is the picture I have with me, always: looking up from the vehicle at a ridge, for this desert undulates. There was nothing but the great expanse of the desert floor, stony rather than sandy, unrelieved by any vegetation, a place that to my eyes, to most human eyes, contained absolutely nothing whatsoever, not even a hint of green. And yet looking up, skylined, the washed-out blue behind it unbroken by a cloud — not even the traditional African offering of one the size of a woman's hand — an oryx: tall, almost white, twin tall horns rising from its head, almost straight, just faintly curved back. In profile, it seems sometimes that the animal has but a single horn. The face wears a black bandit-mask.

The oryx is one of the hippotragus antelopes, the horse-like antelopes that include sable and roan. They are credibly horse-shaped, but finer, less clumpy, more elevation in their non-walk paces. And those paces are all wonderfully horse-like: as they walk, trot, canter and gallop across the desert, it is as if you were watching a glorious exhibition of dressage.

A single white animal, looking like a horse, moving like a horse, with apparently a single horn on its head: is this an oryx, or the last unicorn? I have always been haunted by a cartoon of Charles Addams: the ark sailing away, the world flooded, but there, on the last patch of dry land, a place soon to be submerged by the rising waters, stands the last pair of unicorns, watching sadly as the ark sails away for ever. And many a real extinction has come about in the same way: not from malice, not from greed, but from the sheer absent-mindedness of the planet's most powerful animal.

But it is not just the extraneous imagery of the oryx that matters to me, wonderful though it is. It is the oryx itself: majestically and beautifully making a life where nothing else can. It speaks of the wild world's lust for survival: its wonderful ability to do so anywhere that humans will permit, and not just in minute and cryptic forms, but in glory and majesty.

I love the teeming places, the megafauna of Luangwa, the hidden plenty of the rainforest, the crowds of birds that gather on English estuaries in winter. But this scarcity has a beauty of its own. In Luangwa, you see a big mammal, or fine bird, every few minutes: here, you can drive for an hour, for more, without seeing a sign of life. But then, sometimes a single oryx solving life's problems with a supreme pale grace.

What's the best animal you have ever seen? I get asked that sometimes. And perhaps that's the answer. Unicorn.

50

If we are all wild, we are also all musical. It is very unusual to find a person who is totally music-deaf: a life in which music plays no part whatsoever. There are all kinds of cultural barriers that people create for themselves, shutting themselves off from this kind of music or that kind of music: but just about everybody responds to music in some form or another.

But there is a question of depth. Me, I love music, but I am not at all musical. I can't tell you about key changes, I can't tell you the musical structure of every piece I listen to. I lack the ear, I lack the education. That doesn't stop music from being hugely important to me: and it hasn't stopped me being unbearably moved by the great pieces: pieces that hold an elusive and eternal truth, a truth I might almost grasp and understand if only I was good enough. That mystery is itself a part of my enjoyment: I know that music holds more truths than I am capable of reaching, still less understanding.

I wish my ear were truer; I wish I had learned more; I wish I could sing in tune and read music properly and then I could join a choir, and sing the B Minor Mass. Alas, that is beyond me. But I love my music very much, on the level I am capable of reaching. Musicality is a gift, and if I have it at all, it is in a very tiny extent. For musicians, music is a different thing altogether: musicians hear it differently, understand it differently. But that doesn't put it out of my reach. Far from it.

I suspect that wildness is a bit like that. There is a sense in which wildness is a gift. (Religious people say that faith is also a gift.) We all have wildness: but we certainly don't all have it equally. Partly this is because of the cultural barriers we put up: I don't want to look at birds too hard, because I don't want to be a thought of as a train-spotter. Perhaps more importantly, an awful lot of males inhibit their own response to wildlife because they fear that they might be thought of as soppy. Many men believe that the enjoyment of wild things is somehow girly, unmanly, undignified. When I wrote a column on butterflies for the *Times,* I received letters congraulating me on my courage – I had come out as a lepidopteraphile.

Cultural barriers. Many people believe that the entire world of what they call "classical music" is inaccessible: not for them, unnecessary, outmoded, unfashionable. Their loss: just as those who cut themselves off from wildness are losers.

But also there is the question of gift. Some people simply have a better understanding of what they see and hear, not because of education, but because they are more gifted at the business of watching. It is like musicality, and I have noticed it many times in wild places with people who are simply better at what they are doing than I am. Not because of book-learning, but because they have a gift for it, a feel for it, that is beyond me. This is the diary of a nobody: the wild places are full of people that are better at wildness than I am. And do you know what? That doesn't affect my pleasure in wild things the slightest bit, any more than I like music less because John Eliot Gardener understands Bach better than I do.

51

Cindy and I once visited a Jain temple when I was travelling in India. There was a single monk in charge, a delightful old boy who showed us round and talked a little to us. His English wasn't bad, certainly better than my Tamil. He was an unselfconsciously beatific man: five minutes in his company and I felt I would never do another impure deed for the rest of my life. The temple contained the gnawed remains of food offerings that had been set out by the faithful earlier in the day. We happened to have a couple of coconuts with us, planned for refreshment further on down the road, but it seemed appropriate to offer them to the monk. He accepted them with great pleasure, and took them about twenty yards away, to the sacred heart of the temple. Then, with brisk, efficient strokes of a machete – strangely violent actions for so peaceful a man –

he opened them. Even as he turned his back to return to us, there was a sort of heaving of the ground: and a grey wave engulfed our offerings in holy delight. For several minutes the monk watched all this, entranced. Then he threw his hands up in pleasure and gave us a huge, gap-toothed smile, also of holy delight. "So many rats!"

52

At Badminton every year the world fills with swallows. The lake in front of the great house — the event takes place on the Duke of Beaufort's estate — is the centre point of the big day, the Saturday when the horses set out over a course of fiendish and terrifying jumps; and as someone who has competed in eventing and cross-country, admittedly at the lowest possible level, I know all about the terror. Crowds gather around the lake to see the action; photographers gather vulture-like to record the crashes and splashes — and all the time the swallows skim the lake, feathered bellies an inch or less above the surface, hawking for tiny scraps of life: constantly in motion, yet never going away, always there, for the lake is never empty, constantly swooped over. A horse splashes in, jumps out, the crowd applauds, the swallows skim. A horse hesitates, stops, a rider is jolted from the saddle, slips and falls, the crowd gasps, the cameras go into a feeding frenzy, but the feeding swallows never cease their skimming, not for a 500th of a second. It is a vision of spring: not one swallow, but a summer made. The summer is yet to come, this is still a time of promise, but for sure, summer's fulfilment is almost upon us. Me, I watched the horses, talked horse-talk with friends and colleagues, wrote my stuff for the *Times* and admired the swallows: savouring both the now and the promise of the summer ahead.

53

My May fortnight off began, and my father came to join me for the first few days of it, for a spot of walking and birding and eating and drinking and talking. We went from Blythborough to Eastbridge: sometimes a good day in the wild acquires a theme. This was the day for the Ministry of Silly Flights. Those with long memories will recall Monty Python and the Ministry of Silly Walks, with John Cleese doing the silliest walk ever performed by a human: well, this was May in England, and every bird that can do a silly flight was out there doing it: outCleesing Cleese.

First the curlew: a big, serious-minded wader with a huge decurved bill. You generally see them at vast distances across the mud of an estuary in winter, or a group of them in a field in autumn, resting up soberly, all facing the same way, backs into the wind. They are dignified birds for the most part: but in May, they get silly. We saw a curlew run through his full repertoire of daftness: a flight low to the ground, a sudden rise, very steep, not with the usual regular, deep wing-beats but with a delicate look-at-me flickering of the wing-tips: then into a finicky hover, with wild whistling as he parachuted downwards: at the last, moving into an extraordinarily powerful bubbling song. All this is about territory, sex and the propagation of his immortal genes, but it's not the science of the thing that gets to you: it's the gut-wrenching strangeness of it, the way the bird's excitement becomes the observer's excitement.

I don't think I feel this is because I am a birder, because I am saying: ah yes, territorial display flight of curlew *Numenius arquata*, how frightfully intriguing, must make an ethological note. It's more that the bird's heart is full and the observer responds to something out of the ordinary in an utterly spontaneous way: finding something thrilling in the thrilled nature of the bird.

The meadow pipit can strike a claim for being the dullest bird in Britain: a background bird, a little brown job or LBJ. But in May, even meadow pipits are exciting birds, as I had seen back at the very beginning of spring on Southwold marsh. Time and again as we walked, we saw a meadow pipit filling his heart and his lungs, climbing high and swift and then parachuting down, piping at the top of his voice. Spring turns the drabbest bird of Britain into a polychrome explosion.

More silly flights: the whitethroat, singing his scratchy song from cover as usual: but every so often, the spirit moved him to take the song a level higher: and so he left the shelter of the brambles and rose vertically, singing his scratchy song as if it were the Sanctus from the B Minor Mass.

Lapwings are special favourites: no longer the chilled, preoccupied feeders from the largesse of Aubrey's plough, but the ecstatic oboeing angels of May. This was the full version of the sketches I had seen a couple of months back on the chilled marshes at Southwold: the full wig-wag flight, the full butterfly flight, the hypnotic strobing of the big wide wings.

And skylarks, to make a fifth silly flight, to complete the day's irrefragable theme. A skylark, whose job from April to May is to glorify the commonplace: to proclaim the eternal mystery of the fact that ordinary is also wonderful: that every aspect of life (and for that matter, death) is enthralling: that everything that lives is silly. A dot in the sky, moved almost beyond enduring by the forces of the spring and the beauty of his own song.

54
Wildness was discovered at the beginning of the nineteenth century. Or rather rediscovered. It was the Romantics that did it. Of course, nature has always been celebrated in different ways across the centuries: you can see that from cave paintings, you can read it in the earliest poems that survive. But the Romantics were revolutionaries: and nature – wildness – was at the heart of their revolutionary fervour.

Before the Romantics, nature was mostly celebrated as a well-tended, well-organised garden, or as an Arcadian idyll, full of nymphs and shepherds frisking about in unsuitable clothing, without worrying too much about getting thorns in their bottoms. But for the Romantics, wild nature – nature without the hand of man – was what mattered. The wild world was the place to find beauty: but more than that, it was the place to find truth. For the Romantics, wildness had a religious importance: in the wild world, you could find the truths that established religions had mislaid.

Before the Romantics, the terms "human" and "natural" were seen as absolute and obvious opposites. In Shakespeare, a "natural" is a fool. But the Romantics believed that you were more truly human when more truly natural: that involvement in the natural world conferred a profound moral understanding of the world, something that could not be found by other means. The natural world had a moral rightness that could not be found in civilised life. After all, the natural world knew nothing of the injustices of inherited advantage and institutionalised oppression. This was a profoundly subversive notion. In nature, a person with the right eyes could see revolution. And this apprehension brought about a revolution in the way we see and understand the world.

102

Everything that lives is holy, said Blake, the great vision-ary who summed up the Romantic movement before it even began. The most famous outburst of joy at the wild world is from William Wordsworth, who (all at once) saw a crowd, a host of golden daffodils. The Lake District was once an inhospitable wilderness. It was seen as ugly, fear-some, barren and terrible: but Wordsworth told us that it was the place where you could taste the bliss of solitude. Once, a place without humans was by definition bad: now, Wordsworth said, such a place was by definition good. The principle of the Jain stories was turned on its head.

One of the reasons why the wild world began to attract so many admirers was because the wild world was in the process of being destroyed. Well, in truth, destruction has been going on since humans first walked upright: but the point here is that once industrialisation began, the pace of destruction increased exponentially. The world was no longer the same. It was more efficient, safer, more prosper-ous, and much uglier: and so naturally, people turned their gaze from the factories and lifted their eyes to the hills. The Romantic movement was history's first realisation of the Joni Principle: that you don't know what you've got till it's gone.

And also, with a more advanced society, the wild places became more accessible. As communications got better, they became a good deal safer. You could reach the wild world, or at least the semi-wild world by train. It was a perfect contradiction: the industrialised world made the wild world more vivid, accessible and desirable, even as it accelerated the processes of the wild world's destruction.

One thing has not changed. Loving the wild is still an act of revolution. In some ways, the Romantics are bang up to date. Certainly they affect our thinking to this day: the countries in which the Romantic movement was strongest are those that lead the way when it comes to natural history and conservation: that is to say, Britain, Germany and the United States.

Romantic is a good word spoiled. It has come to mean silly, soppy, cut off from reality. The Romantics themselves sought a deeper reality than that offered by a class-bound, tradition-bound, city-bound society. They saw that looking beyond humanity makes you richer and more profoundly human. Certainly, I felt all that and more on the day when my father and I witnessed the five silly flights.

55

A touch of nightingale on the same walk. Singing from cover: nightingales don't need to do a silly flight. Their singing is too good to require visual ornamentation. Though in point of fact, this was not a great bit of singing, as nightingale singing goes. Rather, it was a sort of throat-clearing from a bird not really ready to let rip. Still, it is always good to hear nightingale. And I was reminded of Keats. Keats was another Romantic, and he wrote "Ode to a Nightingale". These days, scientists suggest that the male nightingale's song carries such force that it affects the female's brain. Physically affects it, I mean, like a drug, making her ready to mate. It is as if the song acted on her like a love-philtre, rendering her lovelorn, full of desire, wishing to give herself to the brain-altering singer. It sounds to me like the same sort of thing that affects a male human when he catches sight of an uncommonly attractive woman: one who makes his heart stir, or for that matter, sing. It is a physical stirring, certainly, but it is not the same as a literal sexual arousal. It is more like a thump in the gut, that moment when your stomach goes into freefall on some enchanted evening, when you see her laughing across a crowded room.

And Keats wrote that as he listened to the nightingale, he felt the same thing himself. He wrote that the nightingale's song affected him physically, as if it were a drug: that his heart ached, and a drowsy numbness pained his senses, as though of hemlock he had drunk.

The natural world reaches out and touches us: not just as a series of pleasant thoughts, but as a powerful, almost violent physical sensation of personal involvement. That is because we are part of the natural world: human and natural are not opposites at all. Despite our civilised natures, we too are affected – powerfully and physically – by the wild world. The Romantics told us this: and we retain that truth to this day. Perhaps we have it more than ever, thanks to the Joni Principle. Perhaps this is a generation uniquely rich in its ability to respond to the wild world. The pace of destruction has made the wild world more vivid than ever it was before. We are a uniquely privileged generation: we have destroyed so much of the wild world that we are able to love it more than any other generation in history.

56

A hobby is the exact opposite of going to confession or buying petrol. A hobby falcon, I mean, not a hobby-pastime. So Cindy tells me, anyway. Her view is that when you wonder if you should go to confession, it invariably means that you should go to confession. The same rule works with filling up the car. That is to say that *if* only and always means *is*.

But with a hobby, or for that matter a tern, *if* invariably means *isn't*. When you see a falcon, and your heart jumps and you think it just might be a hobby, it is always a kestrel. Nothing *wrong* with kestrels, nothing wrong with any dapple-dawn-drawn falcon in his rising. But a kestrel isn't special in quite the same way as a hobby. Hobbies only come to Britain in the summer, and so they always have a touch of exoticism. They are subtly and daringly different in shape and behaviour. And you don't see them very often. They have that scarcity value that always thrills.

In the same way, if you think it just might be a tern, it is always a black-headed gull. Black-headed gulls are, like the poor, always with us, with or without their black heads (they only wear them in summer). Terns only come here in summer and do so reliably in four or five species: they are sleeker, suaver, infinitely more dashing than a poor old jack-of-all-trade blackhead. And if you think you've seen a tern, you never have.

Now I am normally shy about making strong claims for identification with other birdwatchers, especially those of the serious telescope-carrying kind. This is for a good reason: I am pretty poor at identification. I lack the skills the good identifiers have: I don't have the close painterly eye for detail, the card-index mind for diagnostic principle, the intuitive flair for jizz, the exhaustive vocabulary of sound. I tend to say "after you" when any non-obvious bird comes into view.

So there were my father and I, on the top of Dunwich cliff, involved in the much-about conversation with a pair of passing 'scope-bearers, when I interrupted the exchange with a hoarse cry of utter certainty: "Hobby!"

If you *know* it's a hobby, it always is a hobby. So it was, too: turning into the wind on slim, tapered wings and riding down a rushing upslope of air into the marshes to have a dart at the sand martins. Seen for maybe a second. Got the bins on it, too: the impossible length of the wings, the general impression – that's what jizz means – of being a giant swift. And it was gone: leaving in the air a memory, an after-image: a faint fizz of danger.

57

That is what a silly flight is all about. Danger, I mean. When a whitethroat rises in ecstasy from his place in the hedge and flutters above, scratchily singing his scratchy heart out, he is visibly courting danger. He is saying to every sparrowhawk, or for that matter, hobby: here I am. Come and have a go, if you think you're a billion times told lovelier, more dangerous, O my chevalier!

It is the highest form of excitement: risking everything, risking death itself for a song. But for a whitethroat, a song is so much more than a song: it is also sex, a hen, a nest, a family, the survival of his immortal genes. This wild, high-risk behaviour spells out the message: I am a really great whitethroat cock. My song is loud, vivid, scratchy and certain: and I am so confident in my powers that I risk the wrath and the hunger of all the sparrowhawks in Suffolk and still I don't get caught. A cock like me will give you a nest full of hot chicks: and I will be able to guard this fabulous food-rich territory from every other whitethroat for miles around. I am the one: look on my song flight and surrender.

A lot of humans do dangerous things: not because they have to, but because they want to. Sometimes they will pay huge sums of money for the privilege. This is not because these people suffer from a death wish. Nothing could be further from the truth. The thrill of danger makes you intensely, vividly alive. The motivation for seeking danger – actively seeking it, rather than accepting it as a routine hazard of life – comes from the same reason as the whitethroat's silly flight. A love of life: and profound wish that life should continue in its glorious and thrilling way. The whitethroat and the skydiver are both suffering from a life wish.

58

The day after the walk of the silly flights, my father and I walked to Eastbridge again, but from the opposite direction: this time from Snape. The first part of the walk was deep, fecund, green and still: inland Suffolk, as opposed to the windblown reed-beds and the soft coast. And it was here we heard a bird that every reader of this book will be able to recognise by call alone.

Cuckoo!

Another of those birds to worry about. This is no longer a bird I hear every year. These days, it is almost worth writing to the *Times* when you hear a cuckoo at all. I hadn't heard one the previous year: but on this still, warm, soft morning, we had the rare treat of a virtuoso performance from cuckookind. It was the more joyful because you can no longer take cuckoos for granted.

You can't take anything for granted.

How many? Definitely one: maybe as many as four. Cuckoos move fast, and their voice carries far. That is the point of being a cuckoo: the secret of their being is in those two loud, clear syllables: the nearest that a British bird gets to a human voice.

The voice matters because cuckoos are thinly spread birds, even in the best of cuckoo years, even in the rosiest of long-past cuckoo-springs. They don't have a domestic life: they don't hold territories for feeding and nesting. Instead, they have the wild, country-wide summons, male calling to female in a voice that stands somehow for all males of all species, as the apparent willingness to keep him waiting stands for all females.

Then, if he is lucky, loud and skilful, the one brief and gorgeous consummation – a one-day stand – after which, the male cuckoo moves on, to try his luck again, while the female feels an egg grow within her before she deposits it on some luckless host.

The brief song is the way cuckoo civilisation works: it is the heart and soul of cuckoo life.

59

"Me?" said my father, over pints at the Dolphin. "Cetti? If-you-don't-like-it-fuck-off!" Quoting my own much-quoted (at least by me) mnemonic for the song of the Cetti's warbler. We'd been hearing Cettis again. Not a bird you encountered very often, a decade ago: now very much a bird of the soft Suffolk edge. Loud. Explosive. From an exoticism to an annual fact of spring. Actually, they stay around all year: but they are not birds for the seeing. In spring – and for that matter, off and on throughout the year, for they are birds that love to announce their presence in strident tones from deep cover – you can hear them, they insist above all on being heard, and on making it abundantly clear that they are part of the way the modern world works.

But they were not much seen here before 1970. It was only after that date that they began to spread, and over the past decade, they have become full-on Suffolk, full-on British birds. The reasons for this are not fully explained, and are likely to be complex. But it will come down to climate change in the end. The birds can now survive a British winter, because a British winter now asks fewer unanswerable questions. Father Francesco Cetti was an eighteenth-century Jesuit priest and zoologist, by the way; there is no record of any bird named for his manservant or his mistress.

I didn't count the number of little egrets we saw over two days of walking. That's because there were so many. There used to be none. Before 1957 there were only 23 records of little egret in Britain; before 1990 there were still fewer than 600. These days there are up to 1,000 little egrets on the British and Irish coast at any one time. You can see the odd one from the train at Manningtree on the way from Ipswich to London. You can see them in big numbers on the train between Exeter and Plymouth.

Lovely birds: dainty, a beautiful clean white, a striker of statuesque poses, a knitting-needle bill, and, on the end of long black legs, yellow feet, which they are said to use as a lure to attract fish to their murderous beaks. They first bred in this country in 1996: now they are established and enthusiastic breeders. Again, the full reason for their success is not fully explained: again, it is, beyond question, something to do with global warming.

Global warming giveth and global warming taketh away. The cuckoos and the willow warblers are struggling under the stresses of climate change: the little egrets and the Cetti's warblers are thriving. Does that make everything all right, then?

Well, I'll tell you the first thing that the egrets and the Cetti's show: and that is the extreme resilience and opportunism of life. If conditions change, there will always be creatures that find that the new way suits them down to the ground. If the world floods tomorrow, most of us will drown, but it will provide a wonderful opportunity for ducks and turtles. That is probably not, on the whole, a sound argument for flooding the earth overnight. The same argument holds for a nuclear winter.

But it is this miraculous ability of life to find a way of living that gets to you: that brings each of us, again and again, in reach of the archetypal Attenborough moment: on a mountain top, in a desert, in a balloon above the earth, in a submarine in the benthic depths of the ocean, the great David Attenborough has brought us the breathless and undying message: "And... even here... there is *life*."

Opportunities present themselves and a creature leaps in to take it: and as the world changes, and as the cuckoos' call is less and less often heard, and likewise the lovely lisping song of the willow warbler, so we have the gorgeous sight of the little egret picking its fastidious way across the marshes, and from the marsh's edge, the glorious sound of the Cetti, loudly telling us to fuck off. It is indeed wonderful, inspiring, cheering. But I ask again: does that make everything all right, then?

60

In Dublin, I went looking for James Joyce. I walked everywhere that his characters walked in *Ulysses*. I walked down Eccles Street, where Mr Bloom and Molly lived; I visited the Martello tower where Stephen lived with Buck Mulligan; I bought a cake of lemon soap at Sweny's the chemist, as Bloom did (they have a large container of lemon soap on the counter to please the whims of such foolish pilgrims), I drank a pint of Guinness at the Ormond Hotel, where Bloom listened to the singing; and like Stephen I walked along Sandymount strand thinking great thoughts. And it was all very fine.

But when I visit wild places, I do not look for people. I look for something greater: I look for life, I look for plenty, I look for scarcity, I look for common, I look for rare; I look for everything but people. But there was one exception. Just one.

I was in Borneo, and I was invited to "look at some caves". I went there from a cheerful curiosity: a tramp through rainforest, trousers tucked into socks to stop the unpleasantness – a thing I have never learned to take in my stride – of leeches crawling up your inside leg. And there, a massive limestone cave, like some artist's Gothic fantasy of

111

what a cave should be: high-arched opening, strange shapes of outcrops and pillars of rocks: the promise of darkness and silence and a coolness within.

Not much silence, though, once the cave was entered. A high, incessant, nerve-jangling twittering. And as my eyes got used to the twilight of the cave near the entrance, I could see that the lofty vaulted roof was alive: shimmering, undulating, twitching with life. Near the door, birds; further in, bats. All twittering in agitation at the invasion.

And the stench. Goodness, the stench. Nothing to compare with the stench, not even a seabird colony, not even the week-dead hippo on which hyenas still feasted. That ammoniac stench, like a million cans of Ajax, tickling the back of the nose, the back of the throat, for you could taste the stuff almost as well as you could smell it. Hundreds of thousands of birds; millions, millions of bats. And life-changing amounts of shit.

The caves have been home for generations of these creatures, from one millennium to the next: and I was standing on the accreted shit of one of the stablest environments on earth. And with sudden understanding, I dropped to the floor, squatting on my heels, for that floor, too, was shifting and crawling with life: huge cave cockroaches.

And I thought not only of the wonder of life: but of the wonder of the man who had, more than any other, taught me how to love it. I recalled my bad impersonation – a bad impersonation because the real thing is inimitable – of a television programme based on the ecology of this very cave in Borneo, or another one so similar (for there are many) as to be beside the point. "I – am now standing –", (breath, wave of the arms, expression that hints of an immeasurable delight just behind the eyes) "on the biggest heap of shit in the entirety of the known world." (Breath, pause, stop, double handful of imaginary turds.) "And – it is teeming with life."

112

You will presumably get the impersonation even without having me there to perform it. I remember another impersonation of the same man: in Bali, climbing a volcano (a gentle, if rather huffy stroll rather than anything actually difficult) and above the treeline, started a pair of large birds that whirred unidentifiably away. I was with my wife and two Swedish couples we had bumped into. And I, for some reason at the front, turned, and spoke: "And – even here – there is life." The Swedes laughed gratifyingly: "*Ja, ja*, very good, David Attenborough."

Attenborough has shown me, Attenborough has enthused me, Attenborough has inspired me. I caught *Life on Earth* when I lived in Asia, when I was in the process of refinding the faith, relearning how to be wild. I, and a good few others, went to visit a friend in possession of a television with religious fervour every Sunday night for thirteen weeks: and had our eyes and our minds opened.

But that vignette, that one-off programme about the cave, the echo-locating cave swiftlets, the bats, the cockroaches, the snakes that eat the cockroaches, this simple but instructive ecology of the cave, the extraordinary ability of life to find a way of living, and above all, Attenborough's unfaked delight in this mountain of shit: this was *echt* Attenborough.

We all have wildness in us: but sometimes we need to be told, sometimes we need to be shown, that it is all right to express it. Attenborough did it for me: and I, and millions of other humans are in his debt. And perhaps also, billions of non-humans as well: for what Attenborough teaches us to love, we also want to save. But first comes the love: and that's Attenborough's business. So there I was in Borneo, standing on the biggest heap of shit in the entirety of the known world – and, even there, there was love.

61

How does a whitethroat feel when he is about to make his song flight? When he is about to leave the sanctuary of the hedge and to fly above it, singing look-at-me-look-at-me to the Suffolk sparrowhawks? I have a pretty good idea of how he feels, because I have often felt that way myself.

Now it will be noted that this is not a scientific question. Or even a scientific speculation. With any scientific question, the possibility of verification must be there: if not now, then at least at some future date, either by direct proof – as in the law of gravity – or in overwhelming and incontrovertible evidence, as in the theory of evolution by means of natural selection. But no one will ever *know* – in the scientific sense of knowing – how a whitethroat feels.

For that matter, I will never know how you feel: and science will not be able to tell me either. However, there are still plenty of circumstances in which I could make a jolly good guess. If you fell over on Liverpool Street Station (on your way to Suffolk to check out the marsh harriers, perhaps), you would probably feel shocked, upset, embarrassed, in pain. You would probably appreciate it if I helped you gather your scattered belongings and asked if you were all right; you would probably prefer that no exaggerated further solicitousness was offered.

I could make a guess at how you felt if you met someone you loved and hadn't seen for a long time at the same station, or if you hadn't eaten all day and bought a Cornish pasty at that place by Platform 10. I could make a guess at how you felt if your train was cancelled. I could make a guess at how you felt if you bumped into an old friend just after the cancellation was announced, and filled the time by having a drink at the Terminus Bar and talking about old times. And my guesses would be pretty good ones, in a

114

rough-and-ready way: for all that, I couldn't *prove* that you felt ecstatic, deeply relieved, furious, frightfully jolly.

I know how I would feel in certain circumstances: therefore, I can make a reasonable assumption that you will have not dissimilar feelings in the same circumstances. Humans can empathise with each other: and thus, in a rough-and-ready way, we know how other people feel. This is the basis on which society works: by assuming that people feel roughly the same way as we do about certain basic matters of life. It is but a small step to extend this empathy to other creatures.

I don't know in any scientifically provable way how my dog feels when I see her after a few weeks away. But I can guess, from her tail-wagging, hand-licking, whimpering, bum-down scuttling behaviour, that she is pretty happy. I don't know precisely how she feels when she thinks she is going for a walk, but I'd guess that she is cheerful, mildly excited and just a touch anxious, in case it's a false alarm and I'm only going up the drive to collect the post. These are not hard guesses: I'd be a fool to say my assumptions about my dog's feelings were entirely imaginary and nothing at all to do with the way the dog actually lives her life.

Animals are not clocks: soft machines that merely respond to stimuli, as Descartes insisted. (The English philosopher John Cottingham commented: "To believe that a dog with a broken paw is not really in pain when it whimpers is a quite extraordinary achievement, even for a philosopher.") Being an animal myself, I am entitled to have some kind of understanding of how a whitethroat feels when he is about to set off on a song flight. My guess is that he feels as if he were suffering from rather bad peritonitis. He is full of funk, and this is made worse by the fact that he knows, even though half of him is saying "don't do it", that he damn well *is* going to do it.

I can make this guess, because it is exactly how I felt

myself when about to ride a horse in cross-country events: a wild gallop over alarming obstacles, in which a fall would be extremely, perhaps even terminally unpleasant. I remember those times with great vividness: I would be saying all kinds of stupid things to myself: honestly, this is not funk, this is sickness, I'll have to tell the starter, I'll have to withdraw because I don't feel good and besides, it would be irresponsible to carry on, and besides, it wouldn't be fair to the horse. All the time knowing I was damn well going to do it.

This seeking of danger is a natural urge for the whitethroat. That doesn't make him an automaton. I have felt several natural urges in my time: and on many occasions, the responding to them was distinctly pleasant. Some of the greatest experiences of my life – perhaps all of them – have been something to do with natural urges. The greatest books ever written tend to be about the natural urges – love, for example, and hate. War, for example, and peace.

Argue it how you like. You can say that our selfish genes get their host body to respond to natural urges by rewarding it with good feelings. Perhaps that's so: I have had all kinds of good feelings from natural urges: and I don't suppose that the whitethroat is any different. Why would he fly his courageous and silly flight, if it wasn't something that he felt good about?

And danger is something we are drawn towards. Oh yes it is. Danger is something that completes our lives. Different people, to differing extents, at different times of their lives, seek danger: or at least accept danger and find their lives richer for the experience of danger. The whitethroat is, of course, seeking a mate and territory and to put the wind up his rivals: so his reward for seeking danger is pretty direct. But humans also seek danger. To seek risk, adventure, excitement is part of the human condition. Why else do we have a National Lottery and a multi-billion-quid betting industry? We bet the odd quid: the whitethroat bets all, and is, no doubt, the more greatly fulfilled. At least, he is when the sparrowhawk doesn't get him.

62

The cow parsley was waist-high: the stuff seems to come from nowhere, almost as a fungus does, growing three feet with wild ambition more or less overnight. And the butterflies: the sunken path was alive with them. There seemed to be almost as many of them as there were midges, more, at every step, more: practically all of them small whites, one or two large whites among them, every one of them fluttering about with that fussy, preoccupied air that butterflies go in for, full of the great matters of their own lives, delicately insistent that their own affairs are of overwhelming importance. And who could say they are wrong?

In its fecund, rainforest air of plenty, the dog tunnel in May reminds me of Darwin's entangled bank. At the conclusion of *The Origin of Species*, Darwin gets all lyrical. His vision of life, he says, is not only right, but beautiful. "It is interesting to contemplate an entangled bank, clothed with many plants of many kinds, with birds singing on the bushes, with various insects flitting about, and with worms crawling through the damp earth, and to reflect that these elaborately constructed forms, so different from each other, and dependent on each other in so complex a manner, have all been produced by laws acting around us."

This was a passage of glorious defiance. The printing of *The Origin* shocked the world. (For that matter, many people still refuse to take it on to this day, and many more shy away from the essential implications of its truths.) Many of *The Origin*'s first readers rejected outright what they saw as an unacceptably bleak view of life: they could not be

117

persuaded to believe that such a vast and momentous thing as life could have happened by a series of accidents, rather than by means of divine inspiration.

Darwin anticipated this. After all, he had sat on his theory for more than twenty years without publishing it, because he dreaded the furore that he knew would greet the work, mostly because it would upset his wife so much. But he was not a man to apologise for truth, still less back down. Truth was not to be apologised for, but celebrated: and so, piling defiance on defiance, he concluded his book with the following glorious sentence: "There is grandeur in this view of life, with its several powers, having been originally breathed into a few forms or into one; and that, whilst this planet has gone cycling on according to the fixed law of gravity, from so simple a beginning endless forms most beautiful and most wonderful have been, and are being, evolved."

Endless forms. Still needing my Jain gauze mask to protect them all from the crushing force of my breath. The faint danger from the buzzling. The song of blackcap, even though it may be a garden warbler. The dog's hopeless pursuit of the bunnies. Grandeur.

63

The *Origin* is the best book of popular science ever written, as well as by a million light years the most important. Darwin deliberately wrote it for the intelligent lay-reader, rather than the scientific community, understanding that his amazing, civilisation-changing ideas were the property of all of us, rather than a specialised few. He promised a more forbidding work for the scientific community on the same subject, but he never wrote it.

The Origin is a great read to this day: telling the tale of a man's remorseless, lifelong search to demonstrate the truth of a single great insight. Many young are produced, not all survive. Why do some survive, and breed and become ancestors, while others die without issue? Answer: because they are better suited to the conditions presented to them. These breeders, these victors, will then pass on these advantages to their progeny. And the better suited of their progeny's progeny likewise find greater breeding success. And on and on.

There is a huge, a gourmandising appetite for good popular science: for books that accept that the reader is both intelligent and quite possibly untrained in science: for books that tell us that scientific truths are of interest and concern to all humanity, not just a specialised portion of it. This is Darwin's principle: and in recent decades it has been followed by some writers, some scientists of extraordinary brilliance. Those seeking to understand – rather than merely to live – wildness have been extraordinarily privileged to have so many great writers putting out so many mind-intoxicating, head-spinning ideas.

Stephen Jay Gould, Richard Dawkins, Edward O. Wilson, Matt Ridley, Jared Diamond; plenty of others, all writing on evolutionary biology. Stephen Hawking, not a biologist, had outrageous success with his book on time. All these great writers: all these great ideas: all these people reading them, seeking out answers.

Answers to what? A glimpse at the titles is significant. *A Short History of Time*, *Wonderful Life*, *Life's Grandeur*, *The Blind Watchmaker*, *River out of Eden*, *Bully for Brontosaurus*, *Rock of Ages*, *The Origins of Virtue*, *Why is Sex Fun?*, *Nature via Nurture*, *In Search of Nature*, *The Diversity of Life*, *The Future of Life*.

These are books that ask and seek to answer the seriously big questions. The God Questions. Questions about the meaning of life. What are we here for? What is life all about? How did life begin? Why are elephants big? Why are mice small? Why is life good? Why is life bad? Why are there so many creatures in the world? Why do so many of them go extinct? Why do we live? Why do we die? What is the world coming to?

These are legitimate concerns, and we can seek the answers in a thousand ways, and a thousand books. I can find some of the answers to the great questions in books all around the room I am writing in: in *The Jungle Books* and in James Joyce, in the *Narnia* books and in Marcel Proust, in Darwin and in Shakespeare, in Gerard Manley Hopkins and William Blake, in Gould, Dawkins and Wilson.

Not one of these great works is a guru book. I think that is a very important point. None of these is a book that contains all the answers. Rather, they are books that between them contain all the questions. A good few of them, anyway. They give you deeper and better questions to ask: questions that come from a greater awareness, a more profound understanding.

Science cannot replace religion, still less God. That is not the job of science, despite all the fuss made by Dawkins, the proselytising atheist. But science can at least address the God Questions: and give us a deeper and more vivid understanding of life. And as I read about life, and as I walk along my own entangled bank, I can feel very deeply that there is grandeur in the deep, puzzling, buzzling, complex nature of life that these great books have shown me.

64

I have been to the Luangwa Valley many times, so naturally I have a good few friends out there. Some of them started life in England, came out to the bush and failed to leave. Love had undone them. By no means all of them are great experts on wildlife. In fact, some of them have said that I come out to the Valley after a year's absence and start teaching them the call of red-faced cisticola, when they couldn't tell any cisticola from an orange-breasted bush-shrike. True, this is mainly a tease, a friendly gibe at my own sometimes-too-insistent delight in the whole business of birdsong, but there is something behind it. The truth of the matter is that the naming of names is not what being wild is all about.

And these friends will sometimes ask me, when we sit up after dinner and the gulping of Mosi turns to the sipping of J&B, how much I miss the bush when I am away. It is clear that I love it out there: feel happy, confident, fulfilled, excited. Surely everything must be stale Mosi when I am back in safe old Suffolk. As if the Tabasco has been removed from the bloody Mary: and perhaps the bloody vodka as well. No lions to disturb the morning walk; no hippo, no leopard, no elephant, no buffalo, no crocodile. A safe country: tamed to within an inch of its life. A place with too many people: a place where the wild things are not.

And so, when my father had returned home, I got on with my wild fortnight in Suffolk in May. Into a time of danger. Not great danger, certainly: but more than a whiff. A good shake, a decent slug. I gave the time up to my horses. In particular, to my young horse, Dani. Feeling, every time I tacked her up, a faint remembered stab of peritonitis. I took deep, calming breaths: keep the respiration slow, ditto the heart rate. She'll know. Slow, calm, easy, confident movements.

Because she was but five, she was unpredictable, volatile, fit and fast. A horse is a prey animal, a flight animal: if you induce a moment of doubt, it will relapse at once into its atavistic state: and jump, twist, turn, run, casting the rider aside. I have wilderness all around me when I am at home: and most of it is in the hearts and minds of my horses.

Most of the animals that humans have domesticated are

selectively bred for their tameness, their easiness, their bulk, their biddability. But when we breed horses, we deliberately keep in a touch of wildness: a touch and more. (Incidentally, Darwin investigated the way we breed our domestic animals as a crucial first stage in understanding the way a creature can vary so dramatically from its ancestors. Who would think that a terrier and great Dane, a collie and my Labrador, were all the same species? If humans can breed selectively for such things over a few generations, then what can non-human forces do over millions of years? Everything, is the answer, everything, and still more.)

But we have selectively bred our horses for that touch of wildness. We want an animal that will gallop, jump, dance: and as I sought to tame my young horse, I sought not to lose the wildness but to canalise; to explore the extraordinary affinity between our two species, and to establish that intoxicating co-operation, that sense of two wills working as one.

And it frightened me, just a little. The previous summer, I had taken a spill from the horse, suffered compression of the lower spine and whiplash at the top. Small deal, as these things go: a good fall. But I had good reason to be careful, and I was. And as we carried on through May, she came to me, and we rode out on my easy local ride — around the block — and she expanded and relaxed and strode out and went forward: and it was wonderful, and my wild heart was full.

And that danger. That little touch of danger. That touch of Tabasco, that single — or was it a double? — measure of vodka, those little things that make life so much more interesting. Not seeking pain: just seeking that spice, that velvet kick. That feeling of being alive: untaming myself: rewilding.

Being wild is not all about identification skills. It's about reaching beyond the limits of the human condition: the limits we impose on ourselves by our strange notion of what being human is really all about. Other species: we need other species: to savour our affinity for them, and to savour the wildness they give us: and above all, to find some greater understanding of the fact that we can, if we choose, live our lives among creatures that are not human: rather, they are a billion times told lovelier, more dangerous.

65 If you took Occam's razor to a definition of wildness, you would probably end up with something like "the human need for non-human life". The fact is that there are not two worlds – human and non-human – but one world, and we humans are in it, along with oak trees and lesser whitethroats and horses and nematode worms.

All the same, it is becoming more and more easy to set wildness aside. It is not too hard to find yourself in a routine in which non-human encounters are reduced to a minimum. Take the life of a commuter in winter: hard pavements, trains and cars, office or factory: home, telly, bed. You might see a pot plant: no wonder some people lovingly cultivate African violets and spider plants in their workspaces. Even when you shop for food, it is more and more easy to avoid the suggestion that food is anything to do with a non-human life form. Meat comes cut, ready to cook, cellophane wrapped. It's not a bit of a dead animal: it's meat, food, fuel, and that's somehow quite different. The freezer cabinets are full of meat and fish that look nothing like animals. Vegetable matter comes without seed case or foliage, and cleansed of the offending earth from which it sprung. Often it is pre-sliced, or pre-cooked.

In my Asian days, I lived briefly in a fifteenth-floor flat on Hong Kong island: my foot never fell on anything that was not hard and man-made for weeks on end. It drove me nuts: I ran to the islands and a wilder way of living (white-bellied sea eagle from the ferry, the sound of the koel in spring, and, sometimes all night long, the Indian cuckoo singing "one more bot-tle"). But for many, from sheer necessity, from economic ambition, and, who knows?, perhaps from genuine inclination, living without non-human contact has become an acceptable way of life. In the mind-numbingly crowded city of Hong Kong – you get people-jams on the pavements – children go to school in tower blocks and their brief playtimes are spent on the roof, if their school is lucky enough to have a roof and access to it. An outing to a shopping mall is like a trip to the country.

New York – or at least, Manhattan – has something of the same feeling: and the traditional hysteria of both cities is an aspect of their isolation from the non-human world. They are both thrilling places to visit: and very hard places to live in. And if you have money in New York, you at least have a view of the park.

The more we leave the non-human world behind, the less human we become: and the more fearful we become. It is not the thrilling fear of the kind I have experienced with horses, it is more a soul-deep, dislocated sense of anxiety. We lose our sense of trust in the wild world: we begin to forget that we need it. We impoverish ourselves and then we begin to consider it an enrichment.

66 All of life is a miraculous cosmic scheme designed entirely for the benefit of humanity. That is because humanity is the supreme creation of nature, and it is only right and proper that all things should come to us. Humans are the centre of life: nothing less.

That has been the traditional view across the ages, dressed up in a thousand different ways. Freud took another line. He listed three colossal blows that humanity had taken: "Humanity has in the course of time had to endure from the hand of science two great outrages upon its naïve self-love. The first was when it realized that our earth was not the centre of the universe, but only a speck in a world system of a magnitude hardly conceivable... The second was when biological research robbed man of his particular privilege of having been specially created and relegated him to a descent from the animal world."

These lines are quoted by Stephen Jay Gould, one of the great scientists and writers that we have been blessed with in recent years. And he added: "In one of history's least modest pronouncements, Freud then stated that his own work had toppled the next, and perhaps last pedestal of this unhappy retreat – the solace that, though evolved from a lowly ape, we at least possessed rational minds."

How does humanity deal with such colossal blows to its self-esteem? The answer is simple enough. The first step is to ignore all uncomfortable truths: the second and more important step is to create a new set of mythologies. All right, we now accept that the sun does not go round the earth, that the earth is not the centre of the universe, but just a speck in a mind-fuddling expanse. We know that the universe is vast, and the earth is small. But all the same, from our planet and our species comes a constant flow of heroes: we are plucky cosmonauts, we are boldly-goers, we are the explorers, the pushers-back of frontiers. We took a small step for a man and a great leap forward for mankind. Humans have begun the exploration – no, better call it the conquest of space: and that is a glory that Galileo and Copernicus could only dream about. All our stories of cosmic adventure are about humanity bestriding space and time. How can our planet, our race, our time, be insignificant when we can produce Neil Armstrong and Doctor Who and Obi Wan Kenobi? Wherever and whenever humankind has a need, humankind will create a comforting myth. If Jedi did not exist, it would be necessary to invent them.

67 So let us examine a wonderful thing that human beings have done, a great achievement across vast expanses of space (certainly Suffolk) and time (certainly my lifetime). I once shared a flat with Simon Evans: and he came to pay me a Maytime visit. Never a great birder, but always a man with plenty of wildness in him. Brought up in Cornwall with the sea in his eyes. A few years ago, he had a kind of Damascus-road experience with wildlife when canoeing up the Fal in Cornwall. It was the vision of a mythical bird, a mystical, heavenly creature, an impossible angel come to earth. White bird, as the one of the shared songs of our youth went, white bird, white bird, white bird.

Good words, good birds. It was a little egret, of course, one of the birds on the leading edge of the colonisation. Ever since that transcendent revelation of the wild world's possibilities, Simon has looked at birds just a little bit more, and enjoyed them a great deal more. So we walked, Blythborough to Eastbridge again, not a walk I get tired of, and I lent him a pair of binoculars and tried to fill his ears with birdsong. And yes, we saw egrets on the Dingle and saw terns – definitely terns, not possibly terns, little and common and Sandwich – along the sea and over the lagoons at Minsmere.

But it was as we came towards the end of the Dingle marshes, with the Ship almost in sight and the lunchtime pints almost poured, that we shared a moment of perfection. A marsh harrier. A male: his silver, sable and copper wings available for long and leisurely inspection as he made a long and leisurely flight in front of the tower of Dunwich church. Some birds just love to pose: see, look, admire: the wings held, as always, in the shallow vee, the dihedral, banking to one side, to show off his three colours, turning head on, to show us the full elegance of the vee, banking the other way to show us that triple-marked mantle once again: and I lowered the bins (I had kept the better pair for myself) and revelled in the full context of the day and the season and the time of the century: a great bird, the reeds of the marsh below him, the village behind him, beyond, the slope, rising briefly to what in Suffolk we call high ground, and all round the wild wet expanse of the marsh: and he its master, its supreme, and supremely vulnerable master.

How many nests did he have? The best of male marsh harriers might have as many as three, each with its own attendant creamy-headed female, each with eggs hatching out ugly and famished chicks, to be fed by the incessant patrolling of the females, with contributions from the nonchalant triple-timing lord of the marshes. Only the best of the marsh harriers can ensnare three females: only the supreme marsh harriers can see to the raising of three nestfuls.

These birds were once close to extinction: now, this season, it was announced that they had reached their highest numbers in this country for 200 years. Most of the 200 years have involved persecution by shotgun, habitat destruction by the draining of the marshes, and then accidental poisoning by means of insecticide. Now, in the space of my own lifetime, they have gone from that single pair at Minsmere to a population that raised 800 chicks in 2005. These days, a Maytime walk in the right places will bring, not as an astonishing revelation, but as a matter of

127

enchanted routine, the sight of a marsh harrier. Here at least, the processes of destruction have been put into reverse: here at least, the human world has let up its intensity for a moment and allowed the non-human back in. A conquest of space and time: and the world and its most vociferous animal is better of as a result. Ship ahoy.

68 Humankind suffered a grievous blow from *The Origin of Species*, but we have recovered. We have done so, inevitably, not by absorbing and coming to terms with the truth, but by making a myth. That's what humans do. At one time, humans believed that they – that we – were specially created by God: made in God's image, in order to be God's special favourite bit of creation. Therefore it was obvious that the planet – all the rest of creation – was our playground, ours to do with as we liked. Humans were a kind of amphibian: more than animals, not quite angels, capable of living in both heaven and earth, because, unlike the rest of creation, we had immortal souls. Humans were, above all, special.

In the eighteenth century, human rationality became at least as significant as souls: perhaps the two were even synonymous. An immortal soul and a rational mind – either or both – were considered clear and obvious proof that humans were distinctly different from, and a distinct improvement on anything that was non-human.

But then, in 1859, came *The Origin of Species*. And – though Darwin went to very great lengths to keep humans out of it – the implication of the great work was thunderingly obvious. If all of life works by means of modified descent, then humans, too, must be descended from "lower" forms of life. That is to say, some kind of ape: an animal that was generally seen as a kind of vicious parody of humankind. "Is man an ape or an angel?" Benjamin Disraeli wondered, and added: "I am on the side of the angels."

But it was impossible to continue this particular myth: that of the divine provenance of humankind. Humans urinate, defecate, ejaculate, parturiate: we are manifestly mammals; we are, unswervably, something to do with apes. The implications of this are ferocious: that humans, like sponges, like red-faced cisticolas, are the product of the blind chance of evolution. This was a truth not to be faced. It was wholly unacceptable. What was needed, then, was a new myth.

And so we have one. It is best encapsulated iconically: in the famous sequence of silhouettes: the monkey on all fours, the knuckle-walking ape, the stooped and slouching hominid, and finally, the great and glorious uprightness of Man. (never, of course, Woman: silhouetted breasts would get in the way here. This is a Man thing.)

All right, says the myth: man evolved from the apes. (This is not exactly the case: more correct to say that humans and modern apes have a common ancestor. Never mind: this is mythology, not science.) But Man is much better than the apes. Therefore, it is obvious that evolution has been a matter of progress. Evolution is about things getting better and better and better: leading, logically enough, to perfection. Welcome, then, to the human being: the crown of creation.

Next step – and easily made by a subtle slip in logic – it becomes clear that Man is what evolution is for. Now it all makes sense: the purpose of billions of years of life on earth, of the 100 million-year period in which dinosaurs were the dominant large animals on earth, of five separate extinction episodes, of every one of the untold millions of creatures that evolved, thrived, and died out, was one thing and one thing only: the bringing about of the creation of

Man! A new and a false Eden was at once created.

There is a good word for all this: teleology. Moving towards a goal. It is primarily a religious word, a theological word, used for the notion, for example, that the goal of all existence is the revelation of God. It is a valid concept for religion: it is not a valid concept for science. The story of Man as the crown of creation is a myth that is used to prop up our colossal sense of self-esteem: to build up our species-pride: to confirm our belief that we have rights over every other form of life on the planet, to keep us cut off from the non-human world, and to allow us to lead lives less wild than they might be. If we seek to be wild, we must embrace a new kind of humility. And one way of doing that is by coming to a better understanding of evolution. Or to put it another way, life.

69

Now they were back, and the sky was full of them, scything and sickling and showing us triumphantly and precariously that the globe was still working. The swifts, the longed-for birds, were now back in numbers, and their cheery screaming had become a part of daily life once again: as if nothing could possibly go wrong ever again: as if the darkness of winter could never come again: as if nothing to trouble a wild-loving human's heart could ever again be a part of the world and the way we live in it.

Bad weather in England might knock the aerial bugs out of the sky and give the swifts nothing to feed on: but what do they care? They will surf on the weather fronts and make a 300-mile round trip without giving it a moment's thought. If they don't like the weather here, they will find weather more suited to their lives elsewhere.

Anything rather than perch. For swifts simply don't do

that. They are born for life on the wing: they fly as no creature has ever flown before. They live, feed, sleep, make love
and have their being on the wing: *volo ergo sum*, I fly,
therefore I am. One of the many reasons that birds are so
attractive to human beings is because they fly: and our own
observing hearts take wing at this daily miracle, just like
Hopkins' heart in hiding.

And since swifts are the finest flying creature that the
forces of evolution have ever come up with, the swift must
be the ultimate heart-stirrer. Will they ever come down?
Why should they? They like it up there. The earth is nothing to them, a mere backdrop to their aerial lives. Their
reality is not rocks and stones and trees: it is cloud and wind
and light.

The young birds hatch, take wing, fly to Africa, spend
their winter there, return, feed, grow, learn about the
nature of swifthood and swiftkind, return to Africa, and
then return to England, perhaps this time to mate and raise
a family: perhaps to wait one more season. And in all this
time, they will never once touch anything other than air.
They will not perch: for they have no need to. They live on
the wing: flight is everything to them, the ground holds
nothing for them: only death.

When they nest, they seek out caves, and with their tiny,
almost vestigial feet, they can cling to ledges and crevices,
vertical surfaces, and shuffle along on their bellies. In most
places in Europe, however, they have given up caves and
taken to using the roofspaces of buildings: thus a smart
adaptability to human ways has given them a chance to
spread and expand. You can see them, in June and July, land-
ing awkwardly on roofs and belly-shuffling out of sight
beneath the pantiles.

A friend of mine told me one of the great memories of
his childhood was the young swifts' annual emergence from
their nesting darkness into the world of flight: and how

some of them failed to negotiate the tricky bit between dropping from the nest exit and rising to the skies. They found themselves belly-down on the ground: legs too short and wings too long to get a decent flap going and get airborne. He remembered picking them up and throwing them skywards: launching them into their life in the skies, sometimes racing the cats to set the wild wings free.

And over my fields, sometimes so high that they looked like a sprinkling of pepper on the sky, sometimes skimming the treetops – they don't go in for the crop-dusting low-level runs that swallows specialise in – the swifts were preparing for the great breeding putsch, the annual climax of the swiftian year. Could anything be more lovely? More perfect?

It is quite clear that swifts are the crown of creation. The reason that evolution took place was to produce the swift. The end of all those millions of years was to produce this flying creature, a beast of such staggering perfection that it need never descend to base earth save to make more of its own self. What human can stay aloft by his own power for three years? What human could fly from continent to continent with a shrug of his shoulders? What human could make love in the skies? What a piece of work is a swift! How noble in flight! How infinite in faculty! In form, in moving, how express and admirable! In action, how like an angel! In apprehension, how like a god! The beauty of the world! The paragon of animals!

70

I worked a miracle for Simon Evans. Marvellously sweet, marvellously loud, marvellously joyous. Evans and I have never touched hemlock, though we have indulged in one or two distinctly dodgy pleasures in our time. So it was as though of red Leb I had smoked: cheerfully befuddling.

Nightingale, of course. Always from cover: you hardly every set eyes on a nightingale: they are by nature lurkers and skulkers. But despite that, they are tremendous show-offs, and when they sing, it is as if the trees and the skies rejoiced with them. They sing through the day, they sing through the night, hence the name. No bird takes the Maytime frenzies with such seriousness as the nightingale: it's a 24-hour shift. They are impossible to confuse with anything else, unless you happen to be in bed with your beloved and wishing that the night would never end. In such a case, you might be excused for making a wilful confusion: It is not yet day: it was the nightingale, and not the lark that pierced the fear-ful hollow of thine ear: nightly she sings on yon pomegran-ate tree: believe me, love, it was the nightingale.

She? Never mind. Juliet, being female, no doubt assumed that the ecstasies of love are primarily a female concern. It is the cock bird that sings, of course: and he splits the heavens when he does so. He whistles a crescen-do of ever sweeter, ever louder notes, till you think that he might burst with the strain of it: and then he breaks into a frenzied percussion accompaniment to his own song, a deep jug-jug-jug drumming. He will mix in rich fluting phrases, sharp rattles, phrases of startling inventiveness and beauty, sometimes soothing, sometimes challenging, sometimes throwing in more modernistic grating and scraping, and then a sumptuous whistle once again. It is the song of everything: it is the song of all birds: it is the song of all life: it is the song of the earth, and of the heavens, too.

Nothing sings like a nightingale: and even if you didn't know what you were listening to, you would have to stop

133

and listen and let your wild heart sing in response, just as the same organ takes wing in response to the swifts. This is a song beyond compare. It is one of the great treats of England and Maytime and the great season when the year and the nightingale both express themselves in a glorious crescendo: and it is the self-same sound for both.

There is no ducking it, you know. Nightingales are also the crown of creation.

71

Simon Evans and I have been talking bollocks together since January 1971, so there was no reason to stop now. Evans, being a bit of a crown of creation himself, can do just about everything in the world. He has, at various times, worked as a master-chef and a potter, and now designs websites. He has never been formally trained for any of these careers. He just does stuff. He is also interested in just about everything. I have often described myself as a bad birdwatcher: if so, he is a bad stargazer. A good bad stargazer, it would be fair to say.

He may be a lapsed master-chef, but he doesn't make it embarrassing to cook for him. He also eats stuff. I'd done the soufflé that night, and made it with the kind of cheddar that hurts your lips, adding a spoon of English mustard to reinforce the point. The meal had been eaten and praised, the bottles, some of them, put away. I was about to pour some malt whisky, when I felt the need to go outside and check the horses.

Lord, it was a good one. No moon. No cloud. No mist, not a trace. And, above all, no light.

And so the sky was not black. It was white. There were more stars than there was background. Everything was a star, a nebula, a galaxy: and the thick, creamy streak of the

Milky Way ran right through it all. The word galaxy itself means milk: and there it was, curdling in the firmament. I poked my head back through the door: "Evan Evans! Come and look at the universe!"

"All right." Evans has always admired the work of Douglas Adams.

Each an elbow on the gate: neck cricked, regarding the heaventree of stars hung with humid night blue fruit. You don't get a universe like that in town.

Evans was brought up in Cornwall; I went there every holiday. And I remember the teenaged wonder of the moonless nights: as if Cornwall and holidays were so special that you even had a special kind of universe to live in while you were there. And it's not about the beauty of Cornwall or for that matter, Suffolk. It's about darkness. Only when it is dark can you see. Only when there is very little ambient light can you see the universe in any clarity. In cities is it impossible to see any but the brightest stars: and they, in the surrounding glare, look like little light bulbs. Out in the countryside, on moonless and cloudless nights, you see the immensities of space and time in all their incomprehensible splendours.

If you live in a city, you are not just cut off from a nice view. You are cut off from the most obvious thing that such immense views bring with them: that sense of human smallness. In the brilliant newspaper cartoon Alex, the eponymous hero, yuppie and obnoxious, was asked to contemplate the stars: "Doesn't it make you think how insignificant you are?" "Not particularly. I'd like to know how many 25-year-olds there are up there with a brand new BMW."

In a city, you are cut off from the sense of wonder. The fuzz of lights blots out the rest of the universe. Humans are alone. We are Masters of the Universe, because there is no longer a universe capable of fighting back. We have

135

switched it off: switched it off by switching on. A great moon is nothing but a circle in the sky: a frosty night is merely no weather to hang about in, so let's hope the bloody train is on time. Starry, starry night: Vincent's picture of the night sky looks to a city-dweller like the mad figment of an overheated imagination. A country-dweller can see that he painted it from life: understands at once that as he painted, the candles dripped their wax onto his brilliantly improvised night-painting hat.

Many people who talk about moving from the city to the countryside are worried about how they will cope with the dark. Cindy was among them, for her family has a long tradition of spirits and spooks. But the transition was not nearly as painful as it might have been: for with the lack of omnipresent light comes a feeling of reverence. A reverence for the immensity of things. And with it, a certain far from disagreeable thrill of fear.

It is not terror that comes from the country dark: it is perspective. Beneath the stars, there is the certainty that we are not alone. And this is not because the sky is full of alien beings: but because the earth is.

It is a different sort of fear to the one the would-be country-dweller imagines, as he or she considers life away from the comforting light-shield of the street lamps. It is not the chills or the collywobbles, or a stricken can't-leave-the-house frozen terror. Rather, this is fear as a good thing: fear, in the same category, though not at the same level, as I felt when working with my young horse: a feeling of being slightly outside the comfort zone. The city is everybody's comfort zone. That's what it was built for: even it doesn't always work, even if the urban terrors that resulted from it are genuine and serious. The point is that in a city, the universe dwindles: it becomes manageable: humans are so much more in control.

But out in darkest Suffolk, sensing the vast universe

revolving around me, I felt that familiar touch of wildness: feeling both comfort and dread. Good. Good things both. It is better like this: better because wilder. Not just a matter of occasional glassy-eyed, boozy contemplation of the heavens, but as a permanent, more or less subliminal awareness of life's immensities: of life's grandeur.

But come. The Glenmorangie was waiting. It was Evans who told me how to pronounce the name properly – stress on the second syllable – so naturally, it was the right whisky to drink on this occasion. Cassiopeia, he explained, Adams-like, is always exactly where the Great Bear is not. Helpful thought. I poured two large ones: to life, the universe and everything.

72

The previous summer, I had made a trip to Belize: one of the world's great mammal sightings, fabulous birds including keel-billed toucan, and some of the finest mosquitoes I have ever encountered. A few days after I returned to England, I broke out in hives. In a panic, I went to the doctor, convinced I had some thrilling tropical disease. But no: I had just been bitten so many times that my body was having a reaction to the epic quantities of mozzie-spit I had taken on board.

I realised then that the crown of creation is in fact the mosquito. Is there anything in all evolution, quite so elegant and perfect as the mouthparts of a mosquito? Consider the upper and lower lip: inside these, you find hypopharynx, maxillae and the mandibles. There are two mandibles and two maxillae that act like the teeth of a saw, and are used to penetrate the skin. Then the upper lip – the labrum – becomes a tube and enters the wound. After that, the hypopharynx comes into play: this is a canal, and it is linked to the salivary glands. As the mosquito feeds, the hypopharynx pumps saliva into the wound and prevents the blood from coagulating. The blood is then shifted inside the insect by means of the pharyngeal pump: an enlargement of the pharynx then expands and contracts, and so does the pumping. It is the mozzie-spit that makes bites itch: we can spare the blood, but the being-driven-mad part is less tolerable.

If you are thinking of the ultimate achievements of creation, how can you look beyond the insects? There are 3,500 species of mosquitoes: strength, versatility, resilience are to be found not in uniqueness but in diversity. How many species of humans remain today? Insects, in their endless and head-spinning variety, are without rivals in the world today: and the mosquito is one of tens of thousands of claims for perfection.

DH Lawrence saw the mosquito as he really is:

> The mosquito knows full well, small as he is
> he's a beast of prey.
> But after all
> he only takes his bellyful,
> he doesn't put my blood in the bank.

(He? Lawrence, being male, thought that the business of predation was an exclusively male preserve. It's the females that bite: they steal a blood-meal and use the nourishment to make eggs. The male has no need to eat: in his finished and final form, his role is purely sexual. Lawrence might have written something equally pithy about that, had someone troubled to tell him.)

73

It was one of the great wonders of the natural world: and when it was over, my belly was aching with laughter. Quite literally: I returned from this marvellous sight, this marvellous place, feeling as if I had been beaten in the stomach with rubber truncheons in an effort to elicit a confession. I really have never seen anything so funny. I can't tell the story without giggling all over again. I was in Borneo this time, invited out to write some wildlife stuff for the *Times*, and I had been taken to visit the orang-utans, a standard tourist destination, and it was all very fine and splendid. But then my host, a clever and quick-minded man, realised that I had more wildness about me than some of his other guests: and so he asked if I wanted to stay till dusk for something special. This was not only astute: it was also very generous, for it meant we had to hang about for three hours at the edge of the rainforest, doing some desultory birding, until the magic moment had arrived, three hours in which he could have been catching up on business or in the arms of his loved ones. So we waited: and we waited.

But then it happened: and I was entranced. For dusk is the time of the flying squirrels. The first one: shuffling up the side of a tree like a squirrel hoping to escape recognition for a rather unedifying reason, wrapped up in a cloak. This furry cape ruffled and rippled with each movement: the entire animal looked like a small bedroom slipper running away by itself. At last it reached the topmost branches,

139

which bent and swayed under his slight weight.

And once he got there, you could see him nerving himself up for the next bit. Oooh-er! I'm going to do it! I really am! Next time! No, time after that. All alright then. Now! Ooooooo — and with a wild, despairing leap, the squirrel left from the tree and spread out his crazy furry membrane that stretched between his legs, becoming in a trice the worst glider you have ever seen. The completed craft was on the far edge of control: there seemed to be no lateral stability whatsoever: the squirrel wobbled from side to side, correction, over correction, recorrection, oscillating wildly, until, apparently more by luck than judgement, it slapped itself onto another trunk and stopped there: regrouping, apparently saying to itself: bloody hell, that was close. I thought I was a goner that time. I'm never going to do that again. Not until... well, I'll try it again. Just once more. I'm going to do it you know... and up he shuffled again, furry cloak aflap, till he was at the top again and ready to try another demented leap into the void.

This was not flying. It really wasn't much better than falling. It was a kind of parachute jumping: completed under some hazy notion of control. A swift can manage a flight of three years: a flying squirrel can manage about half a minute. Swifts fly to Africa and back: the record for flying squirrels is about 500 yards. Flying squirrels are the funniest animals I have ever seen, but no one could call them the finest flying machine ever designed.

Are they an evolutionary mistake? No, certainly not: there are 43 species of them worldwide, including one in Siberia. There are fourteen in Borneo alone: from the pygmy flying squirrels at eight centimetres in length, to the giants, five times as big. They are a successful little group.

Are they then improving? Are the forces of evolution trying to make them more sophisticated, less funny? Again: certainly not. Why should they improve? They work perfectly well as they are. The blind forces of evolution are not seeking to create perfection: they are seeking something that works well enough: well enough to permit the creature to survive, breed, become an ancestor.

The flying squirrels are gorgeous proof that evolution is not about perfection. This is an absurd and glorious jerry-rigged creature: a living, breathing, thriving Heath Robinson device. We humans know the truth about evolution just as well as flying squirrels, for we are flawed and faulty creatures ourselves. Many adult humans suffer from various different kinds of back problems. The back is an area of human weakness: and, it is generally assumed, this is because the mammal body plan is not really designed for walking upright. We have developed the most wonderful tools – hands – by freeing our forelimbs from the task of locomotion: but we pay the price in niggling aches and pains: and sometimes much worse.

The colossal human brain development also comes at a price: and it is one that women pay. The process of human birth is at the far edge of the possible: the hugeness of the human brain, and therefore skull, and the narrowness of the human birth canal mean that problems in birth are part of the human condition. Women give birth in pain and suffering, and before the advances of medical science, many women and many children were lost in childbirth. Cindy and Joe would probably have died together, had there been no possibility of birth by Caesarean section.

Crown of creation? But the process of life isn't about the seeking after perfection. It is about the seeking after even more life. Those squirrels: like the magnificent men in their flying machines, are gallant pioneers of the skyways, flinging themselves into the air once again with a crazy fecklessness: faulty, optimistic, jerry-rigged, jaunty, indomitable, and apparently deranged: perhaps the ultimate symbol of life on earth.

74
My wild May holiday was at an end, and Maytime had done itself and me proud. Every time I left the house, I saw the white bum of a swooping martin, or the neat, swept-back wings and little notched tail of a rising martin, or I heard the sweet farting calls they make when in a good and merry Maytime temper. They had used Cindy's mud and repaired the winter's damage to their ancestral homes beneath the eaves, and were now in the process of refreshing the white trails they leave against the pink walls of the house: a strawberries-and-cream effect that every house in Suffolk should have. In the evenings, when we sat about upstairs, we could hear the domestic murmuring of martins on the nest: an amiable good-tempered chirruping. Our house was, for four months, the centre of the martin's life: they lived and had their being in precise relationship with its pink walls and pantiled roof.

By no means all the nests were filled: but those that had made it were the best, the wisest and the toughest of martins – how else had they succeeded in making the double journey when so many others has failed? – and they were setting about the task of building martin numbers back up again with a glorious enthusiasm. By day, they hawked and hunted for insects all around the house and the surrounding countryside with all the crown-of-creation élan that you would expect; by night they rested and roosted, in physical contact with the house that has stood here for 500 years, and sheltered us for just the last decade. They are the owners, not us.

The year was quietening now: the springtime frenzies were at an end. Quieter for human watchers: but the fact of the matter is that for the birds, the year was hotting up. The establishing of territory and the finding of mates is the easy bit, as well as the noisy bit. Now was the time for what the whole business was really all about: the raising of a brood. The volume of the singing turned down noticeably in all the trees and the hedges: territories need to be maintained, not established, an altogether less strident process. Besides, as much energy as possible needs to be spent on the chick-rearing business.

From a brutally reductionist point of view, it's all about genes. The genes are doing their damnedest to replicate themselves: martin genes do it by means of martins, exploiting the little scraps of fartin' feathers to do the job of passing on the magic genes: manoeuvring the birds into marvels of aerial design and architectural ability. By the same rule, human genes are pulling the same stroke on their human host-bodies: creating intelligence, thought, language and hand-skills as means, not to create a perfect society, but to make more human genes.

Read these things as you will: but no one who has attended the cacophony of Maytime, and seen it merge slowly into the heated-up frenzies of chick-rearing as June approached, can be in any doubt that the purpose of any individual life is to become an ancestor. Put that way, there is no ducking the matter: that the meaning of life is life: and that the purpose of life is living. You can add to that as much as you like: but that's where it all begins: in life, in living. And in May, as the richness of life fizzed and fermented all around, I wondered: how could anyone find that a disagreeable thought?

75
May ended as it had begun: in great life-giving draughts of rain: great purposeful soft douches, stirring up the life, pushing up the grass for my horses and filling up my well. Rain is a bit like the night sky: you don't really get the

hang of it in town. A good downpour in a dry time always makes me think of my mother. She felt the cold dreadfully, but found comfort and relief in a good slug of Scotch. She would take a first sip, pause some seconds to appreciate the effect as it slipped down, spreading warmth in its wake. And then she would smile and would always say the same words: "I can *feel* it doing me good." That's what my fields, that's what the earth was saying as the water fell: *eau de vie*, *aqua vitae*, water of life, *uisque beatha*, whisky. All the same thing. A row of drops on the brim of my hat as I did the outdoor chores: I could almost see the grass growing, and I could certainly feel it doing me good.

76

At the entrance to the Suffolk Show Ground stand three statues: heavy horse, bull, sheep. Each one a Suffolk breed: Suffolk Punch, Red Poll, Suffolk sheep. The pre-industrial history of the county: the three breeds that fed, clothed and powered the place.

Domestication is both a taming and a wilding. The domestication of animals is one of the first steps that humans took as they began to move on from the hunter-gatherer life: a change from a fully wild to a less wild state of being. And yet the link with domestic animals takes us back to a wilder way of existence: wilder, at least, than 21st-century city life.

We made our annual trip to the Suffolk Show, two days of the celebration of domesticity: the domestication of the plants and the animals that are the basis of civilised life: yet they cannot be cared for without a certain amount of wildness. I love especially the grand parade of the champions: an endless succession of horses of every size and purpose, of dewy-eyed cows, of moody-looking bulls, of scatty sheep and alarmingly well-behaved goats. And the people who do the looking after: the stockmen, women too, proud and preoccupied, some of them taking victory in their stride as a matter of annual routine, others bursting with pride at the novelty of it all: people whose life and work is to do with the non-human animals: people who could not exist without a great deal of wildness in them.

We breed our domestic animals selectively, to produce the kind of animals we want: Suffolk Punches and Shetland ponies are the same species, but their shape and disposition has been affected by their carefully selected parentage. I once met a dog called Ziggy: his father was a dachsund, his mother a St Bernard. The two had been left together, despite the fact that the St Bernard was in season, because the owners assumed the practical problems would be too great: assumed, really, that the dogs were so dissimilar that they were somehow not really of the same species. But life will chase after life: and the ingenious and enterprising couple found a way, and a litter of ziggies was the result.

A breed, then, is quite different from a species. People from rare breeds societies will explain passionately that the Suffolk Punch or the Gloucester Old Spot or the Jacob sheep is "rarer than the giant panda". This is not comparing like with like. The breeds are created by artificial selection: the wild species by natural selection. Humans can create new breeds any time, if there are enough people who wish to breed them: nature creates new species in nature's own good time. A Jacob and a Suffolk can mate and produce viable sheep: your most expensive racehorse stallion in the world can mate with a Suffolk Punch, or for that matter, with my old mare. It won't produce what humans want from either horse: but it will certainly be a horse. There are millions and millions of sheep in the world, and not one is rarer than the giant panda. There are very few giant pandas left: and when they're gone, they're gone. There's no option of breeding them back. They are not tame animals: they are wild species on the very edge of survival.

But domesticity never fails to fascinate me, because it is a sharing of human and non-human life. I find living with animals as important and as rewarding as walking with wild ones. This is not a conventional view in wildlife circles: but for many people, living with an animal is a way of bringing an aspect of wildness into their lives: as important for them as birding is for a birder. Me, I like both: so I consider myself doubly blessed.

I have had close dealings with a Suffolk Punch once or twice: most memorably when I visited the Suffolk Stud, which was then part of the prison at Hollesley Bay. This was for a piece for the *Times*, and they had got a horse shined, polished, tacked up and ready, and the head groom drove him on foot so that the photographer might do his stuff. I at once succumbed to temptation, and asked if I could have a go: Bruce Snith, the stud groom, already knew me for a horseman and passed me the reins.

At once, my view of the world was restricted to a vast landscape of ginger arse: Suffolk are always chestnut. The horse was about twice the weight of my own, that is to say, about a ton. Not that it was all that tall: a comfortable eighteen hands, or six foot at the shoulder. It was all in the shape: the great, powerful, muscle-builder's shape of him. But perfectly schooled and mannered: moving forward at a quiet word from my voice, moving this way and that with the gentlest hint from the reins, stopping with gentle pressure from hands and a call.

Seeing my delight at this, Bruce told me: "Only one better feeling than that in the world. That's with two of them and plough between 'em."

It was a power thing, of course. My power over this great ginger giant? Not a bit of it. It was his power that got to me: that, and the extraordinary, ineffable, eternal mystery: that he was willing to share it, that his power became our power, not by coercion but by willingness to agree terms: the sort of thing that can be negotiated by a good stockman. That ability to share is part of the taming of an animal: and part of the wilding of a human.

77

There is a lovely little scrap of woodland to one side of the Suffolk Show ground, and as we passed, I heard the sudden racket of nightingale. Most people walked on unregarding: perhaps noticing it as a pleasant background din, perhaps just letting it all flow by as part of the essential ambience of the annual splendours of the Suffolk Show. There was a blackcap, too (definitely not a garden warbler), singing rich and fruity.

Then I noticed overhead a hawk: biggish, burly, round-winged: making a fast, shallow, gliding descent into the wood: sparrowhawk, female – females are bigger than the males – on what looked to me like a killing run. I had the quiet satisfaction of seeing something that nobody else did, and hearing something that most people would not have identified.

For this was a spot of Unofficial Nature: and that's just as important – perhaps a great deal more important – than Official Nature. Official Nature is to be found at the big sites, where the star species gather and strut their stuff: places like Minsmere bird reserve, with its avocets, its bitterns and its marsh harriers. These places are of vast and unquestioned importance: everybody knows that a place like Minsmere is a Good Thing.

But Unofficial Nature is perhaps an even better thing. Unofficial Nature is the sort of thing you find and see everywhere, if you are wild enough to keep your eyes and your ears open: the blackbird on the lawn, the flock of crows over the fields, the tight formation of Canada geese glimpsed from the train window. And I always love those extrusions of the wild world into civilisation: for example, the birds I have seen when covering sporting events around the world: crested oropendola in Trinidad, lesser kestrel at the Stadium of Light in Portugal, common tern at Middlesbrough, shikra at the Wankhede in Bombay.

Unofficial Nature is to be found in every garden, in every untidy corner of the countryside, in every copse. It is something that needs to be treasured. And there is a change taking place: slowly, these places are being cherished that little bit more. Joni might be able to explain why.

78

Am I showing off by throwing these names of species at you? Am I alienating you, dear reader, by my attention, such as it is, to the details of species? Am I losing you, when I make my vainglorious claim of being able to tell a blackcap from a garden warbler with my ears alone?

If so, you have a good point. Being wild is not the same thing as the ability to identify one species from another. Wildness does not depend on your ability to tell a marsh tit from a willow tit (and I can't do that reliably, not unless the marsh tit sneezes) or a common tern from an Arctic tern (and I certainly can't manage that, alas). Wildness is not dependent on your ability to pass a test of memory and identification skills. I came across some words by John Fowles, author of *The French Lieutenant's Woman*; nature gets into most of his novels: *The Collector* is about a butterfly-nut, the eponymous hero of *Daniel Martin* is an orchid-hound.

In one of his essays, he ponders on the question of

identification: "Any trained biologist will tell you that identification expertise has about as much relation to serious biology as knowing national flags has to do with being an expert in international affairs. I put the blame for this narrow and superficial identification approach to nature squarely on the shoulders of the amateur naturalist. Nothing puts the beginner off the subject faster than the name-dropping conceit of this kind of expert. The tyro thinks nature must be some kind of academic memory test, a quiz show with no prizes, and quite reasonably takes up something that puts less of a premium on 'experience' and know-how (or more accurately, know-what)."

He's right, you know. Trouble is, he's wrong as well. Does it matter, for example, that there is more than one kind of owl living where I do? Isn't it enough to simply say: hurrah, there are owls! Is it mere name-dropping conceit if I tell you that there are in fact three species of owl that I see, or at least hear regularly? And that they have three completely different ways of making a living? Is it not of serious ecological interest that the barn owl hunts at dusk and over open country, while the tawny owl hunts at night and mainly under the tree canopy, and that the little owl is tiny and eats much smaller stuff than either of the others? Three species, three different ways of living, three different solutions to the problem of being alive.

I agree that the identification-bore can put people off: I try not to be too frightfully boring myself, with varying degrees of success. But all the same, the numbers of species is a very off-putting thing, no matter who tells you about them. A field guide to birds, or for that matter, insects or mammals or trees or flowers, is going to bewilder the beginner by its jaw-dropping, eye-baffling collection of names.

Fowles has particular scorn for those who set out on a chosen day, and try to see as many species of bird as they can: a practice he calls "the freakish idiocy of a clam-brained ornithological minority". Well, I have done it a few times myself. It's bloody good fun, actually. Good sport, of the kind not to be taken too seriously. And, you might ask, is it all about accumulating and collecting and possessing? Actually, no. The whole business is a kind of active prayer to the notion of biodiversity.

Instead of saying: oh, there's a greenfinch, a common bird, so bloody what?, you say hurrah! Greenfinch! Greenfinch, I have a special affection for you – a special relationship with you today because you have just made my list that little bit longer. And so you count moorhen and sparrow and crow and pheasant, instead of ignoring them as so much background. And at the end of the day, you have a chance to count up and celebrate two absolutely wonderful things: (1) how bloody clever you are and (2) how bloody brilliant nature is.

Lots and lots and lots of different kinds of things. And if you can't tell a chaffinch from a greenfinch, you are denied one of the essential and important responses to nature: that sense of mind-boggling wonder at the sheer numbers.

And if you happen to be able to tell one kind of small brown bird from another, you have a great deal more opportunity for this form of delight. It's all very well going into poetic raptures about nature and the obvious birds: but there is also a poetry in the vast, unending legions of the overlooked, the small and the brown and the drab: the poetry of numbers, the poetry of minute differences, the poetry of the apparently endless ways of making a living: in the infinite possibilities, and the near-infinite actualities of nature.

79

All of which brings me to cisticolas. Cisticolas are very small, very brown and very drab. They all look more or less exactly the same. Their differences are location and habitat and habit: for each almost identical bird, a genuinely different way of making a living. Boring birds: each one living out the same boring miracle. They are related to warblers, and you find them all over Africa. One of the great adventures of my life (two, if you count the affair of the silent cloud cisticola) has been in pursuit of cisticolas. And it seems to me that the naming of cisticolas, and even more, the active pursuit of cisticolas, is one of the most complex and rewarding and idiotic and joyful ways of praising God, or nature, or what you will. Well, never mind all that: the praising's the thing. Praise God from whom all blessings flow; praise nature from whom all cisticolas flow, along with everything else. But then cisticolas, too, are a kind of blessing.

80

Red-faced cisticola
Angolan cisticola
Singing cisticola
Whistling cisticola
Trilling cisticola
Chattering cisticola
Bubbling cisticola
Chubb's cisticola
Hunter's cisticola
Black-browed cisticola
Lazy cisticola

Boran cisticola
Rattling cisticola
Ashy cisticola
Red-pate cisticola
Grey cisticola
Red-headed cisticola
Wailing cisticola
Tana River cisticola
Churring cisticola
Winding cisticola
Carruther's cisticola
Chirping cisticola
Levaillant's cisticola
Stout cisticola
Aberdare mountain cisticola
Croaking cisticola
Piping cisticola
Tabora cisticola
Slender-tailed cisticola
Siffling cisticola
Rufous cisticola
Foxy cisticola
Tiny cisticola
Zitting cisticola
Socotra cisticola
Madagascar cisticola
Desert cisticola
Tink-tink cisticola
Black-necked cisticola
Cloud-scraping cisticola
Pectoral patch cisticola
Wing-snapping cisticola
Gold-capped cisticola

That lot are all from the would-be definitive *Complete*

Checklist of the Birds of the World. But my *Field Guide to Zambian Birds Not Found in Southern Africa* also includes:

Cloud cisticola
Black-tailed cisticola
Short-winged cisticola
Nedicky
Rock-loving cisticola
Black-lored cisticola
Greater black-backed cisticola
Lesser black-backed cisticola

And meanwhile, *Birds of Africa South of the Sahara* also has:

Melodious cisticola
Lynes's cisticola
Grey-backed cisticola
Dorst's cisticola
Coastal cisticola
Luapula cisticola
Ethiopian cisticola
Pale-crowned cisticola

But alas, none of them give my favourite, the silent cloud cisticola, which is only easily identifiable on call. An awful lot of confusion, an awful lot of disagreement: some of these birds are considered mere subspecies by some authorities, others are given full specific status by this authority but not by that one, and to make matters worse, a good many of them have more than one English or common name – Latin or scientific names are the only way to get to the heart of that particular mess.

But the real point here is that there are an awful lot of cisticolas. And some may seek to make a life's work of seeing them all, recording all their songs, comparing one with another, working out what makes each species utterly and mind-bogglingly unique. Others may choose to wag their heads in bemusement, hilarity and wonder. What? No farting cisticola? But in the ridiculous numbers, in the amazing similarities, and the small, subtle and absolutely vital differences, there is either a quiz show with no prizes – or else there is a kind of wonder, one different from the windhover moment or the daffodil moment or the nightingale moment: but containing every bit as much immensity, every bit as much of a sense of eternity. I wandered lonely as a silent cloud cisticola and my heart in hiding stirred for a genus, the very numbers of which caused a drowsy numbness to pain my sense, as though of Glenmoranjie I had drunk, when all at once I learned a crowd, a host of little brown jobs – the achieve of, the mastery of the things!

81 Please note that our old friend François Le Vaillant has a cisticola named for him, though it is sometimes, to add to the general confusion, also called tinkling cisticola. And while we celebrate numbers, let me point out that there is also Levaillant's barbet, Levaillant's bushshrike, Levaillant's cuckoo, Levaillant's green woodpecker, and Levaillant's parrot. There is no cisticola named for his mistress, though – or should we count foxy cisticola?

82 I love Norwich airport. It's tiny, it's near, and the route is mostly along minor roads through pleasant countryside. A sporting assignment for the *Times* required a start at dawn: in the grey in-between time that is neither dark nor light, neither night nor day. And as my taxi carried me onwards, I gazed vaguely at the countryside as it began to taste the excesses of summer; as it began to make a decision in favour of day rather than night. And a moment of sudden piercing delight.

A white deer. A hind, a red deer not red at all. Just a vision, glimpsed as we passed, not quite quick enough to be imagined. It was real all right: mild eyes staring dark from her snowy head. And I knew a deep and nameless joy. Strange that the heart should thrill so much at this sport, this genetic aberration.

But it felt like a meeting with some ancient magic: a moment of perfect connection with the ancient and rural past: not just the past of humankind, but quite specifically, with the vanished past of England. It was not just the deer's wildness: it also had a great deal to do with the deer's whiteness. This whiteness made it not so much a phenomenon of the natural world, as a fragment of mythology, some human myth come to life. It was as if the normal laws that keep humans and wild things apart had been momentarily suspended. I had a connection – one way, obviously one way – with this white beast, that I would not have had with a great herd of proper russet-tawny red deer.

I remembered the end of *The Lion, the Witch and the Wardrobe*, when the children, now grown-up kings and queens, are hunting the White Stag, the elusive beast that might grant you wishes when you catch him, and instead, they suddenly find themselves tumbling back into the real (or is Narnia really more real?) world.

And then I recalled a passage in the Alice books that I have always, since reading as a child, found almost unbearably poignant: the moment in *Through the Looking-Glass* when Alice enters the wood in which all who enter forget who they are. And then she meets a fawn, beautiful, unfrightened: "'What do you call yourself?' the Fawn said at last. Such a soft sweet voice it had! 'I wish I knew,' thought poor Alice."

Unaware of their own identities, unaware it seems, of each other's natures, the two seek each other out: "And so they walked on together through the wood, Alice with her arms clasped lovingly round the soft neck of the Fawn, till they came out into another open field, and here the Fawn gave a sudden bound into the air, and shook itself free from Alice's arm. 'I'm a Fawn!' it cried out in a voice of delight. 'And dear me! You're a human child!' A sudden look of alarm came into its beautiful brown eyes, and in another moment it had darted away at full speed. Alice stood looking after it, ready to cry with vexation at having lost her dear little fellow-traveller so suddenly. 'However, I know my own name now,' she said: 'that's *some* comfort.'"

Dear me, indeed: another lost paradise. But then our literature and our mythology is full of them: secret, deeply personal places, places where nature is astonishingly abundant, and, most especially, where there is some important personal connection between human visitor – human trespasser – and the nature he finds there.

Sherwood Forest is the most important of these, especially if you happen to be English. I was Robin Hood for years, living the life of Greenwood, robbing the rich to help the poor, defying the Sheriff of Nottingham and then retreating into the forest fastness, where all is good companionship and peace and plenty beneath the green boughs of Sherwood. No doubt it was better still when Marion was in a good temper and in the mood to play.

The Forest of Arden is another: indeed, all of Shakespeare's woods are wild and special places, places where normal rules are suspended (or are the real rules more rigorously enforced?), where lovers traduce one another, court one another, drink love-potions, fall in and out of love, and amuse each other with complex cross-dressing while others debate the eternal question of how much wildness a human truly needs. In the end, of course, love conquers all, as it always must in such a place; Jack shall have Jill, nought shall go ill. In Tolkien, the travellers meet the Elves in the forest of Lothlorien; in *The Jungle Book* it is not Mowgli, or even Bagheera, but the jungle itself that is the star.

The location of these places is easy to find: deep in ourselves. We seek this place – The Sacred Combe, John Fowles called it – which is special, unique in itself and somehow uniquely personal to whomsoever stumbles in. There is a sense of ownership, as well as of trespass: a sense of being there on sufferance, but also of being the beneficiary of a rare privilege handed out by the wild world to the insufficiently wild human. This place represents nothing less than a truce, and its myriad stories and myths are about our soul-deep nostalgia for a time we never knew: at a time and a place in which we can forget who we are and nature itself forgives us.

83

For two months of my life, I visited the sacred combe every day. Not a place in my heart, but a place of unimpeachable reality, with dusty earth and a trunk hard as ebony to make my chair. It was when I lived briefly in the Luangwa Valley: still at the point between one period of my life and another: between life as half of a couple, and life as one-third – now one-quarter – of a family. Cindy, with wild and glorious generosity, told me that if I still had this wild dream of Africa in my system, now was the time to put it into action, before she got pregnant.

And, recklessly taking her at her word, I went. I had a

brief life between lives. It was a bit like living in the Wood Between the Worlds, another sacred combe in the *Chronicles of Narnia*. I used to get up at half-past five each morning, walk in the bush with the wise and the knowledgeable people who ran the camp and the wide-eyed clients who visited it. A night of lion music was followed each dawn by a walk to meet – well, who knew what, on any given morning, we might meet? Elephant, lion, hippo, crocodile, and enough birds to last a lifetime of glory. Then, back from the walk, to mealie-meal porridge and eggs and honey-and-toast – the bread cooked in a hole in the ground – and then a shower and a sleep. And after that, my daily journey into the sacred combe.

Mchenja camp. Mchenja is ebony. Just behind my hut, a glade of ebony trees. I would walk into it and find my spot, back to one ebony tree, bum on the ground. And I would sit, still and silent, and wait for nature to forgive me. Naturally, every time I entered, there was an uproar and a great series of alarm calls: the cackle of the starlings, a crashing of the undergrowth, often the Jack Russell alarm bark of impala, or the whistle of puku, another antelope. It was as if I had shattered the lovely morning into fragments: so now I had to sit and let it mend itself. And within half an hour, I was invisible: morning unbroken.

The first to forgive were always the long-tailed glossy starlings, sleek and shining, with glittering golden eyes, soon picking away at the leaf-litter a few yards from the soles of my boots. Then the birds overhead would start to call again: and I knew them all, then, hearing the crazy call of hadeda ibis in the Luangwa River just out of sight, the orange-breasted bush-shrike singing Beethoven's Fifth, the collared barbets performing their ringing love-duet. And then the mammals would come, for by this time I was myself little more than a tree trunk. If I used my binoculars, I raised them with extreme slowness, as if I was doing tai-chi. And so I became invisible: I became like Alice, while the creatures became like the Fawn, all of us united in a brief and blessed amnesia. Once a warthog and four hoglets passed me like a clockwork train, less than ten yards away, utterly unaware of me, rooting about, feeding, passing on. Perhaps the best moment was the bushbuck. In Tenniel's drawing of Alice and the Fawn, the creature is impossibly limpid-eyed and lovely. A bushbuck, striped and spotted and accustomed to trusting this camouflage in the dappled light of the wooded areas of the Valley, is even lovelier: almost a Platonic ideal of what a sylvan creature should look like. And a male, modestly horned, gloriously painted, walked closer and closer to me, and I sat in perfect stillness, so that he walked to within ten feet, maybe less.

So there I was, with the great Luangwa River on my left, an ebony tree at my back and before me, the glorious mysteries of the glade, lit by occasional violent shafts of sunlight, hammering down almost vertically, the orange-breasted bush-shrike calling sweetly from above, the long-tailed glossy starlings at my feet chattering amiably and interminably to each other, for they are a garrulous species, and ahead, not quite in touching distance, a living creature that out-Bambis Bambi. I could almost reach out and clasp my arms lovingly around the soft and painted neck.

Dear me! The bushbuck, with a doubletake reminiscent of Buster Keaton, realised who I was, or perhaps who he was: "I'm a bushbuck! And dear me! You're a human!" The glade exploded: the bushbuck's furious deep bark was followed by crashing and squawking and screeching and flapping away. It was all over.

And so I had lost my innocence all over again. I went to join Bob for a bottle of Mosi.

84

But then, just as June was getting into its stride, it was time to leave the sacred combes of Suffolk, and set off for a few weeks of concentrated nature deprivation. Let me not complain: I was off to cover the football World Cup for the *Times*, and that was a thrilling and absorbing assignment, which gave me wonderful tales to tell (if not exactly the ones I had been hoping for). It was a great trip: and I am rightly to be envied for it.

All the same, these trips are hard for all of us, in our different ways. We all miss family and friends and routine: and I suspect that we all, in our different ways, feel deprived of nature: even if it's only – but what's only? – the nature we find in June in our gardens, the golf course, the barbie, the pub garden.

So it is inevitable, then, if rather odd, that my strongest memories of my time in Germany are a strange mixture: the action itself, the various pressrooms, the desperate journeys from one corner of the country to the other, the good cheer of Munich, the grandeur and self-consciousness of Berlin, the dinners alone, the rare moments of socialising, the splendid trains, the books I read on them (Goethe, Nietzsche, Clausewitz, Gras), the various grapplings with my laptop as I struggled to tell the tale, and – as important, if not more important than any of them – brief moments of collision with the wild: and of course, the birds that sang with German accents.

The Germans, being romantic, have some splendidly wild parks in the middle of their towns and their cities. They also see wildness itself as a cure for your ailments. It is called taking the waters: you visit a spa town, take the waters, and, emphatically as part of the cure, the physical and spiritual decoke, you walk in pleasant parks. I remember the Kurpark in Bad Homburg, where I spent a surreal two nights quite alone, not knowing a cat in the entire place.

But at least I listened to blackcap, chaffinch, blackbird and nuthatch, with their Germanic stresses and tonalities: swifts overhead, and a buzzard or two. The air was full of fluff: the floating linden seeds, hanging there in shafts of sunlight.

In Munich, they have the Englische Garten: an idealised wild landscape, calculatedly rough at the edges. There were goosander, not a duck you see every day, on the ornamental lake, and in the canopy the chiffchaffs, who, being German, sang *zilpzalp zilpzalp*.

And in Bonn, in the botanical gardens, a squirrel at my feet – red, of course, the greys haven't got here – hopping about with that overload of charm given by the tufty red ears. My old friend Jim called as I sat there, topping up my depleted reserves of nature.

"What are you up to?"

"Annihilating all that's made to a green thought in a green shade."

"Marvellous."

85

Nietzsche's life was a philosophical journey from piety to nihilism to the assertion of the will and the acquisition of pure power. I wondered if this is a journey that would have lead – had Nietzsche lived another hundred years or so – to a return to the natural world. So much of the destruction of nature has been done not because it was necessary, or even terribly useful: but because it was an expression of power. Turning a rainforest into a piss-poor cattle ranch has no serious long-term economic or political advantage. But that's not why you do it: you do it because you can. The destruction of the natural world is in many ways an expression of pure power, unsullied by ideas of personal advantage. I teach you the Superman, Nietzsche said. Man is something that should be overcome... the Superman is the meaning of the earth. Let your will say: the Superman shall be the meaning of the earth.

One look at the graveyard of a rainforest, as I have seen in Borneo, will tell you that all this has come to pass. The Superman is indeed the meaning of the earth.

Superman is something that should be overcome.

86

Access to nature is not to be measured in negatives. It usually is, you know: "absence of stress" is the usual phrase. But the natural world doesn't only remove stresses: it also adds something. It adds wildness, what else? And there are many studies and surveys that demonstrate this point. Sick people heal faster when they have a window to look out of, and faster again when they can see trees from that window. Office workers work better: there was a survey of 1,200 people, and it was shown that those that could see trees, bushes and grass from their workspace showed significantly less frustration, and had significantly more enthusiasm for their work. There have been surveys on those that do detailed work like proof-reading: those that had wilder working conditions did the job better. The point of all this is that wildness is not a wacky idea I have just come up with: it is not a precious little conceit of a bad birdwatcher. It is a profound and essential part of human nature, and what's more, it is statistically verifiable.

87 How could it not be? We have changed the way we live at the most amazing speed: but we cannot change who we are at the same rate. Our hearts and souls and minds have been unable to keep up. Perhaps we will never truly catch up. We have evolved for the wild: the changes have come far too swiftly for us, and as a result, the deeper parts of us are forever missing the wild. We are not dead parrots, no: we are all of us just a little blue: all of us are pining for the fjords.

88 Humans have reached this unique state of affairs because we have found a way to put evolution on fast forward. The method we use is cultural transmission. Before humans invented language, the only way for changes to be made was by means of natural selection: that is to say, genetic transmission. This is something that takes place over the course of generations: if a change is good, the being that inherited the change is more likely to survive, breed, and pass on that change, and so on, and so on, until, in the classic example, a species of sky-reaching mammals became giraffes. There is no evidence to suggest that the process went too fast for giraffes: that they are sad, alienated creatures who live with a permanent nostalgia for the low and the short. Evolution goes at a natural pace: one that the hearts and minds of the evolving creature can, it seems, readily deal with.

But humans have found an additional way of changing. What one generation acquires, the next generation can take on right away. There is no need for the prolonged, generation-after-generation process of testing. Humans can acquire changes within their own lifetimes, implement them and then pass them on. As a result, the human way of life has changed at a speed no other creature has ever experienced.

Over the past 65 million years, since the fall of the dinosaurs, mammals have been the dominant large creatures of the earth. In a slow and inexorable way, the modern fauna of the planet has evolved. From one common ancestor, from times much earlier than the fall of the dinosaurs, the mammals have radiated out, in endless forms most beautiful, to become bats and antelopes, shrews and tigers, foxes and pandas. And from one lineage the primates came to be, bringing the world the lemurs of Madagascar, the monkeys, the apes and the humans.

The monkeys of South America developed prehensile tails, and so they can climb as no humans ever will (so perhaps they are the crown of creation). The humans developed prehensile brains, along with upright stance and hands as precision tools. They went on to create language. That development allowed humankind to reach a kind of critical mass: and so human life began to change at an impossible and ever-quickening rate: a pace unprecedented in evolutionary history.

Of course there were cataclysms and planet-wide disasters before humans came along. There have, as we know, been five major extinction episodes in the planet's history. But the sustained pace of change is something that has never happened before. And while the endless breakneck changing has brought us Joyce and Bach and Leonardo and Dante and Homer and Newton and Darwin, it has also brought us London and New York, stinking pollution, a concrete world from which the heavens are no longer visible, clear-felled forests and an ever-increasing population that yearns ever more fervently with every passing day for some little bit of wildness in our lives.

We are city-clickers with hunter-gatherer souls: we have evolved for the wild and we have created a world of oppressive tameness. We are out of step with our selves and the society we have built with such reckless brilliance. We need wildness in our lives: and the more wildness we destroy, the more clear it becomes: we need it more than ever.

And there is no substitute.

89

The day after I returned from the World Cup in Germany, I rode my young horse out by herself for the first time. This was a great day. Horses are herd animals: they need to be together. One horse is no horse: independence is an alien state. To train a young horse to walk out alone, relaxed and confident, is a wonderful thing. It meant that she had reached some kind of accommodation with the contradictions in her nature: wildness, tameness. She was prepared to trust humans enough to go against her natural desire to be with other horses. And I, the human in question, had to reach out and give my trust to her. I rode relaxed, easy, undemanding, holding onto the buckle of the reins, not nagging and insisting: just trusting. We had reached the no man's land: the border-country that lies between one species and another: between humans and non-humans. It's a pretty wild place, believe me.

And in a moment of glorious appropriateness, we moved through a vast field of poppies: poppies in full bloom, poppies like a multitudinous sea of incarnadine. I have a picture of the event somewhere: a lone rider, hands and heels doing nothing whatsoever, sitting up and looking forward, a horse, slim, light-boned, relaxed, ears cocked optimistically forwards: a small dark point in a vast landscape of red.

The poppy is the greatest of all emblems of the human need for the wild. Even in the horrors — especially amid the horrors — of life in the trenches, with blood and disease and death and misery a daily companion, the sight of something growing, living, thriving in the devastated landscape gave some kind of hope. Now, nearly a century on, the poppy is as vivid a symbol as ever: inspiration for the greatest fund-raising event of the year. The poppy in no man's land stands for the human need to find hope beyond the self-imposed horrors of the human condition.

Stephen Moss gives a chapter to the First World War in his social history of birdwatching, *A Bird in the Bush*. Again and again, he produces deeply moving evidence of the comfort and hope given to the soldiers by the fragments of wild life that somehow continued to survive despite the fact that the end of the world was taking place on a daily basis and the men all around were living in a pretty fair approximation of hell. One quotation must serve for all: this from John William Street:

Hushed is the shriek of hurtling shells: and hark!
Somewhere within that bit of deep blue sky,
Grand in his loneliness, his ecstasy,
His lyric wild and free, carols a lark.
I in the trenches, he lost in heaven afar;
I dream of love, its ecstasy he sings...

The lark above the trenches. Ever since I first read about him, this lark has stayed with me. It has become a kind of personal archetype: a great universal symbol of the human need for the wild: of the way the wild can, if only for a brief second, give humans relief from the hell we have created.

90 Down to Wimbledon for the tennis. As usual, I stayed at my father's place, at Mortlake, down by the river. This gives us good opportunities for eating, drinking, talking and birding.

Lord, but that river always takes me back: back through 40 years, to my schooldays. The Emanuel School boathouse is hard by Barnes Bridge: I used to emerge from its fastness to cox eights: the Junior A, and latterly, the Colts A. After ramming most of the bridges and the moored boats in the river, I gave up, expressing my sporting spirit by going down to the river and then turning my back on the boat-house, to drink halves of bitter at the Coach and Horses in Barnes High Street.

But I can still remember the stench of that river. Unapologetically vile: vile, as if this were the only way a river could be. And lifeless, of course, apart from black-headed gulls who, being adaptable creatures, scavenged for rubbish and quarked. It was a stinking un-living testament to Rachel Carson's great book, *Silent Spring*.

It was seen as a jeremiad, a prophecy of doom, a realisation that disaster had been created, and now could not be uncreated. It was one of the most important books ever written: no question about that. But as I stepped down to the river that July, it was to revel in nature. No stink. Only birds. *Silent Spring* not only told its history: it also changed history.

The waters of the Thames are clean again – cleaner, any-way, than they were when the Junior A splashed and bum-shoved its way between Barnes and Kew and back again, while I shouted hoarsely in the vain hope that by doing so, I might ensure that eight blades entered the stinking waters at roughly the same moment. As a result of this cleanliness, the plants are back, the fishes are back and, as the most obvious proof of all this backness, the birds are back as well. Bring back the fish, and the fish-eaters will surely follow. That's ecology for you. By that token, if you see fish-eating birds by a stretch of water, you don't have to test the water to see if it's good. The presence of the fish-eaters tells you all you need to know.

There is a small, disused reservoir ten minutes away from my father's door. It is one of those stolen places: a wild place in the middle of town. Cormorants strike heraldic poses in the trees; a heronry of half a dozen nests forms every spring, and throughout the year, herons, young and old, roost and fish and preen in the points of vantage around the sheltered unstinking waters while ducks fuss and splash and snooze.

Rafts have been placed out in the middle, to expand the roosting and nesting possibilities of the reservoir. On a raft, the rats can't get you: and a rat-free riverside residence is highly desirable to the fish-eaters. Since the rafts were put in, common terns come and nest here, and have done so for a decade or two now: definitely tern, that is to say, not possibly tern. It is an extraordinary delight to see these sleek exoticisms in the place where I once knew nothing but stench: dashing white birds darting like arrows over the water, or making their melodramatic winged-dagger plunge-dives beneath its surface: all the more lovely for the thought that 40 years ago, the idea of bringing terns back to London was like bringing fairies back to the bottom of your garden.

Conservation works. Rewilding works. A good deal of harm *can* be undone. Spring can be, to a fair extent has been, unsilenced. A good deal of harm has been undone, as the otters will tell you. But never enough, never enough.

91

How swiftly it all turns. The long, slow build-up to spring seems to move into repletion and achievement and change without any moment of celebration. There is no pause between the year's apex and its steep decline. On the bank of the reservoir in Mortlake, four huge, great, fluffy cygnets, asleep and apparently uncaring about where they did so. Any old where will do. At this reservoir, a swan doesn't have to look for a safe place. A swan is a safe place. Meanwhile, two young kestrels were messing around in the treetops, playing at Spitfires and Messerschmitts, or as my father prefers, Sharks and Jets: "When you're a kes, you a kes," he sings, annually, on this walk. They shriek – grown-up kestrels are seldom very gabby birds – and swoop and dart and plunge at each other, expressing all the skills they will need in later life and doing so in the form of sport. They are young hooligans having the time of their lives: *kikiki!*

And it was all as if I had turned over two pages at once. A looking-forward had turned to a looking-back: anticipation had turned to nostalgia, and all in the blinking of an eye. Summer ousted spring like an over-enthusiastic night-club bouncer. Back in Suffolk, the air was full of swifts and swallows and martins: but the trees and the hedges were silent. The singing had stopped: but summers are supposed to be silent. Only the yellowhammer sung with any reliability, carolling endlessly about a little bit of bread and no *cheeeeeese*.

I felt a need for celebration, one that the birds mostly deny you, for they are too preoccupied with the rearing of young and the thoughts of the harder seasons that lie ahead. But I have got better at looking over the years, and I have learned tentatively that the insects will make a very decent celebration for you. The high summer is their time. A walk across the grass brings showers of tiny shards of life briefly into vision: mostly unknowable, mysterious nameless things. Micromoths: each one a small brown speck of life, a single note in the symphony of diversity. There are 40-odd butterflies readily seen in this country: more than 2,000 moths. And I don't suppose I will ever know any of these micromoths by name: all I can do is bow my head as I walk, both to look and to salute the endless wonders of diversity, to salute the small brown legions that can preach an endless sermon on the endless creativity of nature.

But I can at least name some of the butterflies, in a not-too-precise way: along the dog-walk: meadow brown, small white, red admiral, gatekeeper, comma, painted lady. Gaudy bits of life, flaunting, unmissable, inescapably glorious, sipping at nectar to prolong their brief sex-mad lives. The painted ladies are migrants: it seems insane that such pretty and fluttery wings could take these creatures from the Continent over to our own island. If you ever wish to be astonished, take any small speck of life at random, and look, or listen, or learn just half a fact. Each scrap of life is more astonishing than we suppose: more astonishing that we *can* suppose.

92

High hopes and low expectations. When Joe and I set off to look for wildlife, we recite that phrase to each other as a kind of embarkment prayer. There is no point in visiting wild places and setting yourself up for a disappointment. There is a sense, very much a sense, that being in wild places where wild things are is the real experience: that seeing them is an occasional bonus. I remember Joe's delight when we were in the wonderful expanses of the Coto Doñana in Spain, and were shown the fresh footmarks of an Iberian lynx: there we were, in the same place as the most endangered big cat on earth.

I will never forget an occasion when I visited the faintly sinister spaces of Hickling Broad in Norfolk, and saw 30 marsh harriers with three barn owls hunting in constant sight for an hour and a half, and someone turned away at dusk and grumped: "Well, that was really disappointing." He had hoped for another of the specialities of that mysterious place. I wouldn't have minded seeing them myself: but I was well content with the miracles I had actually seen.

So when Joe and I went to Aberdeen to look for dolphins, we very much had it in mind that we might well not see any. But we would be where dolphins are: and we would take the adventure that Aslan sent us.

We went there to meet some people from Seawatch Foundation, a marine charity that looks to the conservation of cetaceans: whales and dolphins. It always impresses me how popular these animals are: because very few people get to see them. People aren't keen on saving whales and dolphins so that they can have the pleasure of watching them. The only conclusion I can come to is that people like the idea of them: feel that life is better for having these wacky beings leaping about in the sea: so like us, so unlike us.

The previous year, Joe and I had been dolphin-hunting in Cardigan Bay: joined a commercial trip, again with Seawatch, and we had seen a couple of dozen, and it was a wonderful treat. This is one place where the dolphins are pretty accessible, provided that you bear in mind the appropriate prayer before setting off.

But this time, to Scotland. There was a heatwave in England: blisteringly hot. We stepped off the plane into a cold and clammy seafret: Scotland, as they will tell you if you ask, is not England. So, in late afternoon, we went to Stonehaven, and set off on a fishing boat with Sarah

Canning, a Seawatch volunteer. We went to look for mammals: and we had one of the most extraordinary birding days I have ever experienced.

The mist was sitting right down on the sea. There was about 100 yards visibility in any direction: no great conditions for detecting a splash of tail, a sharp dorsal fin slashing the surface. But sometimes, often, you don't find the dolphin: they find you. Their curiosity, their apparent affinity for humans, brings them bouncing and curvetting in towards you. It was worth giving them the chance to do it, anyway.

So we chugged out, beneath fearsome ramparts of cliffs, amid the sound and stench that only a seabird colony can bring you. Not optimal viewing conditions for bird-watching, either, not if you wanted to see every detail of plumage: but this wild and strange occasion had something else. In this wierd, spooky atmosphere, you could look up at these cliffs, tan studded white, as white as the night sky I had gazed at with Evans. Kittiwake, guillemot, razorbill: at the top, puffins. An all-encompassing sensual experience: the sight, the sound, the smell, the taste: fish-stinky stench of life.

We left the cliffs and went out to sea, losing sight of land in 30 seconds. Soon it was as if we were travelling in our own personal hemisphere of light, a couple of hundred yards in diameter: a hemisphere travelling very slowly, and very, very bouncily, through an opaque world of shimmering silver-grey: and into its fastness birds would arrive, birds would disappear, joining us in our world for a few seconds before carrying on into the impregnable silver of their own. Mostly, they were auks, razorbills and guillemots and puffins, coming through on madly whirring wings, like tiny flying penguins, swimming birds who had hung onto the gift of flight. The puffins especially seemed scarcely capable of staying aloft, almost as inept in flight as the flying squirrels, but still somehow proceeding gamely. The water is their element: they are masters of the waves and what's beneath them: but their madly whirring wings take them from fishingplace to fishingplace, and up to the cliff summits where their young are eagerly anticipating a beakful of sand eels. And then, every so often, into our hemisphere and out again, a flight of gannets, low to the sea, pointed, black-tipped wings, spear-sharp yellow beaks, ferocious yellow eyes, a visitation from another world. Once or twice, black-caped like a marine Dracula, the sinister shape of Arctic skua.

93 Next day, we saw them. And not from a boat: from the shore, from the Torrey Battery, a five-minute stroll from the heart of town. Sarah saw them, as Joe was clambering intrepidly on the rocks, and I was looking out at the rafts of eider and the scoters, sea ducks that find city life in Aberdeen gloriously amenable. Just 50 yards offshore, proceeding unhurriedly along the coast, two dolphin: cow and calf, as they are rather incongruously termed, mother and child, if you prefer. Risso's dolphin, to be precise: pale, round-headed, and typically marked by scars that heal in prominent white.

An unexpectedly gorgeous little sight: the two of them travelling onwards in that curious dolphin way, a constant undulation, down to beneath the surface to travel: up to the surface to breath, the head breaking the surface, then, as the dolphin seems to revolve like a wheel, the dorsal fin and the lower back appearing in turn. At this working pace, they don't slip their tails high and clear, or leap from the surface: this was a matter of going from A to B, two dolphins going about their business, within a few yards of a city utterly caught up with the hustle and bustle and business of its own.

Aberdeen is like that: a strangely wild place, a place whose life is the sea: to the extent that you find oyster-catchers – shorebirds, wading birds – piping at you from the flat roofs and, I was told, occasionally even nesting on these dizzy and unaccustomed heights. A ten-minute stroll from our B & B took us to the mouth of the Don: and at a small island, just below the bridge where the buses crank up and down all day long, we saw four seals, hauled out and resting up as the traffic hustled and bustled by. On the sea-ward side of the bridge, we saw terns and a female goosander with a massive brood of thirteen ducklings.

It wasn't the trip we had planned or expected. The bet-ter for that. They're not bloody tame, you know. Being dis-appointed is part of the pleasure: and it gives the edge to the moments of privilege when it all goes right. Risso's dol-phin, eh? And those seabirds, flying in and out of our hemi-sphere of light: unforgettable.

94

"Never mind where we bloody are," said our leader. "Just stop if you see a bird." The point at issue was whether we were in Zambia or Zaire. Our leader, insofar as he can be dignified with such a term, was Bob, old friend, old Africa hand, ornithologist, a man more properly known as Baron Robert Stjernstedt. The reason for being there was Pearson's cisticola. Yes, one of those.

The company was Bob, me, Chris Breen, who runs a wildlife travel company called Wildlife Worldwide, and Aaron Mushindu of the Livingstone Museum. We were in the North-west Province of Zambia. At least, we thought so. The border here is a somewhat vague concept, but a thrilling one for all that: it follows the line of the Congo-Zambezi watershed. On one side of a hill, all the streams eventually drain into the mighty Zambezi; on the other side, they all drain into the equally mighty Congo. We had been travelling along the spine of Africa: now we were either on the Zambezi and Zambian side, or the Congo and Zairois side. Bob, vague on location but precise on birds, wished only to stop if we saw a bird-party making its way through the light, moist woods we were travelling through, and to see if Pearson's cisticola was among them. Aaron was keen to stay on the right side of the great watershed, and he was driving. He was only going to stop when he found a village, and someone to talk to about where we bloody were.

Pearson's cisticola had not been seen in the wild since 1936, and you could understand why. This was not easy travelling. We camped out in the wet woods; I cooked vast tangy stews on the gas cooker; we drank Mosi and Jameson's. This, then, was birding – I beg your pardon, science – with a tang of danger about it. That is why it was so good, why it is still so strong in the memory.

But who is bloody Pearson? There are two contenders in the indispensable book *Who's Bird*? It might have been Dr Arthur Pearson, who was at least at the right place at the right time, or, more likely, Edward Pearson of the Australian Museum, a renowned collector of skins – that is to say, dead birds – and a namer and cataloguer of the same – that is to say, a taxonomist. Take your pick.

Pearson's cisticola is also referred to as the slender-tailed or even black-tailed cisticola, which doesn't help sort out the confusion. It is generally regarded as a subspecies of the nedicky: but we knew better. Bob and I had examined three Pearson's skins at the great British Museum collection at Tring in Hertfordshire. We saw for ourselves what other experts had suggested: that the feathers on the leading edge

175

of the wing – on the alula, or bastard wing, to be precise – had a noticeably thickened shaft, or rachis. It had been suggested that the birds – perhaps only the male birds – use this to make a noise: what ornithologists call a "mechanical" noise, like the wing-clapping of pigeons or the beak-clattering of storks. One 30-second glimpse of a so-called nedicky making a whirring or rattling noise as it flew and we would have established beyond doubt that Pearson's was a good species.

I hope I've made that perfectly obscure. But another point of the trip was good craic. Hence the Jameson's.

We eventually found a village, a small collection of huts gathered there beneath the gentle Zambian rains, and asked where we were. Aaron, like all Africans, knew half a dozen languages, for an African is the least insular person on earth. A tall, slender woman detached herself from the group sitting together under the thatch, and walked towards us – unselfconsciously sashayed towards us – with all the grace of America's next top model. It's carrying stuff on your head that gives you that wonderful posture. Her uncommonly pretty face lit up at Aaron's question. No, we weren't in Zambia. We were beneath gentle Zairois rains. We were in quite deep, ten miles at least. We turned round to look for Zambia: for half a second I wondered if I shouldn't jump out and stay there forever with this Narina of the Zairois forest.

Well, we didn't find Pearson's on that trip. We found one nedicky that might indeed have been a Pearson's, but it flew off. The birds had clearly vacated the forest for a while; some inflexion of seasonal movements had undone us. We were too early: we were too late. It's all one, in these time-less corners of the world.

But we still made a contribution to science. While we were there, we made a careful note of every bird species we saw, partly for the good birding craic of it, but also for the science. We kept two separate lists, one for each of the map squares we were in. The map and its squares had been drawn up by the Zambian Ornithological Society: they were in the process of creating a bird atlas for the entire country. One glance at the map of Zambia, divided into 30 km squares – that is to say, 900 square kilometres each – and you would know the distribution of each bird on the Zambian list. To each species, a Zambian map: with the squares in which it had been seen clearly marked. A distribution map. It was an epic, pioneering project, it took years and it required travel into the places where people armed with binoculars and copies of Roberts' *Birds of Southern Africa* and *The Birds of Zambia* don't normally go.

We got back to Lusaka and gave our information to the head of ZOS, Dylan Aspinwall, and after doing the maths, he told us that we had recorded 35 new species for the atlas. Thanks to our intrepid party, the frontiers of science had been pushed back by a distance of half a micron or so.

A miracle took place on our last day in the forest. I had made the evening meal; Aaron had made a fire. It was time for a drink. We knew we had four rather warm bottles of Mosi, and were unsure as to how to divide these between three (Aaron, being wise, did not drink). And lo and behold, the bottles had multiplied over the course of the day, and now there were six. We drank them, then had a large slug of Jameson's around the brave fire in the damp, mysterious and more than faintly dangerous woods. Danger: diversity: companionship: a nice drink.

A good way to celebrate all that is grand and mysterious and wonderful about life. Only Narina could have improved my lot.

95

I've heard it called the Nightmare Scenario. It is the idea that you can remake the wild: that a place – a planet – can be rewilded. So I went out into Bradfield Wood in West Suffolk on a warm and drowsy summer day to take part in the Nightmare Scenario.

Dormice. Ridiculous, impossible little things: you could easily hold a dozen of them in your cupped palms. They live in the canopies of woods: tiny, and, contrary to their reputation, quick as lightning. They used to live in the canopy here, but then they didn't. Local extinction. No one is precisely sure why this took place: but it seemed to have happened after half the wood was clear-felled and ploughed just after the Second World War.

What's left of the wood is still pretty wonderful: a working wood, owned and managed by Suffolk Wildlife Trust, and full of the hazel coppice that dormice love. Coppicing is something people do to trees, especially hazels: you cut them off at ground level, and the tree will then put forth a dozen or so shoots. After a dozen years, you can harvest these: good, strong, stout and above all, straight poles, useful for all kinds of important things. I have a stick, very handy on dog-walks – I said *wait* – made from a wand of coppiced hazel from a wood just outside my village. A patch of hazel coppice is thick and dense and bushy and leafy and full of stout living poles and, in season, full of nuts. Coppicing is a human rather than a wild process: but it happens to make habitat ideal for dormice and, for that matter, nightingale.

So what do you do about a perfect dormouse habitat that

has no dormice? Put the dormice back, of course. Rewild the place. And so I met up with Simone Bullion, self-confident, knowledgeable, a trifle severe, to put the dormice back. She had been running the project since the spring. She had established a series of release cages: places in which the dormice can rest up, recover from the excitements of translocation, get food and water, and, when the door to the cage is opened, begin tentatively to explore the possibilities of a wild existence. We were on a feeding run: my task, as Simone kept her records, was to supply each cage with grapes, a bit of apple, a few sultanas and half a rich tea biscuit. At the beginning, they were fed every day: now, it was every three days. In some of the cages, all the food had gone, showing that the dormice were alive and well and hungry. In others it had hardly been touched. This could mean that the dormouse was dead: or that it had successfully rewilded itself, and was now foraging with confidence and effectiveness. You just didn't know. Simone recorded the data before her: expressed cautious hope.

We didn't see a single dormouse all day. But then you don't. They are not creatures for the seeing. That begs the question: why bother to put them back? This has two answers. They are completely contradictory, and they're both right. The first is that conservation is not about human gratification. It's about doing the right thing by life, by biodiversity, by the requirements of the wild world. The second is that *all* conservation is gratifying to humans: that Bradfield Wood feels the better, the richer, for the knowledge that it has dormice in it. The world itself seems slightly better for knowing that dormice have been put back into it.

But it is certainly true that rewilding is the Nightmare Scenario. We shouldn't be out there checking up on the lives of captive-bred dormice, each one of known parentage, as recorded, believe it or not, in the Dormouse

Stud Book. We shouldn't have been feeding them, watering them, tending to their cages. We shouldn't have been demonstrating to the world that if things go wrong, there is quite often a way of putting things right. No: things shouldn't have gone wrong in the first place. The dormice should have been there all along, they should never have gone extinct, and the other half of Bradfield Wood should never have gone missing. But all these things have come to pass. So we put the Nightmare Scenario into action because there is no other option available. The nightmare is upon us.

96

Cornwall was the site of my first ecological disaster. I have been going down to Cornwall for holidays since I was ten. My father still owns a place down there, and as usual, we descended on him for a week of high summer. For me, Cornwall is a place of deeply layered and highly complex meanings, by no means all of them comfortable. Too much of the place has changed; too much of the place has remained the same. Cornwall is a place in which I am far too conscious of the infinite complexities of time. There is a place, along the rocks, to which I would scramble with boyish fear and intrepidity, there to reach the gully and look down on its boiling waters. Just below the cliff-edge was a ledge. It was the done thing, the required thing, to lower yourself onto this ledge, and observe the gully from its vantage. I always did so, even when alone: it was a curiously satisfying thing to do. I remember making this journey, this pilgrimage some years later. The ledge had gone. Simply vanished. Sheered off. Can't have been very strong, like the dead branch on the Pigeon Tree. It support-ed my seven-stone boy's body well enough, though, as I admired the water, the rocks below, my own daring. Its vanishment was oddly disquieting: reminding me of the impermanence of youth, the impermanence even of rock: my youth and my ledge now at the bottom of the gully, gone for good.

I was sixteen when the ecological disaster happened. The oil tanker, *Torrey Canyon* hit a rock and discharged its cargo into the clean and living sea. All 31 million gallons of it. That was only the start of the trouble. The worst of it was the cleaning up. An attempt was made to disperse the oil by bunging detergent on it: detergent cuts oil and grease, as you know from doing the washing-up. But the detergent was worse than the oil. It killed everything it touched.

I had been an enthusiastic boy snorkeller, dipping into the rock-pools to gaze at the wonders below: the gardens of sea anemones, the moving and far more animal-like sea-weeds, the darting fish, the half-buried molluscs, the skulking crabs. I had loved the through-the-looking-glass moment when one instant you are in one world, the next instant, in another: the way that in the ducking of a head, the cloudy and obscure becomes clear and still more mysterious. But when I returned to Cornwall after the *Torrey Canyon*, the pools were dead. Lifeless. The *Torrey Canyon* was a living experience of the Silent Spring. The mysteries of the life beneath the surface had gone: it was all just plain old salty water.

And I knew for the first time the helpless outrage: the sense that they were ruining it: ruining a place that I loved, ruining everything else. They! They, the great enemies of us all. The term had yet to be invented, but what I was demonstrating here was nimbyism: as in Not In My Back Yard. It is used as a term of abuse, as a way of somehow discrediting opposition to any unpleasant and damaging scheme. The idea is that a nimbyist is perfectly willing to reap the benefits of whatever is being planned, so long as it is somebody else's backyard.

181

Put like that, it is indeed a little contemptible: but then, if we suggest moving the development, another band of nimbyists is always likely to take up arms. And quite right too. We are right to try and protect the places we love, the places that have a personal meaning for us. The wreck of the *Torrey Canyon* taught me a great deal about love.

I had grown used to gazing at these pools and saying, in the manner of old codgers, eeh, but it was all so much better than this when I was young. And I was absolutely right: my memory wasn't playing me false. The rock-pools were much less rich, much less wild, than the mysterious and fecund places I had hovered over, flying so bravely with my Woolworth's snorkel over my face. But at last, with a rock-pool explorer of my own to be responsible for, I was able to acknowledge, almost grudgingly, certainly gratefully, that, yes, the pools are now very much as they were when I first dared to enter them. And now, as I write these words, I make a mental note: make sure Joe has a snorkel next summer. There are things for him to see.

Cornwall was a special place for my family: a magic holiday place where normal rules were set aside. It was here I learned to love one of the greatest pleasures in human life: walking from A to B in a pretty place. It was here I acquired a good deal of my affinity for nature. I had been a bad boy birder; later on, a star-struck (no light pollution here) delighter in the pantheistic joys of it all, studiously vague on details. I had shared Cornwall's pleasures with my oldest friend Ralph, and we had experienced many excesses and austerities together. I had brought beautiful girls down to Cornwall, and played the game of laugh and lie down.

All these Cornish ghosts: all these and many others. And all complicated by Cornwall's wild richness: and by all my concerns about how much had changed, and how much had changed for the worse.

97

No childhood place is ever the same in adulthood. No grove is ever quite as enchanted as it was when you were young, no combe ever quite as sacred. But in hard and literal terms, this corner of Cornwall really wasn't the same. More than anything else, I remember the glow-worms. Evening walks along the track to the old tin mine were always lit by glow-worms: we would go down there as teenagers to giggle and discuss God and Life and all those other important things. But it's years since I last saw a glow-worm here. And crickets: the crickets were infinitely noisier. I remember being deafened by them: a constant ambient buzz. Now the ways and the walks are much quieter. Sometimes I think it's the invertebrates we really need to worry about: a diversity that is being lost without anybody even noticing. And as the insects vanish, so will the animals that feed on them and the plants they pollinate and the soil they aerate. No one does much shouting for bugs: we are normally only aware of them in negative ways: when wasps disrupt a picnic, when a midge gets into an eye, when a buzzling demands a certain caution, when a spider frightens, when a daddy-longlegs spooks us by flying into our face and caressing us with is absurd limbs, when a moth causes distress by his determinedly suicidal behaviour.

Without them, life – human life, all other kinds of life – becomes impossible. But this was to be a vivid trip for insects. In the kitchen, sitting there with the frankness that baffles townspeople, a dark bush cricket, a big and imposing creature identified resoundingly by me with the help of the most basic insect guide. And then I was summoned to the garden by Joe and his cousin Max, who made the trip with us: they had found "a huge grasshopper".

Actually, it wasn't. I looked him up as well. He was sitting on the outdoor table, the one around which my father likes to take pre-lunch Pimm's, and as I peered at him, he made a hop and landed on Max's shoulder. Max dealt with this emergency with commendable calm: and I chivvied the insect away with a careful finger. This one was a great green bush cricket, identified from the same source. Their stridulations – fine word – are audible, I read, from up to 150 metres. Not gone, then, yet, these crickets, though quieter, certainly.

But still no glow-worms.

98

My father and I walked to Porthleven together. For about the thousandth time. It's a wonderful walk: not much more than an hour and half, so long as you don't see too much on the way, some strenuous bits where the cliff plunges to the sea and then rises up again, dramatic views, a generous rhythm of gradually easier uppy-downies as you come towards the end of the walk. It's the exact opposite of Suffolk – perhaps that explains my love of Suffolk, not so much a matter of perversity as of wonder that a place can be so wildly different. In Cornwall, it's all melodramatic transitions between land and sea. But in Suffolk, there's land, and then there's sea, and a load of soft, sandy, marshy, muddy, shingly bits in between – vague places, indeterminate places, places that can't really make up their mind whether they are land or sea. In Suffolk, you have a soft and volatile coast. Before the seawalls and the semi-taming, the Suffolk coast was in a constant state of flux. And now the coast is beginning to change again as the seawall is breached by rising seas, and then breached again. But in Cornwall, the coast has no vagueness: dramatic land meets dramatic sea in a welter of foam.

So we walked the towering way to Porthleven, walked

on the hard, high land above the never-gentle Cornish sea, and there were still fulmar, gliding on stiff wings, very pointedly not being gulls – they are more closely related to albatross and fly with the same insouciance – and there were kittiwakes wailing their names with heart-rending sobs. At Tremearne my father looked at the grazing meadow crossed by the cliff path and said sadly: "Look at the state of this field. It used to be a beautiful, lush meadow." Now it was rough and pitted and its uniform rich green had gone. And just past Treamearne, a tight group of black birds, messing around together in a cheerily pointless fashion. Jackdaws: but then, as I looked, they were quite clearly not jackdaws. Something about the tightness of the group, and the flamboyance of aerobatics: and a hint – they were a distance off and the wind was in the wrong direction – of that very distinctive voice.

Get the bins on them, get the bins on them. Looking for the hint of red that must be there: there's not an atom of red on a jackdaw. And finding it: yes, choughs. A bird so Cornish that it supports the Cornish coat of arms: a bird that is sometimes known as the Cornish chough. And here's a strange thing: there were no choughs in Cornwall when I was young. I looked for them when I first came to Cornwall, in all my innocence, trying to believe that at least some of the cliff-loving jackdaws were really choughs, not knowing that choughs had gone extinct in Cornwall years ago.

And there they were. In Cornwall. Talking to each other: saying not chuff but chowww, sticking enthusiastically to their tight family group: sleek black birds, small crows to be precise, with startlingly bright red legs and red decurved beaks. Their scientific name *Pyrrhocorax pyrrhocorax* translates as fire-raven, or rather, Fire-raven fire-raven. And they were back: had been for two or three years now. A miracle: and not a miracle.

Conservationists had been researching choughs for some time: what do they need? Why did they go? If we put them back again, what do we need to make sure they stay around and survive and prosper? One of the answers to this was rough pasture by the edge of the sea, near cliffs: with the changes in agriculture, there were far fewer meadows around. So farmers were offered the chance to farm in sympathy with choughs for a payment from the government: hence the disimprovements to that meadow at Tremearne. Choughs like to get their beaks in the soft earth and look for invertebrates. They can't deal with hard earth, so they can only live in places scarcely ever touched by frost. But the Cornish cliff-top meadows were reacquiring a measure of chough-friendliness, and conservationists were wondering when to start a reintroduction programme. It was at this point that the choughs took things into their own hands or wings. They came back spontaneously.

No one quite knows where they came from. Perhaps from Brittany, perhaps from Ireland or Wales. But a pair established themselves and bred successfully, established a family group. This year, a female from the band had split off and paired up with another male, again arriving from no one quite knows where. So now there were two families of choughs chowwwwing their way around the cliffs and cliff-meadows of Cornwall.

And that wasn't how it had been when I was young. Rewilding was now taking place before my eyes: and it didn't even need all that much human intervention. Just get the place right again, and the choughs come of their own accord, like air rushing into a vacuum. Light the green touchpaper and stand well back. It works, you know. Conservation really works.

99

I rarely saw a bird of prey when I was young. This was the early 60s: and they were mythical beasts. I peered along the Cornish cliffs looking for the greatest of them all, but I knew I would never see one: and of course I never did. They weren't there. Peregrine! Peregrine falcon! This is a thrilling bird, one of the great imagination-catchers: a great name adding to the fizz and crackle that surrounds the bird. Only seen in the wildest places, it said in the books I read, places to which I would never go, places that weren't in reach of family holidays. Found only in places where no people ever went: I loved the sound of that, too. Imagine: a place so wild that even a peregrine could be content there. I dreamed of peregrines as I dreamed of unicorns.

My father and I did the Porthleven walk again: to meet wife and boys at the Ship for lunch. Buzzards on the way: once near-mythical birds themselves, back in the 60s. Two ravens silhouetted on the cliff-edge: that unmistakable pro-file, the burliness, the bent conk, the beard. I never saw ravens when young either: I suspect because I thought they were crows. That's one of the things that knowing names does for you: it makes a creature from the background step forward and become a star. That's the reason I have always encouraged people to become bad birdwatchers: because turning a crow into a raven, or a jackdaw into a chough, is a fine and thrilling thing. It is not pedantry, no: these are different birds with thrillingly different natures. They fill you with a special touch of wildness: it is worth learning a few small field skills to savour that.

There is a special spot for seeing peregrines on the way to Porthleven. For Cornwall is once again a peregrine stronghold. It's a wonder what wild things can do when we stop killing them. But there was no peregrine on the usual rock. We scanned without luck, while my father told me of the first time he had ever seen one: just a hundred yards further on, at the place where the path hits the top of that steep and dramatic descent to Tremearne. And it was here that a peregrine came up at him as he was just about to start going down. Damn near took his head off. He had, he said, described the moment to Bill Oddie, with whom he has had professional connections. "You'll remember it as one of the great moments of your life," Oddie said. Rightly.

But we reached the pub without a peregrine, though we did have the comic moment of a wheatear jumping off a cliff without opening its wings: remarkable to be so nonchalant about a hundred-foot drop to rocks and the unforgiving sea, but birds don't have the same attitude to gravity as humans. Good lunch: a pint, Cornish leopard bread, cheese.

It was when I was on the beach that afternoon that I saw them. I was playing with Eddie, my younger boy, but I always have at least half an eye open for the passing wild: indeed, I had just seen a butterfly, a large white, land optimistically on Joe's purple water pistol. No, not a flower: flap and move on. Across the beach, swimmers, sunbathers, beach cricketers, frisbeers, rock-pool explorers, picnickers, readers, dozers. August in England: a dramatic place full of undramatic people seeking the wild in an approximate and roundabout fashion.

And above their heads, peregrine falcon. Two of them. Young birds relishing the flex and might of their new wings, chasing each other with a wild excitement. They are the fastest birds in the world when they go into a stoop: but they are pretty bloody fast in straight and level flight. They whizzed over in a few seconds as if powered by jets. I doubt if anyone else on the beach saw them.

Peregrines are birds of hope. Perhaps they are a better symbol of peace than a dove. Because they give out the unambiguous statement that humans can redress some of the mistakes we have made: that rewilding is possible: that the opportunity for an outbreak of peace between humans and nature lies before us. Peregrines were reduced to the status of very rare birds in this country, found only in places seriously remote from humans, for the same reason that the marsh harriers went all but extinct. DDT, eggshell thinning, as mentioned before. The decision to make this cheap and effective insecticide illegal saved Britain's birds of prey.

These days, it's still a thrill to see a falcon. That is partly because all birds of prey are rare: rarer, at least, than the creatures they prey on. Thousands of antelope: one pride of lion. Even if you live in the bush, seeing a lion is a big moment. And here, along these miles of tough and rambling cliffs, many birds: one family of peregrine.

Once it would have been thrilling to see them because peregrines are always rare, always thrilling. Then it would have been thrilling to see them, because they were so desperately close to extinction, because a sighting showed that they were still around, still hanging on by the tips of their talons. And now it is thrilling to see them because they are around again: because they have recovered from near-disaster to a cautious and tenuous stability.

So much so that they are breaking new ground. They have come into cities. It is a rum business. Cities are full of pigeons, because the ancestors of feral pigeons are rock doves, a bird with a taste for vertiginous places. The cliff-scape of a city is just as good for these intrepid and ingeni-ous foragers: and now the peregrines have moved in as well. I have seen them in London, perching in that sultry way that is rather a peregrine speciality, on top of a skyscraper. It was about 400 yards from Baker Street tube.

A great deal has been lost. But this trip to Cornwall was all about recovery: the rock-pools' recovery, after 40 years, from the oil and the detergent, a fact attested to by the loud and splashing explorations of Max and Joe. The peregrines. Peregrine: a name that means stranger, wanderer, pilgrim: traveller to holy places. Well, Cornwall is a place resanctified. A place that has been, at least to an extent, at least to a very clear and noticeable extent, rewilded.

100 But all the same, the insects were the best.

For this was a clouded yellow year. Sometimes the clouded yellows come in numbers: sometimes hardly at all. They are migrants, coming over from mainland Europe. I have never really got my head around the idea of migrating butterflies: their pretty, fluttery wings look next to useless for anything other than a flit from flower to flower or a brief and gorgeous mating dance. But no: the clouded yellows come up from the Continent: and some years they come in numbers. They did so this year all right.

You can argue long and fruitlessly about why they do it and what happens to them. They don't breed here: they only ever arrive. So either these yellow legions are all doomed, or they go back, or they hibernate and nobody finds them. It's a bit like swallows in the eighteenth century: no one knew where they came from or where they went to; many thought they slept the winter through at the bottom of a pond.

It's hard to get the evidence about flying back: you notice a clouded yellow arriving, you don't notice its departure. Perhaps they are pioneers: insects paving the way for a generation of breeders yet to come and establish themselves. But perhaps they reap southern England's plenty and then fly back in unnoticed dribs and drabs.

It's a thrilling little mystery and the insects themselves are gorgeous, painted with every shade of yellow that van Gogh ever had on his palate. Every time I walked the Porthleven walk, I saw them: one yellow flutterer after another. Once, for some reason, I took the trouble of counting each one I saw: 34 between elevenses and a lunchtime pint.

That walk. Fading purples of heather, yellow splashes of gorse, the complex greens of everything else, and away from base earth, the still more complex blues and greys of sea and sky. The restlessness of the sea: the boot-wide path, the awaiting doom at my right, the rocks below.

And butterfly after butterfly after butterfly: yellow after yellow after yellow: a symbol of summer in England: a symbol of hope. Possibly doomed hope, but then again, possibly not. We just don't know, do we? All we can do is look at each butterfly and say: yes.

Good. Very good.

101

There is a contradiction in the high summer. For humans, it is a moment of achievement: a moment of deserved rest. It is holiday time – Tuscany, Provence, even Cornwall – while even those left behind are consumed by holiday humour. No one takes work with overmuch seriousness: the silliness of the season is not confined to newspapers. There is a cheery frivolity about life: a response to that rare thing in this country, successive days of warmth. The English love to shed both clothes and responsibilities, and they do it very rarely, especially out of doors. In the high summer, people are affected by wildness as never before: every garden is full of drinkers and barbecuers, the countryside and the seaside are both full of visitors, Suffolk is full of walkers, cyclists, caravaners and holiday-letters as every one seeks some kind of idyll, some kind of brief and borrowed Eden.

But out in the wild world, the year is already turning, and the urgencies of autumn are already setting the tone of everything that takes place. The winter is already as threatening as the imminent arrival of the Daleks. The strategies for dealing with the winter are already upper-most in the minds of the birds: those that will cope by running away, those that will cope by ganging up, those that will cope by setting up a new territory. There is, even in high summer, a sense of restlessness, or urgency: and with it, a kind of elegy for the vanished spring. The season of promise leads almost at once to the season of survival, with scarcely a second to savour achievement. No bird can ever rest on its laurels.

Returned from Cornwall, back in Suffolk, I saw three green woodpeckers on a single telegraph pole. They were having a high old time of it: but there was an implicit urgency in what they were up to: thwocking away at the pole in search of insect life, and trying to yaffle. Yaffling is the green woodpecker's sound of choice: a wild, maniacal laughter. You hear it most in spring, when the right bits of open woodland echo to the sound of crazed laughter, as if the wood were a set in a bad horror film. But these young-sters hadn't really got the hang of it. They got the laugh all wrong. It was reasonable to suppose they were young, because they were hanging out in a bunch of three, unlike-ly woodpecker behaviour unless they were nest siblings, and because their behaviour was so naïve. They were yaffling just for the heady excitement of being alive in Suffolk, all three together with a world of telegraph poles and beetle larvae opening before them: but the yaffle was squeaky and unpractised and decidedly uncool. Then at once, all three of them flew away: switchbacking flight, green birds with yellow bums. Occasionally, a phrase or a comparison is so stupendously apt that you think about it at every encounter with the thing it describes. Richard Mabey, the great nature-writer, once wrote that flying green woodpeckers looked like little green dragons. So now, every time I see a green woodpecker in flight, they are little Eustaces, from the *Narnia* books, or little Idrises, from Ivor the Engine, undulating across the sky on little green scaly wings and just about to breathe little fires.

This was a triple flypast of dragons: on their way, not to seek a dragonish hoard of treasure, but to continue their education in country skills, to be good enough to pass the ultimate exam: the English winter: a thing more threatening than any dragon, any Dalek. Above the house, a carousel of hirundines, swallows and martins, and absurdly, I felt a touch of personal pride. These birds – just like that fine-boned little horse on the meadow – had been born in my buildings. My birds: performing a dance of delight as a special tribute to me, their landlord and master. Nonsense, of course: but I was quite bursting with prideful delight.

Every time I looked up and saw a swift, I wondered if it would be the last, until, in the end, it was. This looking for last swifts, for all last migrants, is inevitable if you have your wild eyes and ears tuned in: and it is a pastime that adds more than a touch of melancholy, not at all unpleasingly, to the English celebration of high summer.

This is something quite different from the additional sense of cosmic disquiet that attends all natural events these days. When you see the last swift of the year, you feel a pleasant frisson at the year's turning. But you also cannot help but wonder: so much for the last swift of the year: and will there be a first swift of next year? In eight months time, will they be arriving to show us that the globe's still working? Or not? To every sight in the natural world, the ancient haze of permanence is gone. We see things clearer now, clearer than ever our ancestors did. We see the world in all its hideously fragile perfection. In every revelation of beauty, those with ears can hear the faint ticking of the time bomb, the faint whisper of the voice that says: enjoy it while you can. The high summer is the season of ease and plenty for humankind: and all the better, it seems to me, for that faint touch of melancholy: for that subtle sense of disquiet.

102

Of course, we respond to the charm of nature: and also to nature's horror. You can sentimentalise the kindness of nature, and love the fluffy blue tits on your bird-feeder: but that does give you a difficult problem when, say, the sparrowhawk comes and launches one of its signature high-speed stealth attacks on the unwary. Any one who can see an antelope fawn without an upsurge of gushing sentiment is less than human: in the same way, you can't help but respond to the sight of a lion in hunt with a deep, fearful, and deeply admiring thrill. These are unquestionably anthropomorphic responses: that is to say, seeing animals through human eyes, and giving them human traits. This is regarded as a very bad thing to do: as if there were no intermediate step from thinking of an animal as a lower thing, as a kind of living clock, as Descartes had it, and dressing the wild world in Peter Rabbit's blue jacket. Well, all that I can say here is that I tend to see at least some parts of the non-human world in anthropomorphic terms myself. I can't help it: I am a human; I am an anthropos.

And if I didn't anthropomorphise, I would very probably be injured or dead. I certainly wouldn't be able to live as I do: that is to say, in intimate daily contact with horses.

Horses are big animals of great strength and speed. They can kill you. I try quite hard to make sure this doesn't happen. One of the most important ways of doing this is to read their moods. If I believed that the very idea of a horse having a mood was unacceptably anthropomorphic, then I would be unable to do this: a potentially lethal omission. But my philosophical/scientific stance is to say: she's a bit crazy this morning, better be careful. Or she is in a right strop today, better do this and not that. If you were a scientific behaviourist or a philosophical Cartesian, such thoughts would be inadmissible. I could only say: she has turned her ears back. There is white showing around the eye. She is fidgeting a good deal when she usually stands still. But I can see the whole picture and say, without even troubling to think about it much: she's in a bit of a mood, I must act with tact and circumspection. The concept of a mood, of emotions, of feeling, is not part of traditional good science. But if I judged my horses entirely by science, I would either do nothing at all, or I would get myself in bad trouble.

So yes, it is inevitable that we respond to animals in an anthropomorphic way, at least to some extent. When I made my long stay in the Luangwa Valley, we had many Italian clients. An impala lamb: *che carino!* How sweeeeet! A leopard: *che bello!* How beautiful! A hyena: *che brutto!* How ugly! It seemed that an animal had not been truly seen until it had been accorded the right Italian adjective.

There is, of course, beauty in a hyena's life. There is a fascinating female-dominated social hierarchy, their extraordinary adaptability, their endurance, their bone-cracking jaws (they leave white turds around the bush, because of the amount of calcium in their diets), their super-sense of smell, almost the equivalent of x-ray vision. They are genuinely wonderful creatures. I once saw a hyena attack a leopard that had just brought down a female impala, seeking to steal the kill we had just seen the leopard work so hard for. In a fit of anthropomorphic rage, my old friend Manny, for we had no clients with us that night, made a mad charge at the hyena in the Land Cruiser, lights blazing. The hyena perceived the situation, and summed it up in a trice. He (or maybe she, both sexes appear to have socking great penises) then performed an act of genius. In a flash of those bone-breaking jaws, the hyena snatched at the impala – and extracted a foetus from the dead animal. In a few bounds, the hyena had vanished with the prize. Such speed of thought, such speed of action, such intelligence: so many admirable things.

And yet: *che brutto!*

How can we help ourselves? If we see beauty in the leopard, we cannot help it if we find ugliness in the hyena's embryectomy. There is beauty in the sparrowhawk's flight: ugliness in the half-eaten pigeon. Nature is not nice, any more than it is beautiful. Nature is merely everything. Nature merely *is*, and we are part of it, whether we wish to be or not, beautiful and ugly as we ourselves are. We can respond to nature how we like: as humans must. The sin is when we use these irrational, too-human feelings as the basis for judgements on how we run the natural world. The nasty parts matter just as much as the nice parts.

103

I went to visit a farm. My near neighbour, Richard Symes, does the farming. It was an education in the changing ways in which we see the countryside. Richard's farm is shaggy. It has eight-foot-high hedges, wide green margins around the field, and the hedge side of the margins is long and unkempt – "the hairy bits", Richard calls them. There are ponds, areas of woodland, messy corners full of brambles. Some years ago, I did an ornithological survey of the farm. It was dawn, and May: and the place was jumping with life. Turtle doves were once common in this country, their gentle purring – turr! turr! – was one of the great ambient sounds of the English summer. They are now much less common, because of the changes in farming practice, the intensification of agriculture. (I have them as a house tick but they've never hung around and bred, alas.) I heard and recorded four turtle doves one morning at the farm. Or, of course, the same turtle dove four times. But really, I remember the morning for hares: hares everywhere, leaping about as if civilisation had never begun and the world was one vast leporine paradise.

Richard has always liked the idea that his farm is a rich and living place. But for years, he was somewhat out of kilter with his neighbours. All over Suffolk, and for that matter, Europe, hedges were grubbed out, trees felled, and every last square inch of soil bullied to within an inch of its life in order to make food. The country was not something to do with people, still less wildlife: it was there to make sure that we never went hungry again. An open-air food factory, and anyone who wanted anything else was a sentimental fool.

Farmers are bloody good at farming. And so their farms grew and grew: the land was brutally tidied, rationalised and organised, and the countryside became a place where neither people not wildlife had much of a stake. Then came the belated realisation that what the new farming practices had done was (a) to create food surpluses and (b) to destroy the countryside. Come friendly bombs and fall on Slough, wrote John Betjeman; it isn't fit for humans now. That was the state of the British countryside: and not fit for anything else that lived either.

But there has been a vast change in our attitudes as, Joni-like, we came to realise what we had lost. There was still

197

Official Nature, in the nature reserves: but we were losing Unofficial Nature: we were haemorrhaging our wildlife at an impossible rate. So now farmers are being paid to plant hedges in places where they were once paid to grub them out. Crazy, of course, but better to be crazy in this way than crazy in any other. There is a rewilding of the countryside going on all around us: it is wonderful, revolutionary, cheering, and ever-so-slightly too late. But still worth doing; oh yes, worth doing all right.

And Richard has embraced it. His farm is a business, he works on tight margins, and does not farm organically. But his place is full of the casual, the unofficial, the ambient wild: and we — we who pay taxes — are paying for him to keep it like this. If you like, he is paid to farm for skylarks and crested newts and, farmers being bloody good at farming, he is producing them in hefty numbers. Under the official requirements of the Stewardship scheme he has joined, as laid down by the agriculture ministry, Defra, his field margins are now open to walkers and their dogs, and what's more, to riders and their horses.

The traditional Suffolk greeting has always been "What the fuck are you doing on my land?" But now, in farms that have entered the Stewardship scheme at this level, visitors are positively solicited. A countryside that is better for wildlife is better for people. The government itself has come to terms with the basic theme of this book: that humans need the wild, that we are all the poorer for the wild's destruction.

Richard and I walked along beneath eight-foot hedges: on one of the hairy bits, a clouded yellow. The last I saw that year, as it happened.

104

Sometimes, you can reach out and touch the diversity of life. It can even come to you: a visitation, in response to a summoning. And so it was that I went to Minsmere for a mothing. At Minsmere, you can, on a good day in May, find 100 species of bird. In total, Minsmere has been visited by 328 species of birds. I heard that Minsmere just recorded its 1,000th species of butterfly and moth. Most of them, of course, moths.

The best way to see moths is to summon them, and the best way of summoning is a moth-trap. Moths love a light that shineth in the darkness: and a mercury-vapour bulb brings them flooding in. You make the trap nice and comfy for them with a collection of egg boxes for them to lurk and rest up in. You switch on as darkness begins to fall: and in the morning, you see what has landed.

Among the thousand is a Mediterranean moth never seen before in this country: and so it was given the English name of Minsmere crimson underwing. "You never know what you are going to get," said Robin Harvey, assistant warden at Minsmere, and top mothman. "It's like getting a present every day." So I went down to watch David Fairhurst, another warden, do the unwrapping. He was modest about his mothing skills: but I, mothlike, was dazzled.

With kind, considerate fingers David called one wonder after the next into being. The first of the presents was a hornet, an inch long and striped chocolate and yellow: an encouragement to tact and delicacy in the handling of these gifts. And then, we unwrapped the greatest gift of them all: the biodiversity of the planet Earth. Having apologised for the lack of seriously big moths, he found a convolvulus hawk moth: big enough to be an honorary bird. One moth after another: things of fragile beauty, handled with delicate courtesy, in their subtle colours of earth and dead leaves, silver and grey. I have always loved moths, always been troubled by them: their mad forays into houses, their determination to wipe themselves out against blazing bulbs and flickering candles: the way, when you catch them and try and take them to safety, they flutter so softly against your hands. Even the largest are so gentle, so soft and fragile. I have never felt even a flicker of an arachnophobe's unease with a moth: this is another kind of being, and their gentleness is both pleasing and disturbing. You could crush them in a moment's malice, a moment's carelessness, a moment's absent-mindedness: and they tickle your palms as if they knew that trust was their only option. An emblem, if you like, of the wild world.

All in all, we found 26 species of moth: among them, a pale thing, ginger at one end: a migratory moth called the four-spotted footman. There were seven of them in the trap: a party of them had been passing through. This was another first for Minsmere, only the second time such a moth has been found in Suffolk.

So many moths, as the old Jain monk might have said. So much life, in so many forms! In the Minsmere dark they gathered: and having been summoned, were identified, admired, released: back into the wild.

105

Every now and then, I repeat a mistake and buy a five-million candlepower torch. I can't help myself. They only cost a tenner or so; you plug them in and they recharge, and they last a few weeks and then they fizzle out and I have already lost the receipt. No matter. I bought a new one, big and shiny and yellow, charged it up and took a nocturnal stroll with the dog. The game is to carry the torch and to splash its beam around and see what you can see. It's great sport. What can you find? The eyes of most mammals (primates excepted, alas) will shine in the dark; when you get a reflection, you have found your mammal. (The only birds that have this reflective retina – a tapetum – are nightjars.) I have played this game in Africa and found many wonderful creatures, plucking them from invisibility with a rude shaft of light. It was by this means that I saw the leopard hunt in the Luangwa Valley, with the klepto-parasitic embryectomising hyena.

Mammals are thinner on the ground in Suffolk, but I remember once finding a huge red deer stag at extreme range: another time three does, casually crop-raiding. Plenty of bunnies of course. And always moths, in the warmer months, a perpetual fluttering, whispering presence: pale flecks of the micros, the bigger moths dancing unidentifiably in front of me. The bigger moths hardly seem like insects at all: with their strange furriness they seem almost mammalian. Perhaps, with their crazed suicidal tendencies, there is something human about them. But my first walk with my new torch was rewarded by a pair of gallivanting nocturnal hares. They were spooked by the dog, or perhaps by my intrusive light, and skedaddled in great leggy bounds.

Everywhere you look, there is more life than you can conveniently understand. Taking a bright torch into the English countryside is just one more way of appreciating this great, this absolutely crucial fact of life. You can turn up a stone, you can immerse your snorkelled face into a Cornish rock-pool, you can go marching with a torch like Eddystone Lighthouse, you can lift a clod of earth, you can make a safari through the human body in search of parasites, you can sit in your garden and listen. You can do any of these things and the moral is always the same: plenty.

106

I wanted to see one. I wanted to see one because it was invisible. And so I went back to Bradfield Wood as Simone Bullion of the Suffolk Wildlife Trust faced her year's moment of truth: had the scheme worked? Had the rewilding of Bradfield Wood actually come off? Were there dormice out there in the trees and thickets and coppices, or were there not?

Now I went along with a good healthy interest in what I hoped would be a conservation success story; and Joe came with me. But I must confess that at heart, I had the same motive for making the trip as Joe. We wanted to see one. We wanted to meet one. We wanted to have eye-contact, a meaningful exchange of views. And so we met up with the Suffolk Wildlife Trust people at the edge of the wood and marched on: looking at the nestboxes to see if they had been occupied. The technique here is good fun: you put the nestbox into a transparent plastic sack and then open it up. If there are any dormice inside, you will find them. This is a ticklish and highly skilled job, and you need a special licence to do it. Simone's assistant, Alison Looser, was in the process of acquiring her licence, and to her came the honour of finding the first dormouse.

She plunged her arm cautiously in the sack and the dormouse used it as a ladder, climbing up in an instant of time, reaching her shoulder and leaping onwards, vanishing in the thickets of hazel. But as we worked our way through the wood and the boxes, we found more. A family of four, mother and three fast-growing youngsters: caught them for weighing and measuring and counting. And Joe and I, having revelled in the uncanny speed of the arm-climbing escapee, were now able to do what few people ever do in modern Britain: to gaze on a dormouse. An overwhelming impression of minuteness: a tiny furry face with two oversized boot-button eyes. Quite impossibly minute: vanishingly small, to use an expression beloved of probability experts. As Joe looked on in delight, Simone told him: "It's got lungs and a heart and stomach and guts just like you; it's got a skeleton and muscles and blood just like you." And yet a human hand is too big, too clumsy an instrument for holding one with any ease. The same mammal's body-plan as Joe and me and you: but on an incomprehensibly smaller scale. There was a light year's difference in size: this was a glimpse into the universe of the small, a place were a tree is an empire and a wood a vast unending galaxy.

It is in size that diversity is best understood: because it is so obvious. To be a different size is to live in a different world. A dormouse can go where a man can never dare to step, yet a dormouse need never fear falling. His tiny size will save him every time. As JBS Haldane wrote: "You can drop a mouse down a thousand-yard mine shaft; and, on arriving at the bottom, it gets a slight shock and walks away. A rat is killed, a man is broken, a horse splashes."

In the course of its life, a dormouse will breathe as many times as a human, its heart will beat as many times as yours. But it exists on fast forward: a different speed of life, and a therefore, a dormouse has a different way of seeing and understanding the world. By confronting this, we can begin to understand the virtuosity of nature. Dormice are mammals like us. They are among the 4,000-odd animals we should be able to relate to more closely than any of the million and more others: and yet we are still millions of miles away from our ability to understand them.

107

More than a quarter of the 200 nestboxes in Bradfield Wood had been used by dormice. Of these, thirteen had actual dormice inside, to a total of 46. Eight of these were microchipped animals that had been released into the wild: that meant that 38 of them were Bradfield Wood natives, offspring of the captive-bred animals introduced in the spring. This is not, and cannot be a full census: but it is an important indication of what is going on. Simone, not a woman given to large statements, said it was "very satisfactory". Thanks to her, the world was a little bit wilder – a vanishingly small bit wilder – than it had been six months earlier.

108

We are giants to a dormouse: we are midgets to a whale. And there is a joy, an extraordinary sense of liberation, in finding ourselves as midgets in this shrinking planet: in seeing that, for an instant at least, we are not monarchs of all we survey. Come with me, then, to the Super Bowl, the great occasion in American football, the year it was held in San Diego. The game has gone a little hazy in my mind – Washington Redskins, wasn't it? I was there to cover it for the *Times*, and it was fine, good, great. But what I did the day before has stayed with me for ever.

I went out on a boat to look for whales, for it was the time that the grey whales pass close to San Diego on their annual migration. And I remember the heart-stopping moment when the first plume of breath and atomised sea-water was spotted, and I knew that the trip was not in vain. Then there was the easy, rolling 'ere-we-go motion as the whale dived. I can still remember with complete exactitude, with that rare kind of memory untouched by later additions and subtractions, the most amazing thing of all: the way that the rolling and the 'ere-we-going went on for such a long time, on and on, as yard after yard of animal eased past the boat, as first one bit of whale was exposed on the surface, then another, then another: an incomprehensible length. It would take the fastest man in the world seven full seconds to run from toe to tail.

And then the best bit of all: the breaking of the surface with the two tale flukes as the whale sounded, the tail breaking the water mast-high to our puny boat, two fingers stuck up at the world of civilisation, a great Y, a yes, an affirmation of life and hope. Imagine: sharing a planet with creatures the size of houses. Under the grey waters of the Pacific, there are more grey whales than I or anyone else would ever see.

Another time, another giant – I was sitting in a canoe on Lake Kariba as three bull elephants came down to drink. This is a place known for the size of the elephants: and I was quite literally sitting at their feet, looking up. I was perhaps ten yards away, and yet the elephants paid me no mind: the idea that a threat could come from the water did not trouble them. Each bore a massive load of ivory, each a head with a grey cliff-edge of a forehead, each a trunk like a fire-hose, each two eyes at peace with the world and each other. And so they drank their fill, and I gazed up at this sky-blackening sight, making delicate, nervous, inaudible touches with my paddle so that I didn't drift within touching distance, as seemed likely at more than one moment.

And one more giant, for it is best when giants come in threes. Back, then, once again to Luangwa. I had sat up late at the campfire drinking whisky and talking of old times with my old friend Jess Salmon, and very good it was, too. And as the bottle began to show signs of wear and tear, it gradually became clear that there was Another Presence in the camp, and that it wasn't human. It was the dry season, and we could hear the scrunching of large feet just a few feet away from us. It sounded as is someone was tiptoeing slowly through a field of popadums. So we crouched down and crept to a low grass wall that stood just behind us. We looked out: we looked up. And we saw a head, and it was about fifteen feet higher than our own, and eighteen feet higher than the ground, looking down with that glorious meditative calm that comes only to a giant and a herbivore. Giraffe, of course, right in the middle of camp, human beings on either side, but unregarded as it snacked daintily on leaves from the giant tree that dominated the camp. The shock, the beauty, the relief that it was nothing fiercer, the unbelievable immensity: all these things made us weak-kneed and giggly and thirsty, so we retreated and took our medicine. Later, I was to turn that incident into a pivotal scene in a novel, in which the vision of the giraffe – this revelation of giantkind – was the prelude to an inevitable seduction. For Jess and I, it was the prelude to an inevitable J&B, before we went our separate ways, in still-giggling wonder.

There is a shock on seeing something as big as a whale, an elephant, a giraffe. A giraffe is a mammal with no more neck vertebrae than we ourselves possess: that is to say, seven. It seems impossible, in our dominance and our species-pride, that anything so vast and so demanding of space as this trio of giants should still exist. But this isn't an affront to our human natures – certainly not to mine – because it is accompanied by a great surge of rejoicing. There is a feeling of relief that comes with the vivid demonstration of the truth that we are not the biggest things around: and with it, a secondary feeling of relief that such things still exist. Far from feeling threatened by such sights, the modern humans feel privileged. It is the giants that are under threat, not us. And the fact that these giants, with their strength and their grace and their incomprehensible ways of seeing the world, still exist is one of the most powerful experiences that the world can bring you. And it is not pure fear, though fear is a part of it. The dominant emotion is an awed, almost religious joy: and like many religious experiences, it comes from a sense of our own smallness.

Humans have had a very good try at wiping out the great whale: and have made a pretty good effort at doing the same thing with elephant. The sight of giants brings us an immediate nostalgia for a time when the wild world was fuller and richer: and with it, an amazed thanks that we haven't completed out destruction: not just yet. In the sense of our smallness comes the most vivid sense of wildness: it takes us back to a time when we humans were, indeed, the vulnerable ones. That sense of vulnerability, of humility, of inconsequentiality, touches us as nothing else in the wild can quite manage.

109

I love the surprises: the wild *coups de théâtre* that nature gives us. The better at looking you are, the more surprises you get. First, the dog-walk along the river: and some bloody fool of a farmhand has left a great pile of white plastic buckets on the edge of the bank. A bit closer: and it was clear that this was nothing of the kind. Three white footballs: as white as the whitest thing on earth. But no: not footballs but puffballs: giant puffballs, emerging, as is the spooky habit of fungi, more or less overnight.

Strange things, fungi, neither animal nor vegetable, but in a kingdom all of their own: and giant puffballs are as strange as fungi get. There is a story of workmen at Kew finding a collection of puffballs and calling in the police, believing they had come across a cache of human skulls. During the Second World War, a giant puffball under an oak tree was thought to be a German bomb. Richard Mabey, the dragon-man, informs us in his *Food For Free* that they are delicious fried in thundering great fungal steaks. But alas, I find my wild self too much tamed, too much in thrall to civilisation to try the experiment. I feel nothing but regret about this.

Another coup: another dog-walk: and a dragonfly – a southern hawker – brown and green with a bit of blue – alighted for a moment on my waistcoat. I stayed still, while the insect regrouped and then took wing again.

And another: a weasel, crossing the road in front of me. Weasels are very hard to see. Long and absurdly slim – they are supposed to be able to pass through a wedding ring – they are a blink-and-you-miss-'em species. The best way to see one is on horseback. Indeed, the best way to see quite a lot of things is on horseback: you have total vision, unrestricted by anything in any direction, and your horse makes you, if not invisible, at least much less of a threat. You become an honorary quadruped, and the wild things are that little bit less wary. You are slightly more, or slightly less than human: a weird and rather privileged feeling. And I quite often see weasels and stoats – stoats much bigger, like rampaging furry snakes – as I ride. Here was a weasel, going about its weasely business, and looking, to tell the truth, exactly like my younger boy's toy worm: a furry worm on a springy stick, very good for tickling.

Sunday morning, then, and a noble resolution to take a ride before anyone else was up and about. And another, coup – an especially dramatic one. A heavy dew, a bright sunny morning: and it transformed the field in a magical fashion, because the pattern of vertical lines of the grass was now matched with a pattern of horizontals. From grass-tip to grass-tip, a thin line, like a tightrope. A gossamer morning: strand after stand of cobweb stretching up the shallow hill (we call these things hills in Suffolk). Unnoticeable most mornings: but the combination of the dew and the angle of the sun miraculously called them into being: long strands of silk, used by tiny spiders for the practice of ballooning. They travel vast distances, going where the drifts and eddies of the wind will take them, and by this time, too late to be eaten by swifts – though a few martins were still around, still making their fartin' calls overhead.

It is a beautiful transformation of a landscape: and a heady realisation that every strand – and there were thousands – represented an individual speck of a life, an intrepid traveller, a gallant aviator, ballooning perhaps vast distances in order to touch down in this field. Other forms of silk, too: there were webs between grass stems like tiny trampolines, some square, some round: indivisible things for the most part, but now, this one special morning, called into being.

110

I love gossamer but I find it hard to love spiders. When I was in Belize, some one found a tarantula and there was a happy gathering around this trophy. I am ashamed to say that I hid. I didn't want to see it: still less did I want people to try and jolly me out of my fear and have the bloody thing crawl – ugh – on me. No, not possible.

How ridiculous these phobias are, these ancient, hard-wired, atavistic things. It makes far more sense to be afraid of a ten-ton truck – far more likely to kill you – or for that matter, a mosquito. But no, people in the civilised world fear snakes and spiders, mice and rats, and would willingly face far more dangerous things than confront this fear.

Nor is it a matter of being cut off from the wild world, and so fearing the merely unknown. I don't fear the wild: I fear spiders. I have spoken to many people who daren't travel into anywhere too wild, because they might see a snake or a spider. I remember my first encounter with a six inch diameter wild spider when I lived in Asia, not an encounter I carried off with distinction. But I got better at them: soon, I was able to kill them with some horrendous spray, readily available in the shops. And then I thought I really ought to do better than that, and I progressed to a sort of armed neutrality, giving them occasional queasy glances as they hung, immobile, vertical, improbably, unacceptably large, on the walls of my living room.

This effort of will paid off when I stayed with some friends in Zambia. After a merry and boozy evening, I was dropped off at a guest hut half a mile from the main house. I was a little put out, to say the least, when I switched on the light. So I lay on my back on the bed and counted them: 47. Forty-bloody-seven. All wolf spiders, varying from two to six inches in diameter: coffee-cup to side-plate. There was absolutely nothing to do but deal with it. I took a tautological slug from my bottle of duty-free, raised the sheet over my head, and slept till the morning light. All but a dozen or so had gone. My famous encounter with the lion had been less appalling, less shredding of the nerves.

Fear of wild things comes in many forms, all hard to deal with. And such fears don't make you any less wild.

111

A few years ago, I wrote a book for children about saving the world and so forth. It was called *Planet Zoo*, and was subtitled "100 animals we can't afford to lose". I gathered a good deal of information from the Red Data Books, those books issued by the International Union for the Conservation of Nature (IUCN) that tell you the status of individual species and the extent to which they are endangered. I spent a lot of time shuffling through the pages for good ones: because I wanted more than cuddly pandas and super-sexy carnivores. And I knew that my book was going to be what I wanted it to be when I came across the no-eyed big-eyed wolf spider.

There are many different kinds of wolf spiders, spiders that run down their prey like wolves and leap upon them with appropriate miniature ferocity. In fact there are 104 genera of wolf spiders, accounting for 2,304 species, according to one estimate. A sub-group among them is the big-eyed wolf spider, so called because they have big eyes. There are other distinguishing features, but the big eyes are the most obvious.

But there is a species that has adapted to the perpetual darkness of the volcanic tubes of Hawaii. And while they are unquestionably, so the taxonomists tell us, a species of big-eyed wolf spider, they don't actually have any eyes at all. They have a venomous bite that can kill small creatures. And yes, it is endangered, because water extraction for agriculture and domestic purposes is causing the volcanic tubes to dry out, changing the environment and making it harder for the no-eyed big-eyed wolf spider to make a living.

The gorgeous discovery of this wondrously named animal said many of the things I wanted to say in this book: the awful mystery of biodiversity: and how humans can put into danger creatures that they hadn't even heard of.

My son Joe is fond of saying that he has no ambitions to go out into space and search for aliens, because there are more than enough alien forms of life on our own planet: weirder than we imagine, weirder than we are capable of imagining. We are not alone: and from the depth of the tubes in Hawaii to the top of the Himalayas, and into your own back garden, there are creatures we are killing off: to our eternal impoverishment. We are not alone, as Joe will tell you: but if we carry on like this, we soon will be. The world will be a poorer place without no-eyed big-eyed wolf

211

spiders: it will also be poorer – so I tell myself, anyway – without the wild spiders that did their night-hunting above my whisky-sodden sheet-shrouded head on that black African night.

112

Great good luck: Joe found a hedgehog in the garden. He had gone out for a torchlit bounce on the trampoline – borrowing my supertorch – and had caught a glimpse of the beast, hedgehogging its way across the garden. He called me, and I ran out across the dewy lawn in my socks to enjoy a peer at this preoccupied and prickly visitor. When Joe had finished his bounce, I told him a story.

I was sharing a tent with my old friend Ralph when we were walking a section of the Cornish cliff path, and camping out boozily in fields. Ralph has always showed a justified contempt for my practical skills, for he is a person in a higher category of ruggedness: he is an indefatigable walker, a cyclist of high and lofty virtue, and is inclined to be a bit of a glutton for austerity, something I try to correct when we meet. I woke in the night and called out in shock.

"What's the matter?"

"There's something in the tent."

"No, there isn't." A world-weary voice, on the edge of tolerance.

"No, something scrabbled at my head."

As if to a child: "You imagined it."

"I didn't."

Sigh. "I'll find the torch." Meaning, that he'd show me that there was nothing in the tent, and then we'd all get back to sleep. But he shone the torch and there, six inches from my pillow – a thing constructed from a towel resting on a pair of boots – was the biggest, fattest, prickliest, brightest-eyed hedgehog you could ever wish to meet. We opened the tent flap, and in its own good time, the hedge-hog hedgehogged off.

It was good luck to catch sight of Joe's nocturnal hedge-hog, but if you live in the right place and are prepared to do a bit of looking, you are going to get lucky. That's statistical luck: luck as a reward for hard work, for hours spent, for the habit of looking. I have seen so many wonders in Africa that it would take a separate volume at least to set them all down: but then I have worked for that, too. I have seen leopard hunt and kill on three occasions, for example: but I have taken part in countless lamplit night hunts, so it would be highly surprising if I hadn't. I have seen wild dogs at their den: I have tracked black rhino on foot. I have been lucky in Africa a thousand times: and I have earned every amount of my luck. The wilder you are, the luckier you get. The more places you visit, or the more you go to your own local wood or park or river, the more luck you will have in what you see. It took me years to see barn owls, they were a com-pletely elusive bird for me. Now I see them every week or so, because I live in a barn-owly place and do a fair bit of looking.

But there is a luck that you don't earn: and it's a high and wonderful thing. John Burton of the World Land Trust, aka the power-crazed fanatic, has been to Belize on maybe twenty occasions, because the WLT has been involved in buying up rainforest there. And he had never seen a jaguar. I went to Belize for five days, and visited forest owned and managed by Programme For Belize with funding from WLT. And guess what I saw.

I was in a vehicle with Ramon Pacheco, who has worked as a station manager in the forest for eight years and seen them eight times, and Vladimir Rodriguez, who has worked as a field naturalist for Programme for Belize for six years and has seen them fourteen times. My Belize wildlife book

213

said: "Banish all thoughts right now of ever encountering El Tigre." And as we rounded a curve in a forest road, a great, glorious spotted beast: not fine and slinky, like a leopard, that was the real shock of the thing, but big and butch and burly, with a neck on him like Mike Tyson. Looking over his shoulder at us with an expression of spotted contempt, he turned and slouched unhurriedly into the forest. Not Africa luck, not earned luck, no. This was unearned luck, this was Belize luck: a moment of sudden piercing brilliance, and one of those images printed for ever on the unfading screen of your retina, or your mind.

Burton has never forgiven me.

113

The wonderful thing about wild dogs is how marvellously doggy they are. Strange things to look at: everyone has a different pattern of white, black and tan, with ears like satellite dishes. They are not even in the same genus as the domestic dog, *Canis familiaris*, or the wolf, *Canis lupus*. They are in a genus of their own, *Lycaon pictus*, the painted dog: but whatever their taxonomic status, the world's greatest expert and my six-year-old boy have only to look on them to say "dog!"

I saw a family group of them at their den on the Lowveldt in Zimbabwe: a party setting off to hunt and in the process of leaving the little ones and their minders behind. It was a ceremonial occasion, it lasted a full hour, and it was full of all the sniffing and licking and romping that dogs go in for. The puppies were all given a lovely play. Every dog greeted every other dog. It was a scene of great jollity, great content, great stability. Ethologists will no doubt explain, and rightly, about the function of such behaviour in maintaining the integrity of the group bonds, how the pack dynamic depends entirely on such rituals, how the dominance hierarchy is strengthened, how friendly relations are made possible across the hierarchy.

It's fascinating stuff: but for all that, I saw only dog: saw only cousins, however distant, to the beasts I have shared my home with and patted and been licked by on a million occasions. There was a deep sense of familiarity in this strange and wild scene: almost a sense of cosiness. Wild though they were, the dogs looked organised – most social groups look organised if you are used to lions – efficient and effective. Everything was sorted: and so at last, the hunting party set off, tails high, ears up, eyes bright, as if they were going for walkies. They set off with unmistakably doggy exuberance in their step, and we followed them until they lost us in the bush.

I wanted to take one home: he'd have fitted in a treat. Sometimes the wild looks so familiar, so easy, so comfortable: a place where even a modern human is completely at home.

114

The level of understanding between human and dog can be startlingly close. With any dog: but most especially with your own dog. Sometimes, with heavy-handed humour, I speak to Gabe, my black Lab, in French: "*Assieds-toi!*" She sits. "*Reste-là!*" She waits. "*Va-t'en!*" She doesn't understand French, she understands me and the rhythm of our lives: where the drive meets the road, she is always told to sit and wait, always does so, and would do the same if I gave the orders in the language of the Khoi Khoi people. "*Viens ici!* Come back here, you bloody dog!" But she's caught a scent, as I knew the instant her body language changed, and I've lost her, and I won't get her back till I

215

hear a great kerfuffle in the long grass and a pheasant has taken to the air with that loud noise she finds so gratifying. She has no serious expectation of catching one but she loves making them shout. Then she comes back, looking slightly embarrassed at having let me down, but more than slightly pleased with herself for making the pheasant go "tikkup, tikkup, tikkup!", and knowing that I'm annoyed with her, but not punitively so, since she came not much later than too late. All things I know and she knows because we live together and are in sympathy with each other. This is not anthropomorphic nonsense: this is how any human gets on with any dog. I understand her – to quite a considerable degree, considering she belongs to another species, another order. She understands me. It's an enjoyable, even a fascinating business.

But there are other animals whose fascination comes not from their comprehensibility but from their incomprehensibility: not from their kinship but from their distance from us. I remember seeing a crocodile, a massive fellow, and then passing that way again 24 hours later, saw that he had not moved. Not a muscle. I wondered about the mind in there: was there even a concept of boredom? What was going on inside this eternally waiting crocodile, remote from the rhythms of hunger as we mammals know it, remote from the impulse to move and be up and doing?

I have seen crocodiles again and again: sometimes in phantasmagorical numbers in the Luangwa dry season, as they gather in groups of more than 100: as if we were back in the Jurassic and reptiles ruled the world. The crocodilian body plan has survived for more than 100 million years. And almost always, they are still. Stillness is their natural state: they stand stiller than the human beings who dress up as statues to solicit loose change from tourists. Crocodiles would win any statue competition with a human: with any mammal.

Sometimes you see them walk: ungainly, but capable, legs all stuck out at the sides, not designed for long journeys.  Sometimes you see them slither into the water, where they shift from awkwardness to sleek purpose in a stride. In the water they cruise: a log-like snout just visible.

Only once did I see one move quickly. Or rather, I didn't see it. One moment a vista of Luangwa peace: the low river, the long sand beach exposed by the retreating waters, a small gathering of puku – a foxy-red antelope – coming down to drink. The next moment: there was a rifle-crack splash and one puku fewer on the bank. A crocodile had struck much as a whip cracks. On another occasion, I saw a small breeding group of elephants in a state of horrible distress: a human-like distress quite disturbingly comprehensible. It was clear that horror, misery and grief are not the exclusive preserve of humankind. It seemed we would never know the cause: until we saw a grey thing like a big sack in the water: a croc had seized a baby elephant, as in the Just So Story, the one called "The Elephant's Child". But this time there was no Bi-Coloured-Python-Rock-Snake to come to its aid. The elephant was drowned, and awaiting consumption: the elephants beside themselves with grief, and it was horribly obvious which one was the bereaved mother. The elephant females were an embodiment of grief, grief as we humans know it. The crocs, in the waters of the lagoon, still again, log-like snouts on the surface, yellow eyes caught glittering in our spotlight, stood for every sinister thing in the world. Sinister, because so remote from humanity.

But my most vivid crocodile moment came on the Grameti River, which crosses the Serengeti in Tanzania. It was a narrow thing, I could have crossed it in a dozen strides. The place we stopped was overhung with trees: an arcadian spot. From the canopy, I could hear black-naped oriole and his sweet call, and the still sweeter call of orange-breasted bush-shrike: details I recall because the scene is so perfectly recorded in my mind. It was another sound that I remember still more clearly.

The crocs were far too big. They had no right to be so big in so small a stream: you can't get to the eighteen-foot size of these champions just by eating fish in a narrow stream. But they didn't eat fish. They ate mammals. They ate mammals just once every year: and it was eleven months since they had last tasted any. They were hungry. Very hungry. The wildebeest migration would be crossing the Grameti in a week or two: I had seen the migration front myself, just twenty-odd miles off and heading this way: heading towards sweet grass for the many and a horrible splashing doom for the few.

I got out of the vehicle and walked just a pace or two towards the river. And the crocodiles saw me, and uttered the strange gargling crocodile growl. I have never heard it before or since. It was a hideous sound. Come and paddle. Come, cross here: it's lovely once you're in. I tell you, it's not the most relaxing sensation in the world, being prey.

But a very rich feeling nonetheless. Sometimes, the beauty of the wild lies in finding a humanity there: in the song of a nightingale, in the eye of a deer, in Wordsworth's daffs, in Hopkins' kes. There is a joy in our kinship with nature; in nature's kinship with us. But there is also a deep meaning to be found in the lack of kinship: in the alien nature of the wild. A human can't understand what it's like to wait eleven months for a meal — eleven months in a small, shallow river between the last pudding and the first hors d'oeuvre. We can't begin to know how a crocodile thinks, feels, imagines. Did they, for example, know that the wildebeest were coming? Did the nagging of their bellies give them the joyful news that soon, the bleating, splashing, long-legged panickers would be scrambling madly across the place where the crocs have their being, most of them scrambling to safety and the vistas of long grass that await them on the far side. The wildebeest do so at the cost of the annual tithe of failures: those who are taken as they enter the river, those who get half way and no further, those who get within a stride of the far bank and are seized a hoofprint from safety.

Me, I stood there, reduced to the status of prey, and stared, enthralled, at creatures whose lives and thoughts and rhythms were as different from mine as if they had come from another planet, another galaxy, another universe. And all of us just vertebrates together. I climbed back into the vehicle. On a day of blinding heat, chilled.

115

Winter may be the enemy, but it comes in stirring forms. An early sign: several squadrons of geese flew over in the evening. I was alerted by the honking: and on they came: in the first wave, 60-odd in a double-arrow-head formation. Then came another flight of a dozen, followed by three stragglers, looking rather ill at ease in such a small gathering. After a pause, yet another flight: and this time, I risked dashing inside to fetch binoculars. All greylags, so far as I could tell – the mellow sound of the birds was a good clue – but with one pure white farmyard goose among them.

Every winter, around 80,000 greylags come honking in from Iceland. This lot were flying south-west, away from the coast, seeking some safe roosting-ground for the night. I had been in no hurry to see them: but now they had arrived, they were welcome enough.

Flocks of southing swallows continued to pass overhead, frequently in curves and spirals and circles and arabesques as they fed while they travelled: how many airmiles do they travel, I wonder, as they pass from here to southern Africa? And then the robins started to sing again: setting up their winter feeding territories. They would hold them, all being well, until the spring, by means of their soft, sweet song

116

The wind across the fens can cut like a razor – after all, there is not much to get in its way – but I was properly clad, and besides, deep winter was still some way off. But the prospect was bleak all the same. God, I love bleak. I remember a surveyor's report on a Suffolk seaside property I once owned: it suggested that the value of the place was somewhat diminished by its "bleak aspect".

I loved that bleak aspect. A shingle beach sloped down to the North Sea, and er, that was it. That, and an awful lot of sky. I wrote *Planet Zoo* while gazing at it; migrating Brent geese passed in front of me six feet above the humpy grey-ness of the sea as I rootled though my pages of the Red Data Book and chortled: long-footed potoroo! That one goes in for sure. Pygmy hog sucking louse! Can't resist. Usambara eagle owl! That goes in for the name alone. Out there on the Suffolk coast in January the east wind never blew. It sucked. There was nothing to see but sky. There was often a Mediterranean gull on the roof. The bleakness was inspir-ing: it was quite uncompromisingly wild. The view lacked the comfort of the savannah, the heartland landscape of humankind: but its forbidding nature was an aspect of its charm. I felt as if I had given civilisation the slip. Iowa Pleistocene snail!

It was the same here, at Lakenheath Fen. I had last been there a dozen years earlier: the place was full of bulldozers and a man called Norman Still was yelling at the drivers: "Not straight! Crooked!" Meaning not tame. Wild. Before the bulldozers, this had been a carrot field: part of the ferocious landscape of the fen country: a place of monoculture where nothing lives except carrots, and there is not a tree to break the hideous man-made monotony of the landscape. Now that's what I call bleak.

Before the carrots and the drainage and the ditches and the wind-pumps, the fens were a wet, wild, spooky, sinister, and really rather alarming place. A couple of relict fens remain: odd scraps of ancestral landscape, islands in a sea of carrots. The tide of carrots had more or less overwhelmed the fens: but then the RSPB sent the bulldozers in.

And so here, the Fenland has been recreated: the carrot land rewilded. Norman pointed out a great ancient lump of bog oak, a hunk of timber that had been preserved in the peaty soil for centuries, dug out as the new meres and reed-beds and channels were being excavated. He had asked his bulldozing crew to set this on end and dig it in: where it makes a rather sinister eminence over the flat vistas of reed and grazing marsh and generously supplied quantities of sky. One day, Norman said, as he admired the ancient and newly vertical lump of ancestral timber, one day there will be an osprey sitting on that oak. And last year, an osprey sat on that oak.

Osprey: the great reckless fishing-hawk, the bird that plunges talons-first into the water and emerges with impossibly large fish. Osprey, extinct as a breeding bird in the country – a conservation cause célèbre of the 50s – now returning in scarce but increasing numbers. It was a moment of complete vindication.

For the fen lives. That summer, seven pairs of marsh harriers had raised 25 chicks. There was a bittern booming in the reeds. And in front of us, with the great bog oak behind him, a marsh harrier got up, a male, tri-coloured and sumptuous, and turned insouciant circles before flipping onto one wing-tip and dropping shuttlecock-soft into the reeds.

We are back at the counsel of despair: the idea that if we destroyed the natural environment, well, hell, we can always make it again. But of course, we are long past the point of despair: and that counsel works better than anything else. The option of putting Time on fast rewind is not, alas, available.

And it can't be done, not perfectly, and what is destroyed is always destroyed: that is what the counsel of despair stuff means. It can't be done at all with rainforest, that's the bloody tragedy of it. But all we can do is the best that we can: and if rewilding is best for such wildlife as remains to us, then rewilding is the way forward. And here, at Lakenheath Fen, there is a spectacular example of what can be done in just a decade. The marsh harrier got up again, flew unhurriedly away, wings in that careful dihedral: a sight that always thrills me, because it always shouts of the possibilities of rewilding. Ten years: "You're a magician," I said to Norman. "What a place!"

"Should be ten times bigger."

Perhaps it will be. Talking continues about the Great Fen Project: the possibility of turning endless acres of carrot-fields back into fenland: the ancient, wild and wet places where the sound of booming bitterns was once as common as the call of a sparrow. Lakenheath Fen is one and a quarter square miles: there are fourteen square miles more that could follow Lakenheath and become rewilded fens. Discussions continue between the Wildlife Trusts, English Nature, the Environment Agency and Huntingdon District Council. Think of it: all those talks, all that paper, all those meetings, all those vested interests, all those points of law and procedure: and the conservationists, whose souls would far sooner be out with me and Norman among the reeds and the marsh harriers, sitting in windowless rooms at long tables with the doodlepads and the water glasses, listening and listening and talking and talking: all with the aim of forcing the toothpaste back into the tube. A lot of modern conservation is like that.

O let them be left, wrote Gerard Manley Hopkins, wildness and wet, long live the weeds and the wilderness yet. But they weren't left. They were drained, smashed, destroyed, obliterated. They were turned into carrot fields, the most desolate landscape in Britain. O let them be put back: o let them be rewilded. Let us attend to the counsel of despair while we still can.

117

I had a drink with Julian Roughton, director of the Suffolk Wildlife Trust and all round good egg. He talked about the otter he had seen in his garden, a protracted visit, apparently snacking at length on great crested newts. This is a rather scarce amphibian that the Trust has done a good deal to help. No irony, when you think about it: conservation is not about conserving one species and not another: it's about absolutely everything. He also talked about the progress of plans to release white-tailed sea eagles in this part of Suffolk: restoring the long-gone monsters of the airways to our soft and volatile coast. Rewilding once again: another pint, on the strength of that.

118

My father came to Suffolk for his birthday, and after a nice lunch at the Swan in Southwold we changed our footwear and set off for Dunwich: windswept, brisk, autumnal: a day to keep moving, hope you don't see anything too exciting and have to stop and look at it. The reeds were jumping with pingers, or bearded tits. Handsome little things, normally seen as a small group of tiny birds just above the seed heads. In this strange other world of the reeds, their jauntiness very slightly diminished the threatening aspect of this landscape. The reeds, armpit height and higher, stretching out like a nightmarish cornfield, the ground beneath your feet reaching up to grab and hold, and above, the endless acres of sky, the landmark of the old red-brick wind-pump.

It was a teal day. It generally is at this time of year: aerial groups spinning away, relatively easy to pick out even at extreme distances, because of their inexorably duckish silhouettes and the frantic whirring of their wings. Tiny ducks, they must work flat out every second they are aloft. Teal in number, especially teal in flight, have ridiculously busy wings, giving them an impossibly preoccupied air. They, more than any others, are the birds of the Suffolk coast in winter: tough, elegant, indomitable little survivors. The drake – easily seen, because teal also like to sit about in numbers – is one of the most handsome birds in Britain with his chestnut head and green wash over the eye. I remember a former rarity-seeker, telling me of a Damascene moment when he was birding with a friend and feeling somewhat disgruntled at the lack of rare birds. His companion said to him: "Aren't teals *fabulous?*" He looked at a drake teal and had to agree. He never looked at birds in the same way again: never again felt that there were birds worth looking at, and then again, birds not worth looking at. He went on to become an RSPB warden, and a bloody good one.

As you get towards Dunwich and you find yourself within sight of journey's end, the going gets harder, though you have only yourself to blame. It's all loose shingle at the top of the seawall, at least, it is in those places where the wall hasn't come down, breached and hooshed away by rising sea levels. And you want to be on the seawall, in order to see the sea on your left and the marshes on your right. You scorn the easier, inland way, for all that each step requires added effort, as the ground shifts beneath your foot. It's a route that rather needs a nice bird to reward you. On we went, pausing more than was strictly necessary to scan the marshes for teal. And looking back, we saw a white bird that had not been there on the last look. An egret: jolly good. How splendidly and newly familiar. No it's not. Yes it is, surely. I really don't think it can be. Well, it's not a bloody swan is it?

But it held a hunched, round-shouldered, un-egretlike position, its beak immersed in the water. After a pause: "I reckon that's a spoonbill."

"Bollocks."

The only way to resolve an academic discussion on this level is to go and have a look. So we retraced our steps, crunching our way through the shingle – more or less wading – and pausing every few yards to peer at the bird.

And do you know what? It was a spoonbill. Perhaps the most improbable of all the regular-occasional visitors that come to this country, with its absurd wooden spoon of a beak, one of the most bizarre affectations of any bird in the world. We remembered the African spoonbills – a different species – that we used to see in the Luangwa River, for my father once paid me a visit there, and the way that the birds moved in a constant, dashing-here-and-dashing-there frenzy of feeding, creating a good flow of water through their beaks to make the filter-feeding work efficiently. It reminded us of my brother-in-law doing the hoovering.

However, this Suffolk spoonbill was happy with a less frantic approach, moving gently around the small brackish lagoon, as if being a spoonbill in England were the most natural thing in the world. Delighted by his cheerful absurdity, we turned and for the third time, attacked the shingle. Back home for a good meal, then, but before that, a cold and fizzy birthday bottle from the fridge. And a fire to drink it round. Yes, certainly a fire tonight.

119

Is it possible to suffer from wonder fatigue? Is it possible that the glories of the natural world begin to grate on your nerves: and you say, for God's sake, enough, Give us a break. That's enough wonders: that's enough of the most moving and amazing and glorious things that a human could possibly see. The very idea reminds me of that primordial Pete 'n' Dud sketch – Peter Cook and Dudley Moore, in the 60s – when the mackintoshed cloth-capped topers discuss their sex lives. Do you know who was ringing Pete up at midnight? Bloody Brigitte Bardot! "I said, 'Look, Brigitte, we've had our laughs, we've had our fun, we've had our kicks, we've had our thrills. We've quaffed deep of the cup of love… But now it's over. *C'est fini!*' But she wouldn't take that for an answer…"

That's wildlife on television for you. Every time you watch a wildlife programme, there are lions, copulating as only a lion can . Or if not copulating, killing. Or if not lions, something fabulously rare doing something fabulously exciting. And I say, Oh come off it, seen it all before, we've had our laughs, we've had our thrills. Now it's over. *C'est fini.*

It's not like that, you know. Out in the real world. Out in the real wild. Lions don't spend all their time copulating and killing. They spend at least nineteen hours of every day sleeping. Most times I've seen lions, they've been snoring away, occasionally lifting a sledgehammer paw to swat a fly. Television wildlife documentaries no more represent the real wild world than a soap opera represents marriage. Marriage is not all terrible rows and orgies of reconciliation. Of course these things happen, but most days in most marriages are comparatively humdrum. That is the joy, that is the point. The same principle works in the real wild, when it happens before you in real time. As opposed to the edited highlights.

It's the same when you watch sport on television. You can see just the goals and the sending offs: but that's not a satisfying experience. It's different when you watch the whole thing: when nothing might happen, or it might be the greatest match ever played. You just don't know. You never know. You are not supposed to know what happened next: until it does.

These days, there are wildlife programmes trying to bring that out: that all-important don't-know-what-happens-next feeling. That creates at least something of the joy of being out there. The programme *Springwatch* has been a great success: and it was followed that autumn by a programme following the same format, called, not surprisingly, *Autumnwatch*. The scene-stealers were red deer in rut: roaring their defiance at each other as they tried to get best access to the best hinds. And we all watched the programme and enjoyed it.

But then Joe and I made an early morning visit to Minsmere: to see the red deer rut. And we found ourselves out in the real wild, with the real coldness of the wind, the real smell and taste of the wet, wild world, and all around us, on every side, there was a 360-degree roaring. The great gut-deep passion of the stag in his autumnal frenzy; the wide-eyed sexiness of the hinds who watched so solemnly; deer everywhere and us in the middle; and it was, despite the excellence of the television, a completely different experience: ten times more vivid. We didn't have anything like the views you get on television. We didn't get a fight, we didn't get to see a stag covering a hind, we didn't know who was champion, who had won and who had lost. What we had was the wild: us out there, the stags out there – big, well-fed, crop-raiding stags with up to twenty points on their antlers, heraldic beasts fit to grace the shield of an emperor – and all around, the wild world. The first white fronted geese of the season flew overhead, and the faint squeak of redwing, also arriving for the winter.

120 It was a week that confirmed my status as a

rain god. This is something I have known about for some time. For example, I made a trip to the Spanish Steppes, the driest place in western Europe. There, among the bonsai vegetation and shrivelled grasses, Martin Davies of the RSPB and I went to look for Dupont's Lark, a rum, scarce little bird that revels in the driest of the dry. (Leonard Puech Dupont was a nineteenth-century French naturalist; so far as I know there is no bird named for his mistress.) Anyway, it pissed down, which explains why we never set eyes on Dupont's bloody lark. The hard, tightly tamped dirt roads broke up under the onslaught of the rain, and the expedition vehicle, a hired Seat 600, got stuck more than once. We had to rip up great handfuls of priceless and ancient vegetation and stick it under the drive wheels to get out.

On another occasion, I reached the Kalahari Desert

shortly after the most massive rains in living memory. My desert birding was mostly about ducks and wading birds; the air was full of African fish eagles, turned for a brief week or so into African frog eagles, flying into the desert to feast on the sudden bonanza of frogs. These are the kind of frogs that sleep ten years beneath the sands wrapped in clingfilm, only to come to life for a few weeks in the sudden, occasional and dramatic rains, there to croak and roar and breed and produce young frogs able to bury themselves for their own long sleep before the waters are quite gone. It seems a hard thing, to sleep ten years, to wake in the newly made splendour of the fresh and soaking desert, only to be scoffed at once by a cruel and handsome hook-beaked bird, but as I said before, nature is not nice. And you should have seen – or rather felt –the mosquitoes.

So out we went, *en famille*, all four of us, for a week of late autumn sun: to revel in Spain, Catholicism, horses, wildlife, and the whole art of sitting out in cafés eating specially nice olives and drinking specially nice drinks. We went to El Rocio on the edge of the great park of the Coto Doñana: and it pissed down. The place, drought-ravaged, exists always on the edge of possibility. Here, life struggles on a daily and yearly basis. And then, all in a week, came a ten-year benison of rain, and no one had the decency to say so much as *gracias* to me. All week, the streets were foaming torrents, and planks were laid down for a safe crossing. The sky was black, the waters before our window ink, the flamingos, who usually gather there in hundreds, were gone. It was, to be frank, a disaster: one that makes a serious test of the family dynamic. We had a lovely room, huge, looking out over the great wet marsh, and we spent hours in it. I shall never forget the blasted wet expanse, a whiskered tern working moodily along the rim. Rain fell in repeated short, intense bursts. Storks and red kites occasionally crossed before us.

Joe and I at least managed a couple of trips into the park in slightly less wet moments. And unexpectedly, it was the vultures that stole the show. In this vast expanse of the park, a former royal hunting preserve, there are cattle and horses ranging freely. An animal tends to die where it falls: and so naturally, other creatures come in to do the clearing up. On this extreme edge of Europe, the job falls to griffon vultures. We saw them roosting in trees in huge numbers, 30 and 40 to a tree as if this were the African Savannah, as if I were back home in Luangwa. You could see the birds, big and burly, crops full – a sharp protuberance in the throat where the meal awaited processing – all there in a corporate digestive stupor. It hardly felt like Europe: it felt deeply and gratifyingly wild.

There are plenty of big wild mammals here also, red and fallow deer, wild boar. A young stag of elfin mien, wearing two twiglets on his head, large eyes and sexually ambiguous, passed briefly into view. "*Femina?*" asked a fellow traveller. "*No – macho.*" The staglet minced away into cover.

121
But back home, the weather was relentlessly lovely: one mild, sunny day followed another. And morning after morning, I saw butterflies. There was a glut, almost a plague of red admirals. They fed on the juice of the wind-fallen pears, fluttering up distractedly as I passed, only to return for another gorge as I moved on. Many of the red admirals that turn up in this country in spring are migrants flying up from the Continent. As the year turns, many – most of them from a newly hatched generation – fly back south again. It is possible that some of them hibernate successfully in this country. I couldn't ask these dark flutterers, so artfully tricked out in red and white, what their plans

were. All I could see was that the year grew later and later, and still the red admirals remained. Did that mean that the globe was still working? Or that it wasn't? I saw my last red admiral on November 17. Thus, in the gentlest and most beautiful way possible, we see the madness of the world and the irreversible nature of the changes we brought about.

122

Rainforest, rainforest, always rainforest. Why is it that as soon as conservationists start preaching, they talk about rainforests? As a result, rainforests have become a special kind of joke, always used to sum up the excesses of book and newspaper publishing: entire rainforests have been felled to celebrate David Beckham's illustrious career etc etc. We know an area the size of Ireland is destroyed every day, or maybe it's Wales and every hour. Anyway, we know it's bad. Rainforests are something to feel guilty about: a symbol of the way we have buggered up the planet. All rather old hat, really. Rainforests have become something we'd rather not think about. And mostly, it must be said, we succeed.

But what's it like? In a rainforest? To be actually in one?

Well, it's rather like being Tantalus, sunk up to his chin in the river in Hades, with the rich, rare fruit dangling just above his head. Every time he dips his head to drink, the river recedes; every time he raises his head to eat, the fruit is just beyond his reach. He is doomed to suffer throughout eternity from hunger, thirst and the cruellest sting of all, from unfulfillable desire.

I first visited rainforest in peninsular Malaysia before I had refound my way in the wild world: at a time when I was full of unexpressed nostalgia for the wild, without having the smallest idea of what to do about it. Just on spec, on the back of a passing whim, not mine, I went to visit the rain-forest with two or three friends: and it was one of the most moving and powerful experiences of my life. So what did I see? Not a thing. That was the thrill of it: that was the joy of it.

Yes, yes, the cathedral-walks: the mighty pillars soaring up to the endless rolling acres of canopy far beyond reach. Yes, the columns of huge and vigorous ants, the occasional leech. Yes again, the thrill of a flying lizard. Above, the sounds of birds: not melodious or chattering and complex: clear liquid whistles, the better for piercing the dense acoustic of this world of endless vegetation.

Plants growing on plants growing on plants. At dawn and dusk, the wild, heart-stirring chorus of gibbons: one of the few mammals that has a territorial song, as if it were an honorary bird. On the wide, swift river, the occasional flash of a birdwing: unidentifiable, but at that time, I found most birds unidentifiable. At night, great rumblings of mystery: and always, the hum and zip and buzzling of the insects. There were walks, along courteously marked paths: and all the time, everywhere you went, a sense of vast, impossible reservoirs of knowledge and understanding always ever-so-slightly out of reach: receding every time you moved clos-er.

There are more different forms of life in rainforest than in any other habitat on earth. Why, then, don't you see any of them? Because it's bloody hard to see: because there are an awful lot of trees, an awful lot of leaves, an awful lot of vines and epiphytes, and most of it a very long away up. On later visits to Malaysia, I did better, meeting people with better knowledge than me, bringing binoculars, acquiring information: but rainforest birding is still on the edge of the possible: neck-cracking at all times, with occasional frustrating, fleeting glimpses, overmuch cover, ambiguous calls and unfamiliar species.

232

It's like being at sea. At sea, there is a world of vast and endless life below you, but never seen, save in sudden, stolen glimpses: a fin, a pair of tail flukes, a splash — but mostly, you have to take it on trust. In the rainforest, the ocean is above your head: you are down in the benthic depths of the forest, while life goes on at the surface level at the great reef of branch and leaf that lies for ever above you and out of reach.

You hear brief, enigmatic sounds: crashes in the canopy, far-carrying whistles, rustles in the leaf litter. But you don't see much: not in the way that you see life out in the savannah, where the big mammals have their being in full view of every passing vehicle. Here a moment's glance is a lifetime's work: and that is why my jaguar was so outrageous, why Burton is still anatomising his melancholy.

Oh, I have seen things in rainforest, every now and then. An outrageous whirling overhead, whistling wings, a mad pursuit along dodgy paths, and then, glimpsed for a long and glorious moment through a rare gap in the canopy, a pair of rhinoceros hornbill, birds almost as big as the mammal for which they were named. Those hilarious flying squirrels, that flying lizard. In Belize, I had good long looks at howler monkey and spider monkey: the howlers, who make that wild, far-carrying din across the forest (not Burton snoring, as I first uncharitably supposed) and the spiders, who climb five-limbed, arms, legs and tail, and really do look like huge arachnids as they make their nonchalant way across the highways of the canopy. And of course, the great bull-necked jag. But it's the sense of teeming that matters. Not the one but the many: not the individual but the totality: the sense that you are there, and that absolutely everything else is there too. Rainforest comprises six per cent of the landmass of the earth (and shrinking): it contains 50 per cent of its known species. And shrinking. And of course, many, many more unknown ones.

The creator certainly had an inordinate fondness for rainforest creatures.

So why should we conserve these wacky places where the wildlife viewing is so dodgy? One answer: perhaps there's a cure for cancer out there. Hell, there *is* a cure for cancer out there. The rosy periwinkle of Madagascar provided a cure for Hodgkin's disease, which mostly affects young adults, and also for a form of leukaemia, one that invariably killed the children that got it, but no longer. There are many more plants that will repay exploration for medicine. And then there's all that complex but important stuff about the carbon bank and the carbon-dioxide absorption of these great swathes of forest, and their vital role in the control of greenhouse gases. And it's all true: and do you know what? It's all bollocks so far as I am concerned. I don't care whether the rainforest is good or not. If the rainforest was positively bad, I'd want to see it conserved. Yes, it's true all right: the what's-in-it-for-me argument for conservation stands up to the most scrupulous examination: strong, powerful, utterly persuasive. And yet I reject it absolutely. I am not even terribly interested in it. Perhaps I should be, but I really don't give a stuff. When it comes to the rainforest, when it comes to every other aspect of the wild world, I don't really care whether it's good or bad, whether its profitable or not profitable, whether it's advantageous to humans or disadvantageous. I don't care what's in it for me. I just care about what's in it.

123 I missed three weeks of the advancing autumn by making a trip to Australia to write about cricket for the *Times*. The sport was good: so was the sun: the wild times were minimal, as usual. Three moments need to be recorded. The first took place at the outdoor bar of a hotel in Brisbane, when I was waiting for James Lawton, my old friend from the *Independent*, to join me for dinner. I noticed one of the bar staff scattering peanuts, abandoned by previous drinkers, beneath the tree that dominated the courtyard. As I watched, a small furry beast slithered down the trunk and ate them, as sure of herself as the rats in the Jain temple. She was a possum: a small marsupial. There are over 60 species of possum: this was, I think, a common bush-tailed possum, a self-certain little animal fond of life in the suburbs. As I watched it, I saw the waiter bend down and stroke it, an impertinence the possum took in good part. Naturally, I had to join in and have a go myself. She was carrying a baby on her back: the baby was too shy for any such interspecific interaction, but the mother was remarkably relaxed about the whole thing. It was the way you got your peanuts.

Inevitably, possums, being such bold beasts, are regarded by many as pests. Many creatures that find a way of living alongside humans are called pests, which gives us a licence to despise them and to kill them. If you try and gather information about feral pigeons, for example, you will get loads of stuff on how to kill them, and very little on the way they live and how they got to be that way. But possums are protected under Australian law, which seems a good thing to me. I always like those moments when wild and civilisation touch, in this case quite literally. Most especially, I like them when I am living between hotel rooms and sports grounds and city restaurants. We need, I think, to feel more at home in our own world.

In Adelaide, thanks to some curious organising by my newspaper, I found myself not in fact in Adelaide at all. I had been placed in a hotel 45 minutes outside town, miles from the cricket, miles from the story, miles from my colleagues. Never mind, I thought: maybe it will turn out to be rural and exquisitely beautiful: a glorious country-park hotel, surrounded by wonderful wildlife. The hotel turned out to be a gambling hell for trailer-park trash. I kept myself sane during the four days I stayed there by taking long walks along a dusty track that led around the back of the Australian bungaloid suburbs. It was a dust-track lined with eucalyptus trees, and whizzing from one tree to the next, the birds of the suburbs, the Australian equivalent of black-birds and blue tits. Parrots.

There were rainbow lorikeets, sulphur-crested cocka-toos, and, sitting in the trees like great pink blancmanges, the galahs. How odd I must have looked to passers-by: solemnly observing through binoculars the multi-coloured common-as-sparrows nonentities of Australian suburban life. But they were all thrilling to me. By means of the galahs I kept semi-sane until at last I managed to get a room downtown. A touch of the wild always tends to keep me that little bit nearer sanity.

After I left the cricket to its now-inevitable disaster, I went to visit some friends outside Sydney. They breed hors-es, and much of the talk was about drought. Much of the talk in Australia is about drought these days. This was, in many regions, the fifth year of drought: the worst drought in a thousand years, said some. I visited a new property my friends had bought: 40 acres of dust. It was a heart-break-ing sight. You could see the horses, picking at what little grass there was. They were kept going with imported hay, not a cheap option. This is a parched land dying for a drop of rain.

And no one knew if this was a climatic blip, the sort of thing that happens and then stops happening: or whether it was the beginning of the end. It might be a temporary aberration: it might be the start of a long-term shift, some-thing to do with global warming, the planet-wide changes in climate that are caused by the greenhouse gases. In

Britain, these changes are happening in small and subtle ways. But in Australia, the changes – if, indeed, they are part of long-term changes – were startling, dramatic, obvious: and seriously bloody frightening. Will the rains come? Or must Australia – this great, big, lovely place that is thrillingly still in the middle of inventing itself – prepare for hydrological bankruptcy?

I have had marvellous times in Australia, and always felt that thrill of the new country: that glorious notion that here, a person might be anything he chooses to be. In *Voss*, Patrick White's great Australian novel, the explorer-hero says: "But in this disturbing country, so far as I have become acquainted with it already, it is possible more easily to discard the inessential and to attempt the infinite."

Is Australia really on the cutting edge of climate change? If so, then human life, in the way we understand the term in the 21st century, may be no longer possible there. It is a frightening thought. Because if that is indeed the case, who will be next?

124

Away, then, from the black swans on the Torrens River in Adelaide, and the purple swamp hens lurking in the grasses at the river's edge: fine city birds, but willingly abandoned for Suffolk. As always, after the cosmic dislocation of long-haul travel, a need to touch the earth: and so a walk along the Suffolk rim: finding a homecoming in the exotic hissing of the landscape, as the wind soughed in the seed heads of the reeds. We love the strange, we love the familiar: we have a deep need for both, preferably at the same time. The changing seasons fill that need for us: the most familiar walk is never quite the same as it was last time. The winter crowds of waders along the Blyth estuary, the greylag geese on the Dingle in their cold season gatherings, along with straggling groups of teal and mallard: and the now inevitable numbers of egret. I counted twelve, a homely exoticism, both semi-strangers and an integral part of the English winter.

Across the heath, the gorse was in fine yellow show: meaning, of course, that kissing's in favour; kissing's out of favour when the gorse is out of bloom, my mother was fond of quoting. Good to be home, for the gorse and the kissing both. There is good reason for the perpetual flowering of gorse: British gorse generally comes in three species, outside Scotland. Common gorse flowers mostly from January to June, while dwarf gorse and western gorse both flower from July to November. Richard Mabey, the dragon-man, quotes the old gorse saw as "when gorse is in blossom, kissing's in season," adding that the "when" seems to imply a "where", since thickets of gorse frequently offer a room-like, almost womb-like privacy (of a kind unavailable in rural habitations crowded with three or four generations all together) to those with kissing on their minds. But this was December with the Suffolk wind showing its teeth: not a season for playing that game of laugh and lie down.

At Minsmere, more gatherings of waders, and none of them with love on their minds. And, in a sudden start, all the lapwings – but only the lapwings – took to the air and performed a lengthy ballet of alarm, sweeping across the Scrape and back, making as if to settle, and then feeling the need for another circuit or two. There were a couple of hundred of them: what, if anything, had disturbed them? And if disturbance it was, why had it disturbed only the lapwing? The redshank, the natural alarmists of the marshes, were unmoved by the lapwing frenzies. Was there some kind of species solidarity in this alarm, and in the lapwings' sustained response to it? Was this not so much an escape from danger as a celebration of lapwinghood, a closed vannelline ritual that kept the redshank and the dunlin out of it?

It was later that same day, back at home, doing the mucking-out, that a group of 500 crows flew overhead: to be precise, rooks and jackdaws, the jackdaws saying "jack", the rooks mixing their gentle caws with strangulated bugle notes. And I wondered again: why the need for this aerial solidarity? Why, this time, were there two species rather than one? There seemed to be a hint of joy, perhaps the joy of safety, in this loss of individuality, this celebration of being one of many. It was a celebration of being not a single crow, but a fraction of a battalion. The jacking and the cawing was balm to the souls of the jackers and cawers, promise of a peaceful night for a black bird in the midst of a black throng. Perhaps there was an element of recruiting in this flypast: come and join us, the more the merrier, the more the safer. But more than anything else, the crowded and complex aerial manoeuvres had the feel of a ritual, almost a touch of religion. To be part of this congregation was a form of salvation, and the privilege of dancing the duskdance of the crows gave a meaning to the short days and the long dark nights of survival. It was, after all, a long while before the time of busyness and love and breeding would be back.

I put the horses in their boxes, hayed and watered, gave them their feed. Walked back down the gentle slope to the place where the most important part of myself lives: not as an individual but as a quarter of a battalion.

125

Another garden tick: siskins, natty, busy little finches, working the seed heads up the drive. Exotic and homely: new and familiar: part of the winter hanging on and part of the promise for the coming spring. Preoccupied, utterly taken up by the delights of this new food source, completely ignoring me as I led my old mare out to her field. There were harder times coming for these little birds: harder than they knew, harder than they could dream of. And these times came with thunderclap suddenness.

126

Dramatic: beautiful: really rather eerie. But strangest of all, it seemed to impart a sense of privilege: as if I was lucky to be alive on such a wild day: as if this were the first day of spring.

But it was nothing of the kind. It was winter's deepest and darkest throw of the entire year. It was a sudden and profound freeze. It lasted for a week, and every day seemed more beautiful than the last. There was scarcely a cloud to be seen in all that time: ice-blue days, blue-black nights wildly freckled with stars. I adopted seven layers of clothing for vigorous outdoor activity (I sent a detailed itemisation of this to my drought-suffering Australian friends enduring their "stinkin' hot" summer). And all along I wagged my head at the beauty of it all: the almost absurd beauty of it all.

It began with a hoar frost: the forming of crystals in every possible place. Mostly, this meant the twigs of trees and bushes, with the result that every tree was etched in white against the almost-white sky: the darkness of the tree within to set it off. It was a wonderful calligraphy of frost: every twiglet a masterpiece: every tree the life's work, the entire oeuvre, of a virtuoso genius in the medium of frost.

But in some places, it was different. Instead of being outlined in crystals, twigs, leaves and plants were encased entirely in ice: as if preserved in a colourless amber. The seedheads of the docks around the top stable were protected with this magic substance, as if they were museum specimens of incalculable value wrapped in some wonderfully perfect substance developed specifically for their preservation throughout the centuries: as if these stubby stalks with the coarse powder of their seeds were things of high and remote beauty: things of such specialness that they must be coated with this stuff of ineffable magic.

Day after day it lasted: the white byssine crystals on the trees, the glass-clear covering of the docks. Water froze in the pipes, and I had to carry jerrycans up the frozen field in a wheelbarrow, snagging the wheel in rock-hard craters of hoofprints, bouncing furiously along the frozen tussocks. I had to break ice every morning so that the horses might drink: ice, too, in their water buckets in the stables, their breath steaming from their nostrils as they leant over the half-doors to greet me, as if I were keeping a yard of dragons. I wore fingerless gloves and cursed bitterly when they got wet: but never for a second did this feeling of privilege lessen: this feeling that we were living in an enchanted time.

Perhaps, as we are nature-deprived, we are also becoming winter-deprived. Perhaps, in the softness of the ever-warming climate, our northern hemisphere souls cry out for the harshness of the traditional northern winter. Perhaps there is a sense of homecoming in this hard weather: the satisfaction of a nostalgia for a lost time: something we more often associate with kind weather than with the brutalities of winter.

I remember the sense of astonished privilege, almost of disbelief, on those childhood occasions when a beautiful day coincided with a family treat. I remember one particular golden day on the Thames in Berkshire, with my two sisters and a kind and beautiful family friend who gave us all terrible giggles when she referred to the fruit we ate for pudding as strawbuggers. I remember the golden summer of 1976: the parched outfields at the cricket as the West Indies beat an England team that had promised to make them grovel. It is traditionally the fine days in England that are treasured: summer's lease hath all too short a date. Blake's advice on revelling in the good times as and when they come was surely based on the treacherous qualities of the English climate:

He who binds to himself a joy
Does the winged life destroy;
But he who kisses a joy as it flies
Lives in eternity's sunrise.

But I was kissing the joy of the frost as it flew: I was dwelling in eternity's frosty dawn: and it was bizarre and beautiful. Christmas was almost upon us: Joe was longing for snow, and one morning, two cock wrens fought a song duel at the front of the house: tiny birds with welkin-busting voices, and a huge, roaring trill at the end of it. Then, that same morning, the high, thin voices of the gold-crests in the pines, great tits, robins, and a gallant, boun-cing, team-handed invasion of long-tailed tits: little pink scraps of fluff with a preposterous tail, arriving always in a great crowd, sometimes altogether, sometimes in line astern, always si-si-si-inging to each other – I'm-here-where-are-you – I'm-here-where-are-you – in a restless, all-action way, as if they were little feathered mice.

That hint of spring in the midst of winter was something perfect, something that strikes to the heart of the northern hemisphere humans. But it needed that cold to strike from: it needed that hardness, in order for the coming spring to have a meaning, a savour.

127

It happens sometimes that you see your beloved unexpectedly: across a room at a party, perhaps; or a glimpse of her at long-range at a time and place when no meeting has been arranged; or when you are in a crowd, and you half-fail to recognise her, in three-quarter-profile, turned away, the poise of the neck, unaware of your presence; and instead of the moment of easy familiarity, you are smitten with a curiously unspecific pang of tenderness and lust. The cold spell was a little like that. I was seeing my beloved Suffolk countryside in a way I had scarcely ever seen it: white and hard and dry, perhaps like your beloved in a special and sensational and rather uncharacteristic outfit worn specially to please you. That half-suggestion that she is a different person reinforces all the joy that she is, in fact, the same as ever: new yet familiar, changed yet unchanging. I felt a deep and privileged joy at this wild and different place I had lived in for the past ten years, relishing my own sense of estrangement and my deep familiarity with it. The season was the more beautiful for being so fragile, so ephemeral. Every day represented a bonus, a privilege: one I both savoured and cursed as I wheelbarrowed the jerrycans up the rutted hill once again.

All the hopes of spring were hidden in the beautiful despair of this short, intense winter. And then; to great relief and almost too soon, the thaw: the hairy crystals gone, the white trees now all black, the glass-wrapped seed heads now freed. And on Christmas day, as I did the evening chores, I heard a prolonged chinking chorus of blackbirds. This is an evening habit in which blackbirds talk to each other at this time of year: and it is deeply ambiguous. It is both a celebration of togetherness – I'm-here-where-are-you – and a warning, that this is my place, and not your place.

Annually it catches to perfection that moment of the turning of the year, the moment when the days start to get longer, at last. We can all feel, wild things that we are, the minute easing of the darkness of winter, and the blackbirds respond. As they go to roost, to their resting-places of the night, they are caught between two seasons: between the long truce of winter and the brief but life-depending antagonisms of spring. This was not song, this was not alarm call, but there was some element of antagonism in it, just as there was also some element of community, of the enjoyment of flocking togetherness. Hallo for now, but don't you come too close when spring is sprung and my song is being sung. The joyous tensions of the chinking chorus came as the hidden blackbirds prepared to face the long – but not as long as last night – night: one bush, another, another, chinking at each other, the year turning, the juices beginning to stir. Spring: a promise, a threat.

128

When I had that famous, thousand-times-told encounter with the lion, it was not the lion's vulnerability that struck me at the time. When a human looks at a lion face to face, unarmed, unexpected and in the heart of the lion's territory, it is not the delicate fragility of leonine life that occupies his mind. But it bloody well should do.

Even when we are not ourselves being prey, we respond to predators with humility and awe: delight in their speed, their power, their size, their ferocity. We love the teeth, the claws, the talons, the beak. We love that feeling of nature's ferocity. In the National Football League of America, eight of the 32 teams are named for iconic predators: Falcons, Bengals (that is to say, tigers), Panthers, Bears, Lions, Jaguars, Eagles and Seahawks. Wouldn't do to explain to the offensive linesmen that all of these are the most vulnerable creatures in their food chains.

But all the same, these were thoughts that recurred to me as the twelve days of Christmas counted themselves out. The trigger was a brief, and angry encounter between a barn owl and a kestrel. It happened in full daylight and at high speed, which gave all the advantage to the dapple-dawn-drawn falcon: he swooped, yelling at the top of his voice – *kikiki!* – at the barn own, and the owl, for once forced out of his usual hunting cruise, showed that he had a fair turn of speed. In a vivid flash, they were both gone, though the argument continued. The bone of contention was the short-tailed field vole.

Not that I could see any: but it is frequently the invisible, the uncountable, the unknowable creatures that dictate the pace. The birds are the ones we see: but that is something to do with icebergs. The short-tailed field vole is a rather winning little creature in its own right: like a little furry teddy. You are only likely to see one if the cat brings it in. They even look rather sweet dead and mangled.

But they live their lives out of human view: out of the view of owl and kestrels, for that matter. They live and have their being in the tunnels they make through the dense grass of rank, unkempt meadows. So when you see a scruffy meadow you can rejoice for the sake of voles and for their spectacular and vulnerable predators. Barn owls locate these hidden mammals by sound: their asymmetrically positioned ears give them an accurate cross-bearing: the voles help them out by being noisy little buggers, always squeaking and chattering at each other. The kestrel's method is still more esoteric. The voles leave scent trails of urine: these reflect ultra-violet light, and the kestrels can pick this up.

Two solutions: one problem: one battle. The barn owl made his escape, no doubt muttering to himself that he would be back at dusk with his ultra-clever ears, and a fat lot of good ultra-violet vision will do you in the dark. But the real problem is that the fate of these two top predators is tied to that of their voles. And the voles are boom-and-bust species. Every now and then, a population explosion is followed by a crash. It is not the predators that control the population: this is to do with the dynamics of the voles and their food sources. Rather, the voles dictate the number of predators: in a boom year, the predators are in clover; in a bust year, they suffer. It is the furry teddies that dictate the pace: and it is the sleek and the fierce, those of sharp beak and cruel talons, that suffer when the vole population is down.

It is not the lions that are the masters of the Luangwa Valley. No: it is the buffaloes they feed on. The impalas control the leopards. The weak control the strong: and no matter how many brilliant solutions the predators come up with – the teamwork of the lion, the stalking skills of the leopard, the ears of the owl and the vision of the falcon – it is always the hunted that remain in control. They are the masters: it is the hunters that are hanging in on the far edge of possibility, whether they are roadside kestrels or jaguars in the jungles of Belize.

129
The cold slackened its grip. The twelfth day of Christmas was one of rains: I rode out past a big old hedge: raindrops hanging from twig-ends like Christmas decorations, all of which had to come down that day, while small birds were whizzing about, ducking in and out of the hedge, with a sense of renewed purpose. The following day, a dunnock in full song outside the house, and then a distant mistle thrush. A few days later, everything was silenced by

a big wind: and in the calm that followed, a great tit broke out in his teacher-teacher song for the first time... but perhaps you've heard all this before. Perhaps you read the same thing a couple of hundred pages back. Perhaps I am beginning to repeat myself here: but then so is nature. Nature, too, is beginning another chapter, much the same as the old chapter. That is the point. You thought the last spring was something that could never be surpassed? Well, hold on, because nature is about to do it all over again. This endless repetition is the rhythm of life in the northern latitudes. The sound of the first spring singers told us all that the fourth season was almost out, and the first season of the next cycle was materialising before our eyes. A year ending, a book ending: and as ever, a new beginning.

The new beginning is the most wonderful and thrilling concept in human life. We are all of us intoxicated by the idea that we can throw a double six and start again, set off as if the past had never been. Perhaps the notion gets into our souls because the new start is nothing less than a fact of life in the high latitudes: the annual renewal of spring, of hope, cannot help but establish an important principle in our lives. And as it comes, it brings with it the ultimately optimistic belief that the past can be left behind, that we can escape the wrongs and mistakes of the past and their consequences, if only we keep on running. And alas, it is the ultimate error: as the most cursory glance across the landscape – any landscape – will tell you. The destruction and the errors of the past are an irrefragable part of our present: and our future.

130

Tim Hallissey, sports editor of the *Times*, is not a birder. All the same, when he came down to Suffolk to discuss my sporting assignments for the coming year, I took him for a stroll across the marshes at Snape to give us an appetite for the task, for a pint, for lunch. Best way to do business. And across the fierce wintry expanse of the Alde estuary, birds in pretty decent numbers.

I know, because I counted them. I take pleasure in counting: particularly, I like counting birds. There is something wonderful about big numbers of animals: something intoxicating about a multitude. Not just the odd one or two: but hundreds of the bloody things. It is a very dehumanising sight, the more thrilling for that. A deeply wild thing. Counting seems in some way to get them under control: and then to open the doors to greater wildness: to a deeper understanding. There is no special virtue in imprecision.

We saw a huge crowd of small waders get up; probably dunlin, but too far away – for me at least – to say for certain. And they performed that aerial ballet that waders are so good at, making shapes and clouds and spirals, going this way and then that way: so you wonder who's in charge, who makes the decisions, who decides when they should get up, and when they go down, how come they all seem to move as if controlled by a single mind, and anyway, how come they don't bump into each other in the sky? Part of this wonderful illusion of unanimity is to do with the small size of the bodies, hence the short time it takes to convert a message from the brain into action: a process that, for a small bird, is much faster than we lumbering humans could ever comprehend. And so I sought some kind of comprehension, some kind of union, by counting.

You don't count 1-2-3-4, you count to ten, and then superimpose your remembered block of ten over the rest of the flock. Or sometimes, when you are confronted with serious numbers, your block of 100. Real experts can do this to a stunning degree of accuracy. Me, I do it for the sport, and I made it 1,000. It's a standard rule, and a wild

one: you always undercount. We also saw a big raft of avocets: and they took to the air as well: in intense charcoal-
grey light, the black and the white shone out from the
wintry half-tones. I counted 400 this time, and they too
made a series of patterns in the sky, less tight in formation
than the probable-dunlins, with a more languid, almost
ragged approach.

"Why do they do it?" Tim asked.

I gave him a long and scientifically detailed explanation,
which can be summed up here as "I'm not really sure, but
then I don't think anybody else knows either."

Tim thought for a while as we retraced our steps.
Eventually, having pondered the matter with some care, he
said: "I suppose they do it for the same reason that a dog
licks its testicles."

"Yes?"

"You know. Because it can."

We moved on to Guinness and the sporting calendar.

131

As spring began to take a tentative grip, the
nation was seized by terror. There was a bird flu outbreak.
It took place at the Bernard Matthews turkey plant, just a
few miles from my house, so I was rather involved. As
instructed, we moved our own chickens under cover, so
they would be safe from wild birds. And as we did these
tasks, it was clear that the national terror revealed a profound truth about human fears. Because wild birds were
blamed for the outbreak of bird flu: and in the confused
memories of many, wild birds are still the heart of the problem.

The story about the wild pigeon that "must have been"
trapped in the ventilator shaft, thereby releasing the deadly

wild virus into the fat, healthy, contented and civilised turkeys that gabbled and gobbled beneath, found widespread emotional acceptance. And yet it is a nonsense. The H5N1 virus is a problem within the poultry industry, and it has been spread by industrial means. The outbreak in Nigeria was caused by the import of birds from China; the disease spread in China along the rail and road routes, not along bird migration routes.

Work it out for yourself: what is the best way to pick up human flu? Go for a nice walk in the country, or spend some serious quality time in the rush-hour tube? And factory-farmed birds spend their short and horrible lives in conditions far less comfortable and healthy than the tube.

But the interesting thing here was the eagerness with which the wild world was blamed: the way we really rather relished the idea of a cruel and random death swooping down from the skies. We have been taught to fear the wild: one horror story after another shows the revenge of the wild on civilised human beings. *The Birds*, thanks to Daphne du Maurier and Alfred Hitchcock, gets to the heart of the matter, but there are a thousand others, from the *Odyssey* and *Sir Gawain and the Green Knight* to *Jaws* and *King Kong*.

We have a need for monsters. We have a need for fear: and the wild is the traditional place from which fears come. Our nursery rhymes and fairy stories are full of bears and wolves: sometimes three at a time, sometimes dressed as your grandmother, and if you go down to the woods today, you'd better go in disguise. The bear sums up our contradictory attitudes to the wild: bears terrified Goldilocks, and they come to get you with the most fiendish tickle when you go round and round the garden, and yet most children take a bear to bed with them. The bear is a terror, a comforter, a protector.

The dichotomy between civilisation and the wild is celebrated again and again, perhaps most explicitly in the short stories of Saki, in which he introduces a werewolf to the Edwardian drawing room; in other stories, he presents a blood hungry ferret that is worshipped as a god, a child-killing hyena and a horribly indiscreet talking cat. But it is Gabriel-Ernest, the wolf-boy who comes in from the woods, who tells us most vividly about the barriers we humans have erected to shield ourselves from the wild, and the way they can be destroyed in an instant of time. The prim and prissy Van Cheele encounters a naked boy in the woods. They talk, Van Cheele asking the boy what he feeds on, living in the woods: "Since it interests you, rabbits, wild-fowl, hares, poultry, lambs in their season, children when I can get any; they're usually too well locked in at night, when I do most of my hunting. It's quite two months since I tasted child-flesh." The boy next appears in Van Cheele's drawing room: "Gracefully asprawl on the otto-man, in an attitude of almost exaggerated repose, was the boy of the woods. He was drier than when Van Cheele had last seen him, but no other alteration was noticeable in his toilet." It is Van Cheele's Aunt that calls him Gabriel-Ernest. It all ends as badly as you might expect.

We yearn for the wild: and yet we fear it. But then fear is a part of a great many important things: without fear, life is pretty bland. But we are in danger of letting fear overtake the yearning. The less access we have to the wild, the less time we are able to spend in the wild, the more we encour-age our distrust, our fear, at the expense of the yearning and the love. We fear the pigeon in the ventilator shaft: we dread the arrival of Gabriel-Ernest in our living room.

132
And yet even as the country was recoiling from the natural world with fear and loathing, so the

turning of the year inspired everyone in the country to embrace the natural world with renewed fervour: with the fervour of spring's renewal: just one more of the contradictions we humans embrace with wild enthusiasm.

The shedding of a layer of clothing is an annual joy. It is a freedom, not only from the weight and the inconvenience of a topcoat, but also from the dark and the cold. The first day you walk out of your house with a garment fewer than the day before is a day of real meaning: a celebration of union with nature and the turning of the year. Our spirits rise: the sun trips off all kinds of deep responses in us, and we seem to leave our cares – at least some of them – hanging up in the hall with our abandoned coats. The women are suddenly prettier, the men find themselves striding out with a forgotten energy.

And it seemed to me that the high spring sprang in a single day: a single sweet Thursday. I woke to the sound of sparrows: their cheeping reaching a new pitch of excitement and intensity. It was as if the very roof of my house was echoing to the sound of horniness. Then the first blackbird sang out on home territory: not a great version of the song, if truth be told: this was perhaps a warm-up routine, the favourite syrinx-loosener from a great virtuoso; or perhaps it was a young bird who hadn't really got the hang of it yet.

After that, a wonderful song duel from two mistle thrushes, skirling and counter-skirling, a great antiphonal ecstasy of confrontation. It was a grand year for mistle thrush, and the more there are, the better they have to sing. Competition forces the best from them: and the fields and the hedgelines and the garden and the little copse echoed with the thrill of it.

The whole world appeared to be taken over by the most monstrous fit of good temper. I was filled with an urgent need to get on a horse and ride through the countryside.

The birds, the horses, the humans: all of us were in the best of all possible moods, while the sun shone down with real warmth: for the past six months, it hadn't really occurred to us that the sun was a source of heat: it was merely a light in the sky, and a pretty intermittent one at that.

But now it shone, and the stark white blossom on the cherry plums, the great early flowerer of the hedgerows, was now softened with green leaves; there were celandines sprouting up along the drive. I rode out in my shirt-sleeves without feeling even remotely brave: a kestrel stood on one wing and wheeled away in front of me, while skylarks sang their endless song. There were prim-roses in real numbers, new leaves on the hawthorns, sticky buds on the horse chestnuts. From every thicket, the wrens were belting out their ear-shattering trills. Wild birds, domesticated animals, over civilised humans: all of us responding to the same atavistic joy. All of us in our hearts wild.

I got back home from my ride and turned the horses out into their field without their winter rugs on for the first time that year, and their response was to turn to each other in joy. They stood shoulder to shoulder, nibbling each other: nibbling at all the un-get-at-able bits behind the wither, making the perfect horsey picture. This mutual grooming relieves itches and irritations: but far more importantly, it cements the link between the two horses: it celebrates the fact that they like each other, trust each other, need each other. One horse, after all, is no horse. And my heart lifted at the sight: not least because I would soon be seeing the same sight replicated again and again, but with another equine species. I happened to have a ticket to Eden.

133

The river itself is wild. In fact, it had gone on the rampage. A couple of weeks before I arrived, it made a demented charge from its banks and invaded the villages and the camps on either side. The worst floods for 30 years, they all told me, with that mixture of pride and humility you find in people who have got through a natural catastrophe. Only two of the tourist camps were above the water level: everyone else abandoned ship and took shelter at the dry camps and waited for the water to recede. There was a great ceremony of mucking in: it was just like the old days, said the old hands. After that came the real test: and the cleaning up of the epic layers of silt the river had left behind.

The Luangwa River flows across Zambia, at the bottom of a deep trench that runs through the plateau that makes up most of the country: and it is perhaps the wildest river in the world. Very, very few people live on its banks: there is no hint of a town, still less a city. No one has built a dam, no one has tried to canalise it and control it. For millennia, it has lashed itself from side to side like a wounded snake: never in the same course for two years running. Constantly, it makes new oxbows and new courses, while the main channel takes new shapes and abandons old ways. Two camps where I have stayed in the past have fallen into the river, victims of the river's latest caprice. The Luangwa, always different, always changing, always the same.

Like the English year and its slavery to the rhythm of the seasons, Luangwa – the same term applies to both the river and the land – runs to the rhythm of the water. And, just as it was with the beltingly hot day when I walked through clouds of clouded yellows in Cornwall, and when, months later, I grappled through the week when frost and ice made the world so beautiful, the rhythm is one of extremes. I have waded this river many times: sometimes without getting my knees wet, once armpit-deep in an early-season surge that threatened to sweep me off my feet, me wondering, like Sergeant Wilson, if this was quite wise. I was walking second: would not the crocs be stirred into resentful life by the leader, just in time to close their jaws on his immediate follower? It was good to reach the opposite bank.

You wouldn't wade the Luangwa now. It would take a magnificent swimmer, and a fool, even to try a crossing: 400 yards at the narrowest, and moving with a daunting urgency. The craziness of the floods had diminished, and most of the river was back inside the banks, but it was still unrecognisable to anyone who had only seen it in the dry season, the time most tourists make their visits. Meanwhile, the roads were mainly impassable: even the so-called all-weather roads were dangerous, unstable, and in some places where we tried, impossibly cratered. So we took a boat. And I was back with Levy Banda, an old friend met in the first chapter of this book, and Chris Breen, ditto, also my companion on the hunt for the elusive Pearson's cisticola, and a lot of other mad jaunts too.

We were heading for Mchenja: to the ebony glade where I had sat and waited and watched: to the place where I had watched the river flow: to the place where there will always be a piece of my heart lying buried. Heading back to my sacred combe. Looking across the endless stretch of water as we chugged up a river that would very soon be unnavigable: open-billed storks flying overhead like pterodactyls, occasionally a puku or two seen at the river's edge. There were plenty of crocs in the river, some of them seriously big: and every now and then, small gatherings of hippo, sometimes staring at us from the waterline, once or twice involved in concerns of their own, brave yawning exchanges, gaping at each other in big mouthed threat.

And then a miracle. A new Luangwa mammal, for me at

255

least. Just as I had seen on that day on the Walberswick marshes: a sinuous slither, a silent, almost rippleless plop, the smallest possible set of concentric circles. Otter. Otter again: this time a Cape clawless: an animal seldom encountered here, almost never seen. I was the only one who caught sight of it: through luck, through some kind of familiarity with the species: a half-second of perfection.

We reached Mchenja: a place that was much changed and as lovely as ever. It had gone upmarket, reflecting a changing tourist industry: no more the longdrop lavs, no more the outside showers, carved into the living riverbank, no more the sand floors, the laundry-basket huts with a folding bed and nothing more. But the same ebony glade: the same, ever-changing, unchanging river.

134 In the evening, a visit to a cathedral. We went by boat, as if to a Venice sunk beneath the waters of the lagoon. Another ebony glade: the one my romantic old friend Manny always used to call the Robin Hood Glade. The ebony trunks were the pillars, the trees waist-deep in river water, the closed canopy of the ebony trees was the vaulted roof. The transition was distinctly rum. There was a party of us: Chris and I, Levy, a couple of the camp's other clients. We were chatting and laughing on the main body of the river, but the minute we went beneath the roof of the sunken glade, we stopped. We fell silent, as if the headmaster had entered the room. With the engine throttled

back to the most whispering chug – not so much for reverence as because the going was treacherous in the extreme –
we penetrated the glade: always finding we could get in that
little bit deeper, weaving our way between the sky-reaching
trunks.

It was a place I had visited in the dry season on many
occasions, generally at night, in a vehicle, with the spotlight
on, hunting for hunting leopards. It was there that Manny
and I saw the hyena steal from the leopard: and where
Manny had subsequently charged the embryectomising
hyena. It was a place of subtle shadows and hidden surprises.

The great pillars of the ebony rose above all around us,
leading up to the roof, fine-boned and fan-vaulted like the
chapel at King's College, Cambridge. We whispered our
way onwards: at times switching off the engine to devour
the silence. An extraordinary feeling: to travel across the
land by means of a boat: to pass between trees with the
water slapping gently at the boat's sides. Land should be
land, and water water: but the normal rules had been suspended. Clearly, this was a time and a place of magic: clearly, this was the Wood Between the Worlds. A croc, log-like,
apparently slumbering but with a golden eye watching
hard; a hippo, a small oval of back, front of its ears and eyes
just visible; a giant kingfisher; the sound of woodland kingfisher; an African fish eagle, chestnut and a rich Cheery
Blossom tan with a white head, moving ahead of us from
perch to perch. This place I knew as dry was so wet we
were able to travel in for a full mile: this place I knew as one
of danger and death was one of peace and ease; barring the
menace of the croc. We took sundowners near the exit to
the glade, a Mosi, the beer of Zambia. And then emerged
not as if from a wood but from a dream.

135

It's at night when the place is most truly wild: when you don't have the use of your eyes to make sense of a landscape. The only information comes through your ears: and it is a massive sensual overload to those of us used to the quieter nights of the north, or to the never-silent humming of traffic. First the constant jangling of the crickets, a sound we have all heard in a thousand jungle films. Behind it, at this time of year, the tinkling of the reed frogs: frogs have many voices, and the painted reed frogs of the Luangwa Valley clink and chink like windchimes.

You hear these noises at a meal, or around the campfire, but most of all, you hear them in bed. The vast canvas of sound has no perspective, very little sense of distance. The African scops owl punctuates the frogs and the crickets with a neat little prrrp; every now and then, again at this time of year, the sound of a young Pel's fishing owl. This is a beautiful animal, more often heard than seen though well worth a look: a great tangerine-coloured ball of fluff that seems to have been put together without any rigid structure whatsoever. They are improbably huge, and can occasionally be seen squatting at the edge of rivers and lagoons: more often when accidentally flushed from cover in daytime, when they burst out like giant orange moths into the hated sunlight. The young bird makes a call invariabily described as "like a lost soul falling down the bottomless pit".

Every now and then, the whoop of hyena: wild and wonderfully exotic, worth the trip for that sound alone, coming across the blackness of the bush, forever evoking the African night. But then lion. Lions, being social animals, love to keep in touch, and they do so over long range with their earth-shattering voices. The half-hearted snarl of the Metro-Goldwyn-Meyer lion is nothing like the roaring of a lion with an urgent need to trumpet the glory of the pride across the savannah. I have lain awake in a tent between one pride and another, both giving out the full pride chorus to remind each other of where their boundaries lay: and was frankly and unambiguously terrified, not least because of the bedtime stories about the man who was taken from his tent and eaten in this very spot. Terrified: and yet in love with the craziness of it all, with the intemperance of the great beasts.

Mchenja is safer than this: but still the night was filled with lion music, each call rising in intensity and volume before fading away from its peak with ever-softer calls till at last, there is nothing but a huffy breath. And if you can hear that, you have a right to a little unease. It is the sound of too close. That little huff may be the wildest sound on earth: which makes it – slightly queasily – the best.

136

It is a convention, in wildlife travel-writing, to imply that I, as the writer, am having an experience that you, the reader, can never hope to share: that what I am doing is something beyond your scope and your hope. My vanity strongly desires to keep it this way, to roar, lion-like, and proclaim my own specialness before you. But I must resist this temptation. What I am up to is special enough, but nothing special, if you see what I mean. I must force myself to abandon the convention of specialness and explain that I got to Luangwa the way most people get there: by buying a ticket. You can do the same thing. You can go to Africa, to Minsmere, to Belize: to anywhere in the world you fancy, if you can scrape together the price of a ticket. You can see it as a luxury, or you can see it as a necessity; downgrade the car and blow the money on something that lasts. What you do with money – at least in the developed world – is all about priorities.

Should you make the trip? What about carbon debts and all that? Of course you should. There are strong counter-arguments, but they don't stand up. If places like Luangwa are not visited by rich westerners, they will have no dollar-value for a poor nation. What will their future be, if they became, in fiscal terms, valueless? And as for guilt about carbon footprints, ethical wildlife travel firms are these days getting involved in schemes for offsetting this. You can find all kinds of firms that offer wildlife travel, if you look at the ads in BBC*Wildlife* magazine, or the RSPB's *Birds* magazine. You can even find Chris's company: an outfit that has launched me on more than one adventure.

Go. It is the only way of keeping the wild places wild.

137

For years, I kept trying to go to Africa and failing. I kept losing my nerve. More than once, I booked a trip, and then bailed out.

I was deeply afraid. I was afraid, not of lions but of humans; not of elephants but of vehicles. I dreaded the idea of surrounding a lion in the company of two dozen other jeeps. It was, I think, as much a religious thing as anything: the notion of sanctity, and more especially, of violating sanctity, seemed terribly vivid. I wanted to meet Africa, I wanted to meet the bush, I wanted to meet the beasts in a meaningful way. I didn't want just to see them: I was seek-ing something more.

I ordered yet another brochure; read, mostly skimming in a dispirited way, waiting for the catch: for the give-away phrase that said it would all be terribly comfortable, terri-bly easy, terribly safe: and that there would be dozens of others sharing the experience with you, all insanely clicking their cameras.

One word changed everything. The word was "walk".

In the Luangwa Valley, you can walk. I remember thinking: "My God, there are lions and hippos and elephants and buffaloes out there. Walking? That's got to be insane." So naturally, I booked. Leading the trip was a young fellow by the name of Chris Breen, who told me, one evening around the fire after a day of wonders, that, while his day job was flogging plane tickets at Trailfinders, his ambition was to start his own company and specialise in wildlife travel.

Anyway, I walked. I walked in the bush. The system is simple: at the front goes a game scout, carrying a gun, whose job it is to keep you safe and make sure his gun is never needed. Behind him, the guide: qualified, knowledgeable, and these days generally, like the game scout, a Zambian. Behind them, in single file, follow the clients.

Walking changes everything. Walking is one of the most important things about being wild: not just in the bush, but everywhere. Walking is the wildest form of travel: the most ancient. When you walk, you are part of the landscape. Your vision is omnidirectional. You can hear, smell, taste, feel. When you walk, you cease to be an observer, and become a participant: just like our ancestors when they, too, first walked on the floor of Africa.

Chris and Levy had got involved in a conundrum of identification: distant small birds in distant large trees, while John Saili, the scout, lounged at his ease, leaning on his rifle, his fingers making an oddly delicate pattern around the foresight. Was it, then, a yellow-breasted apalis? Or was it a burnt-necked eremomela? It was high in a tree, rather distant, and I kept losing the bloody thing. I confess my attention wandered. And my binoculars. "Come on," Chris said. "Don't you have an opinion to offer?'

"I do," I said. "It's a lion." It was, too: a big male, lying under a bush, about a hundred yards away. We tried to walk around him, attempting the cosmic courtesy that every walker in the bush seeks to employ: but he got up and snarled crossly at us before setting off to find a more private kind of bush. We sat down and had a cup of tea.

138

A puku – the foxy red antelope found everywhere along the Luangwa – seen from the boat at the edge of the river, a male, its horns covered in hay like a bizarre hat. It had been horning the vegetation, demonstrating its power and aggression by means of an assault on the innocent grasses. It had clearly established a territory, and now needed both to lure in the females and to keep out the rival males. It was a fine animal, sleek, muscular, and – at least in puku eyes – fearsome and impressive with its daft hat. Puku ram, I thought. Handsome, young, prosperous; owner of desirable riverside property, WLTM 20-30 puku ewes for friendship and fornication; GSOH not essential.

139

There are no people in the Luangwa Valley. Not in the three national parks that dominate the valley, anyway. People only go there if they are tourists or are looking after tourists. People have never had much to do with this area. That's because you can't keep cattle here. It's the tsetse flies that do it. Tsetse flies are famous for giving humans sleeping sickness: but the wider truth is that they are vectors for typanosomiasis, a suite of diseases, some which are certain cattle-killers. There is no sleeping sickness in Luangwa: but there are no cattle either. So every time you get bitten by a tsetse fly, you have to give thanks: difficult business, because the tsetse's bite, though it does not linger and itch like a mosquito's, is disconcertingly sharp. (They can take a blood meal as heavy as themselves, a small miracle which possibly qualifies them as the crown of creation.)

Humans have mostly kept clear of the valley, certainly in numbers. These days, there is a little agriculture outside the park: and a fair bit of fishing, most of it legal. There is some illegal meat poaching, mostly for commerce rather than subsistence, but this is policed by the game scouts and is a high-risk activity.

It is a place in which humans play very little part. At the time I made this visit, the park was much quieter than usual, for the full tourist season was not yet upon us: the roads had yet to go through their annual repairing and regrading. The life we saw was not directly touched by humanity: rather, we humans fitted in around the margins. The fascination, the joy of the place came from the absence of humanity. Indeed, there are times when I even feel resentful of the baboon communities for being primates, for being too closely related to me, for spoiling the purity of the bush. I always feel slightly put out when I come across the baboons' too-human handprints and footprints, and their altogether too-human turds.

But for most of the time, you can bathe in the feeling that you have escaped not civilisation but humanity itself. The entire order of primates is mostly absent, bar the baboons and vervet monkeys (the males of which have bright blue scrotums) and the occasional fragile, acrobatic bushbabies. As you observe the life going on around you, you do so without reference to your own kind: something that frees the spirit in the most extraordinary way. At Mchenja, I sat and watched the river flow, as ever: taken up by the small comings and goings, the small details of life. When I spent my two months at Mchenja, every day I observed the same prospect: and each day, it was ever-so-slightly not the same. An extra yellow-billed stork fishing in the river; the usual spoonbill for once absent, a giant kingfisher uncharacteristically present; a pied kingfisher uncharacteristically out of sight.

These small details became utterly engrossing: I felt like Great-Aunt Leonie in Proust, who was on tenterhooks for an entire Sunday because she did not know whether or not Madame Goupil had got to mass in time for the elevation, and was briefly horrified because she had looked from the window of her sickroom and seen a strange dog – a dog she did not know – walking in the streets of Combray.

140

I was there precisely on the cusp of the seasons. The year was turning beneath my feet, beneath the boat I sat in. The wet season was ending, the dry season beginning. For the herbivores, the time of plenty was ending; for the carnivores, the time of plenty was about to begin. For the camps and lodges of the valley, the migration of the tourists was about to start: in Luangwa, the dry season is best for communications, for travel and above all, for seeing large mammals, especially predators. That is to say especially lions and leopards. The vegetation is lower, the ground is harder, the travelling is easier, the views are clearer. The best time of all is right at the end of the dry season, when the days are stinkin' hot, unforgivingly dry, flash-bulb-bright: when the plant-eaters are craving serious nourishment and longing for the rains, while the carnivores, sleek, fat and well-fed, are cashing in on the last of the time of plenty.

Chris and I have seen all the wonders a thousand times, and God willing, we will see them again. For us, the sense of urgency has gone: we can savour each small thing, in the sure and certain knowledge that the spectacular will come our way in its own good time. For us, freed from the first-time tourists' tensions – will I feel cheated if I don't see a lion? – we could enjoy each nuance without any of the said issues.

And the river was falling every day: some days by as much as a metre. Someone had pulled the plug out, and the Luangwa River was emptying at breakneck rate, pouring its waters into the far distant confluence with the Zambezi. There are many tributaries to the Luangwa along its length and these were also emptying fast: quite literally emptying, for in the dry season, they would be rivers of sand, some of them punctuated by the occasional waterhole.

There is an elegant paradox about the Luangwa River. The more there is of it, the less it matters. At the height of the wet season – sorry, my loyalties to my friends in the tourist industry mean that I should call this the Green Season, or even the Emerald Season – there is water everywhere, all the tributaries are full, all the oxbows are full, and the ground is soft and yielding beneath your feet. Nothing is fixed, nothing solid: everything is liquid, shifty and likely to flow. You can get a drink anywhere you like. The hippos are everywhere: in small groups in the tributaries and the lagoons; the crocs ramble where they please, forsaking the main channel to explore and to take prey as they find it. The antelopes, the puku and the impala and the rest spread out across the entire width of the valley floor: everything is green and growing and edible, everywhere you can slake your thirst. And in the middle of it all flows the mighty Luangwa, a quarter-mile across, in a good year rushing over the edge of the banks, tearing down new routes as is its centuries-old wont, with very few creatures having very much to do with it.

But then the land dries up and bakes hard: and it was all beginning to happen as we watched. Every morning, the boat was a little bit further away: required that little bit more of a step and a slither to reach it. The level in the tributaries was falling even faster: we could see the change in the river itself: day by day, the hippos were arriving at the confluences, driven downstream by the imperative of the retreating waters, grouping sulkily and reluctantly at the places where the tributaries met the main channel. The clans were gathering. You began to see more crocs. One day, we saw the first sandbank, revealed by the retreating river: and then more. As a result, the very sound of the river changed: we began to hear the piping of the greenshank, one of the great Luangwa sounds, but silent until this moment. One day, we saw a vast flock of birds, resoundingly identified at long-range by Levy as chestnut-winged pratincoles: the sandbanks had drawn them in: and we saw them later, settled, in a long line looking at the river – neat, natty little birds, 800 of them, as I counted. The Robin Hood Glade was no longer navigable: from its edge you could see new islands rising up from the cathedral floor. We began to see impala in large gatherings, confused, leaderless groups: the tight breeding herds and bachelor groups of the wet season had broken up and a dry-season chaos had taken over.

Soon, almost the only water left in the Valley would be the ever-diminishing river. Most of the lagoons would dry out; just about all of the tributaries. All that would be left by the end, in the stinkin' hot, would be there in the main channel, and all the creatures that needed to drink would have to come down and chance it. Life would concentrate around the slim ditch of the river and the narrow strip of land on either side. All that mattered now and for the coming six months would be the hanging on: the getting through until the rains came again.

I looked down as I walked, to see the cloven prints of antelope, much as I see, though less often, the tracks of deer in Suffolk. And I recall vividly hitting a patch of sticky mud, and leaving the prints of the soles of my boots along with those of the impala and the puku: and realising that those prints would last for another six months, cast in concrete, imprinted in the hardening land until the merciful rains should fall again and the river once more start to rise. The year was turning: the carnivores were licking their lips.

141

But as we celebrated wildness, we also celebrated humanity. We returned from an evening boat-ride along the river, sun already down, that remarkable fact having already been marked with Mosis drunk on a sand-bank. Dusk was long past, the lights of the camp shone out as if to mark the end of an epic quest. And we found a second boat tied up at our ever-longer mooring-point. Four old friends: Ade and Jess, Gid and Adrian: they had said they would come, said they would make the long journey up-river, but in Africa, and in the Valley, nothing is quite certain, so every well-made plan acquires the added delight of surprise if it actually comes off. And so we partook of a feast, while the crickets sang and the frogs tinkled, the hyenas whooped and the owls went prrrp or fell into a bottomless pit, and every now and then, a lion crumped in the distance. Fireflies floated around our heads, bottles were emptied, new ones opened. A dozen of us around a table, with yarning and laughter. I sat beside Jess, my old companion from Mchenja days, she with whom I had seen the midnight giraffe. The food was wonderful, as the best camp food always is, and the drink plentiful. Later we sat by the fire, having made a migration to whisky, the talk quieter, gentler. It was a lovely evening, and the wild Luangwa night, with its wild and deeply familiar sounds, made it a thing of perfection.

I tell you this because I wouldn't want you to think that a hatred of one's own species offers any kind of answer. It is good to go to places which human hands have touched lightly, if at all: but that is not the same as misanthropy. True, the main problem facing the world is not climate change but the ever-growing human population, and it is logical, I suppose, to wish a terrible pandemic onto humankind, to rejoice whenever a natural disaster, or a man-made one, reduces the population. But that is a logical step too far for most human beings.

A return to the Pleistocene is not really an option. The real joy of a visit to a place like Luangwa is to get re-inspired: to reconfirm your sense of joy in the wild world: to understand, with renewed vividness, the way that the wild world matters, not just for the lucky few, but to every human ever spawned.

A small party of humans made merry on the banks of the Luangwa: a ritual feast: food, drink, laughter, talk, joke and story. It felt good to be wild, good to be human, good to be there. Jess told the story of when Bob fell off the riverbank, and I told the one about the time we got lost on Lion Plain, and we all had one more. A hyena called in a rare silence.

142

I have looked up the technical term, because I like to get these things right, and it is *utchari*. This translates as "throwing down at the edge of the ring". It comes from sumo, and it is used for that extraordinary moment when one giant somehow flips another giant onto his back and then lands on top of him.

We were travelling up a very narrow, still-water-filled tributary of the Luangwa when two hippos broke the surface ten yards in front of us, in the middle of a furious battle. We came upon them around the blind bend of a watercourse so narrow you could in places touch the vegetation on both sides at once – and so found ourselves in sudden, dramatic proximity in a manner deeply shocking to us all. The hippos, the lust of fighting hot and strong in their veins, did not for a second cease their struggle, gaping and counter-gaping, teeth as big as your head and bared in furious confrontation: but then – had our dramatic appearance caused one to lose concentration for a nanosecond or two? – one seized another, mouth to mouth, and impossibly, outrageously, flipped him: there was the brief sight of four tree-trunk legs poking up at the sky, then a tidal wave was sweeping down on the boat and both contestants vanished. The entire action had taken no more than five seconds.

It was one of the most extraordinary things I have seen: ferocious, genuinely alarming, genuinely dangerous, seldom seen, and faintly hilarious. I had not gone to Luangwa hoping for a great view of hippos: if I'd been given a choice, I'd probably have asked for caracal, a beast I have never seen. But no: the high spot, in terms of drama and danger, was hippos.

If you go out looking for wildlife, you will get many disappointments: but you will be paid back by any amount of extraordinary things you weren't even looking for. A few years ago, I made a trip to Nepal to look for tigers. I saw the grass that was disturbed by the passage of a tiger, but that was as good as it got, though I did have the bonus, as you know, of falling in love with the idea of becoming a mahout. But despite the lack of tigers, the trip brought me one of the great wildlife sights of a lifetime.

In five of the great river systems of the world, there live dolphins. These are not the merry ocean-going Flippers that we see in all the pictures, the stars of a million posters, most of which carry a pious slogan about world peace. Dolphins come in many sizes and forms, and in these rivers, the dolphins are white, blind, and curiously shaped: like dolphins evolved to live on the moon. They certainly don't look like earthlings: they live in the murk and silt of rivers, finding fish to eat by means of echolocation: a life of clicks that gives them a world-view impossible to imagine.

As you'll gather, these are not animals you see very often: they have their being in darkness. And yet I had the extraordinary privilege of seeing three of them, all together, in a moment of high spirits that seemed utterly out of character for a creature of the dark: leaping and plunging, breaching the surface, at times leaping clear: this was the Ganges dolphin, with a long beak, a strange humpy-back, and an unearthly pallor.

One of my textbooks has a picture of a male and female in a face-to-face embrace, beaks tenderly crossed, rapt expressions on their faces, copulating like people. Impossible, even in a scientific publication, for an artist to keep all emotion from his work: impossible, even when attempting the loftiest heights of detachment, not to feel involved, touched, moved by his kinship with the wild.

143

Few people have looked on a bateleur without wanting to be one. The bateleur: a most singular eagle. The name is French for tightrope walker, for that is the way the bird flies, constantly making lateral adjustments with its wing-tips, like a man balancing with his hands stretched out as far as possible on either side. The bateleur seems to have no tail: and though there is, in truth, a vestigial stump of a thing, the scientific name, *Terathopius ecaudatus*, means "tailless meteor": as good a description as you could get. It was first described by François Le Vaillant, no doubt with the help and support of Klaas and Narina.

The bird's way of life involves eight or nine hours of flight every single day. Flight is energy-expensive, but not as a bateleur flies: for it doesn't trouble to flap. It ambles across the sky, holding its wings in a high dihedral: a much sharper vee than the marsh harriers of the Suffolk wetlands, at times close to 90 degrees. The mature birds are sharply black and white when seen from underneath: a bright red beak when you catch them in a good light, and bright red feet that stick out beyond the tail. And here's a rum thing: the young birds do have a tail. But as they grow, so the tail gets shorter with each year of maturation, until they reach the full adult all-but-tailless phase. This is because a bateleur's mastery of the air requires a good deal of practice. The tail on the young bird is like the stabilisers on a child's bike: and it gives the young bird added lift, a lower stalling speed, and greater aerial stability. A bateleur has to earn its right to fly tailless: the lack of tail is the badge of a hard-won mastery.

You see them all the time in the skies above the valley floor. They are not birds of whopping rarity, but they are profoundly special. Once the air has warmed up enough to give them the thermals they need to acquire lift and height, you will see them often enough, and yet every one of them is remarkable, every one worth a second look. They are not birds you ever get blasé about. They feed on birds, small mammals, reptiles, carrion: but it is not their hunting passes that make them vivid. Rather, it is their omnipresent aerial mastery, their casual self-certainty, their wobbling dominance of the Luangwa airways. They are more closely related to the snake eagles than the "true" eagles, with long, bare featherless legs, and a woolly, rather owly head. And no human can look at one without envy.

And that was why I decided that it was nothing to do with bungee jumping. Chris and I left Mchenja and travelled on to stay with our old friends, John and Carol Coppinger, who run a camp called Tafika, further to the north of the park. They also have some select and deeply wild bush camps. And John flies a microlight.

I was staying with him some years before when he first suggested I take a flight with him. It was a scary offer. There is not much to a microlight: a kite with a lawnmower engine, and that's about it. I thought long and hard about rejecting this offer: just a stunt, I thought austerely, just a cheap adrenalin hit. Just a bungee jump without the bungee. But a little more thought told me that this was not a stunt: this was probably the only chance I would ever get to be a bateleur.

This time, John invited me up for two flights, both extended half-hour explorations. John is one of those old Africa hands who does absolutely everything with a calm, easy competence: and when he goes flying, he is not trying to frighten you and show how macho he is. You ride pillion, strapped in but still hardly secure, with a helmet and visor and radio comms with the pilot. You bounce across the grass like a toy, and then a magic trick takes place.

When the river is high, it never looks like a river, not when you are sitting on it. Everywhere you go, you seem to be on a closed lake, one that you never quite come to the end of. But when you take off in the microlight, in a handful of seconds the lake before you turns into the crazy snake of the world's wildest river, and you are bateleuring your way above it. "Not bad, eh?" John's voice crackling in my ears: I must have whooped or cheered or uttered an obscenity. Like riding on a motorbike, there is no frame around what you see, no restriction. You can look through 360 degrees, but unlike a traveller on the ground, your view is not circular but spherical. You are travelling in three dimensions: you are seeing, you are beginning to think, like a bird.

No, not a stunt: this was viewing my beloved valley in a way only a Coppinger or a bateleur does. You need to acquire a new way of seeing: the country and its creatures all look different from above. Elephant, buffalo, the giant antelopes called eland. Eland never let you come any closer than 400 yards when you're on the ground; they have an exaggerated flight distance because of their lack of speed. They didn't mind us cruising by above them, though. All the animals took our passage in their stride: they merely raised an eyebrow at our noise and left it at that. After a brief glance, they carried on with the business of the evening, feeding, socialising, travelling, mooching about. We saw things that no one can ever see without wings: the huge wagon-wheel nest of saddle-billed storks at the very tip of the tallest tree, counting the ungainly sky-reaching chicks within: losing height to cruise easily over impassably treacherous bogs, where crowned cranes were nesting.

But never mind the details: what mattered was the expanse of it, the numbers of the creatures that lived here, the wild river with its lagoons and its old courses, its never-ending changes of mind, the closed canopy over some of the tributaries, the groups of hippos at the confluences, all the meaningful patterns written below in greens and browns and blues, soaring above the world's most beautiful place with the calm joyous insouciance of a bateleur. My heart in hiding stirred for a bird: and I was that bird, looking down for ever on a world that was free, unending, wild. The only man-made thing I could see as I looked down across the endless miles of the Valley was my own boot.

144

There was one last scene to be played out before we left, one of those agonisingly, deliciously, pro-longed farewells, like the clasping of hands through the window of a train, the train slowly, but still far, far too swiftly shuffling into life, gathering speed, the joined palms slipping, the grip now no more than sliding fingers, touching fingertips, hands, alone, waving...

We were to meet Levy back at Mchenja to make the boat journey downriver towards the airport and home: and we decided to do it by canoe rather than stinkboat. So we sat in a line of three, John at the back to direct operations and shoot crocs if they came on board, Chris in the middle, me in front, and we made our way down the shrinking river, not so much paddling as drifting with attitude, with our course directed by stern, decisive sweeps of the sternmost paddle. Me, I used my binoculars more than my paddle, even them not much.

The pratincoles, the sound of the greenshank, the hover and plummet of pied kingfishers, the daily increasing hippo population, the sinister leather logs of the crocs. Every now and then, the river had already drawn back its skirts enough to reveal the beginnings of the long sandy beaches that lie on either side of the the Luangwa in the driest time of all, before the rains come and bring life and hope back to the sun-roasted land. Time ceased to pass, on the whole, and one section of the river looked much like another, and you couldn't believe it would ever end, or that you would ever want it to.

It was my old friend Brian Jackman who wrote that: another man who loves Africa not wisely but too well. At Mchenja, an orange-breasted bush-shrike sang out in the ebony glade. And then a fish eagle called: that wild triple-note: a sound so exultant that to make it, the bird must fling its white head right back onto its chestnut shoulders: a sound impossible without total commitment. It is, as it were, the national anthem of the Luangwa Valley. The eagles that patrol the waterways announce their delight in themselves and in the place they live with this glorious triple scream. Mine, the song meant: and found an echo in me. But does the bird, does the visitor own this place: or does the wild land own us both?

Levy started the boat: the first of a series of engines that would take me back to Suffolk. The sadness of leaving Luangwa pricked me as it has always pricked me: the pleasure, no less keen, of returning to my few acres and loved ones awakened.

The spring singing would be in spate by now.

145

That little bit wilder. Nothing could be easier. All it requires is a little escalation, a little more eagerness to give in to your natural inclinations: and giving way to your natural inclinations is never a hardship. If you can do that, the process of saving both the planet and your soul can continue very nicely: which is something of a win-double, I think you'll agree. So here are some suggestions for a wilder life.

Walk. Break the tyranny of roofs. Get off a stop early,

take a turn round the park at lunch time, walk the school run. Learn to spot the ways in which the civilised world takes you away from the sky, and stops you from moving your own body underneath real weather. Then you can begin to counter-attack in small, gentle, sustainable chunks.

Sit. A five-minute sit looking at trees, looking at water, is a serious assault on the stresses and the upside-down values of 21st-century life.

Drink. The best way of enjoying the wild world is on your own: the second best is with people you like. Share the outside over a cup of tea, a bottle of champagne, a beer, a glass of Rose's lime cordial: they all work.

Learn. Discover how to recognise five more birds, or five butterflies, or five trees or five birdsongs. Doing so will increase your involvement with the wild world, will make you look more, will make you understand more, make you enjoy more.

Read. There are many wild books. Read poems, science, travels, any of the writers I have mentioned in these pages and more.

Make visits. Nice places are accessible: it is easy to find a nice bit of countryside for a walk and a sit.

Have treats. The weekend away, the day trip: such things need to be priorities in your life.

Make pilgrimages. There are many wonderful wild places in the country that are within your scope: that will come as glorious revelations of wildness: mood-changing, life-changing places.

Make longer pilgrimages: travel abroad to see the wild.

Join things. Join one more thing: if you are not a member of the RSPB, join; if you are, join your county wildlife trust (there is one for London, too), join WWF, join Plantlife, Buglife, Butterfly Conservation; there are addresses in the back of the book. And if you are the volunteering type, volunteer: all of these organisations will cherish you. If you don't care for volunteering, just volunteer your money.

Buy up the earth: give yourself and your friends chunks of rainforest for birthdays. The World Land Trust continues its bid for global conquest.

So there you are. There are many books that claim they will change your life: but this one will not only do that, but will save the planet as well. You really can't ask for better value than that.

146

Sometimes, it's almost too much to bear. The musical frenzies of the nightingale are too good, too strong, too passionate, too intense, too wild. One study counted 250 different phrases used by a single nightingale; all of them based on 600 different sound units. A spring, a year is incomplete without exposure to the too-muchness of nightingale: and I was there in the blackness before the dawn. The bittern provided the bassline, booming out memories of times gone by, times when all rivers, not just the Luangwa, were untamed, when the wild and the wet were found more often than they are now: wildness and wet, O let them be left.

And then the nightingale: the only bird with a genuine 24-hour shift, who must sing through the night and then sing through the day: it is his genes, it is his biology, it is heart, it is his art, it is his soul. Delete according to taste.

It was good to be at Minsmere in the pre-dawn: the weather itself certainly wild and wet. The Minsmere site manager, Adam Rowlands, was very decently showing me around: and there, at a place carefully selected, no nightingale, but the gorgeous redstart began to sing out against the

Mr Bassman of the reed-beds. The redstart's sweet, laconic song is soon over, almost muttered, almost thrown away: the bird itself is so handsome it hardly needs a song. This was dawn: the first light came and it was May, and so all the songbirds who were not nightingales flung themselves into song as soon they could see a wing in front of their faces. All except the nightingale, for the nightingale was singing already.

And always something new. Sedge warblers were birds I had mostly overlooked: now, with exceptional numbers of them that year, they were forced into a position from which brilliance was the only option. Competition had driven each bird to sing as it had never sung before: for only the best would keep a territory and hold a hen. And so each sedge warbler dredged into its deepest repertoire of whistles and warbles and imitations, throwing in blue tit churs, and nuthatch whistles and other, more enigmatic impersonations, the whole unstemmable song pouring out with compulsive speed. "Is that a sedge warbler imitating a water rail?" I asked. "Or is it a sedge warbler with a water rail calling behind it?" "Both," Adam said.

On, to a place where competition was bringing the best from opposed nightingales, and once again the air was filled with song: and as the antiphonal duet reached ever greater ecstasies, it was as though of hemlock we had drunk. The song affects humans as it affects nightingales: the nightingale, like a human singer, does all he can to make the song he is singing right now the best song ever sung. Or if not, the best he is capable of singing: and as I come to the end of this book, which may not be much but is at least the best song I am able to sing, I felt a sense of kinship with the singers of the dawn. We humans like to think that our fancy ideas of love and art and beauty put us in a different category from other living creatures: and yet, if you visit Minsmere at dawn, you will find within an hour a thousand arguments to the contrary. We have more in common with the wild things than we like to think: the barriers between humans and the species we share the planet with are not as solid and insurmountable as we choose to pretend.

147

It was a nice evening, so Joe and I went out to watch the swifts. This involves walking as far as the pub, where there is a seat perfectly placed for observing the screamers at their evening rituals. I had a pint, Joe, austerely, stuck to water. The swifts didn't disappoint, zooming over in noisy gangs; the sky was clear, the light very good, and you could see the wing-edges flare and fluoresce as they passed over: the black birds briefly exploding with light like a flashbulb before resuming their usual darkness.

Joe and I talked of many good things: Dr Who, Dad's Army, a clay model he is making of an alligator snapping turtle, his younger brother's latest hilarities, the possibility of going back to the badgers, and maybe – certainly – another jaunt to look for dolphins. The truth is that Joe was drawn to the vesperal swifts more by a willingness to humour me than a burning desire to see the swifts: I am not sure whether I should be especially pleased by this or slightly disappointed. But he is still a wild boy: it's just that on the whole, mammals touch him more than birds. He still has a great appetite for wild wonders.

I say "still" because Joe had just turned thirteen. For all that he rejected the very title of teenager, for all that the wild world is, right now, a very important part of his life, the fact is that people in their teens are less touched by nature than at any other time of their lives. Teenagers are tuned in to each other and their own unfathomable selves, caught up in the great adventure of who they are and who they will become. Some horrible place where teenagers can come together is lovelier than the most beautiful place in the world.

One of the reasons that the wild world plays so little part in fashionable life is because fashionable life is not based around maturity. It is based around the teenage ideal: or rather, around the silliest side of being a teenager. It misses out the introspection and the angst and the exploration of the universe, and concentrates on bad music, parties, changes of partner and urban socialising. Things like family and the wild are never groovy: as the fashionable world apes adolescence – get to the silliest time of your life as quickly as possible and stay there for as long as possible – so it cannot help but fall in with the adolescent's brief period of indifference to nature. The wild world is never trendy.

Joe may go through a period of comparative indifference to the wild world himself, though there is no sign of such a thing happening as yet. But if so, I must accept it, take it in my stride, understand that people will be who they are, not who you want them to be. (My mother wanted me to be an international lawyer, a comparatively rare example of fantasy in her life.) And even if Joe leaves the wild world for a time, he may well come back to it: after all, I did. The point, as always, is to savour the moment: the swifts were flying, Joe and I were watching them, the evening was good, the beer cold, and a sparrowhawk flew menacingly overhead.

We also talked a little about the book I was on the point of finishing, and how the badgers and the dolphins were an important part of it. I thought then that writing this book had been an altogether unexpected liberation. It had freed me from the onerous duties of optimism, and the crushing burden of pessimism. Edward Wilson, the great scientist and writer already mentioned in these pages, has managed to keep his own optimism intact despite a life-time of wrestling with life's most intractable problems. He concludes his dauntingly titled book *The Future of Life*: "I believe we will choose wisely. A civilisation able to envision God and to embark on the colonisation of space will surely find the way to save the integrity of this planet and the magnificent life it harbours."

Amen to that; sometimes I believe every word of this. At other times, I feel the opposite: that short-term thinking, over-population, greed and sheer bloody absent-mindedness will bring the wild world to destruction and with it, inevitably ourselves.

But the thing is that both optimism and pessimism are impossible to live with. Optimism is too hard to sustain, pessimism is so destructive to the pessimist. The answer lies in the third course: the course of wildness, the course that takes you beyond optimism, beyond pessimism. It involves an ever-deepening relationship with the wild world, and an ever-strengthening commitment to saving it, nurturing it and rewilding it: but without any need to feel that what you are doing is of any use. Let us go back to Reepicheep, the gallant martial mouse in the *Narnia* books, and his intervention, in *The Voyage of the Dawn Treader*, when he and his shipmates are confronted with the dark island. (I read all the *Narnia* books to Joe, and great joy we had with them.) And as the horror of the dark island becomes clear to everyone on board the ship, they all seek to turn tail, save, of course, Reepicheep, the only person of the company blessed with a tail:

> "But what manner of use would it be ploughing through the blackness?" asked Drinian.
>
> "Use?" asked Reepicheep. "Use, Captain? If by use you mean filling our bellies or our purses, I confess it will be no use at all. So far as I know, we did not set sail to look for things useful but to seek honour and

adventures. And here is as great an adventure as ever I heard of, and here, if we turn back, no little impeachment of all our honours."

The very question of use is irrelevant. We seek the adventure of becoming wilder, of seeking to save the wild world, not because it is of any use but because it is the right thing to do, because that way, we seek honour and adventures, because being on the right side matters more than mere victory. It matters more because living a wilder life is a better way to live: it has more meaning, it is better for our minds, our hearts, our souls.

Joe and I walked back home across the fields, my mind full of hopes and fears for Joe and for the world he will inherit. I hope his, and the world's choices will be wild ones: for his sake, for everybody's sake. The swifts screamed overhead: which means the globe's still working.

CONTACTS

Birdlife International
(an international
organisation for bird
conservation)
3-4 Wellbrook Court
Girton
Cambridge
CB3 0NA
01223 277318
www.birdlife.org.uk

Buglife – The Invertebrate
Conservation Trust
170a Park Road
Peterborough
PE1 2UF
01733 201210
www.buglife.org.uk

Butterfly Conservation
Manor Yard
East Lulworth
Wareham
Dorset
BH20 5QP
0870 774309
www.butterfly-
conservation.org

Plantlife
The Wild Plant Conservation
Charity
14 Rollestone Street
Salisbury
Wiltshire
SP1 1DX
01722 342730
www.plantlife.org

Royal Society
for the Protection of Birds
The Lodge
Sandy
Bedfordshire
SG19 2DL
01767 680551
www.rspb.org.uk

The Wildlife Trusts
(Umbrella organisation for
the county wildlife trusts)
The Kiln
Waterside
Mather Road
Newark
Nottinghamshire
NG24 1WT
www.wildlifetrusts.org

Wildlife Worldwide
(A commercial travel organisation
run by Chris Breen)
Long Barn South
Sutton Manor Farm
Bishops Sutton
Arlesford
SO24 0AA
0845 1306982
www.wildlifeworldwide.com

Worldwide Fund
for Nature
Panda House
Weyside Park
Godalming
Surrey
GU7 1XR
01483 426444
www.wwf-uk.org

Wildsounds
(a commercial organisation
that supplies recordings
of natural sounds; also
wildlife books)
Roses Pightle
Cross St
Salthouse
NR25 7XH
www.wildsounds.com

World Land Trust
Blyth House
Bridge Street
Halesworth
Suffolk
IP19 8AB
01986 874422
www.worldlandtrust.org

Praise for Simon Barnes's
How to Be a Bad Birdwatcher **and** *The Meaning of Sport*

"A witty, perceptive book, thoughtful, instructive and full of simple wisdom." *Daily Mail*

"A delightful ode to the wild world outside the kitchen window... A book which fills you with that warm feeling that a shared love conquers all." *Daily Telegraph*

"How to be a bad birdwatcher is a work of pure enthusiasm for the cause of birds and us. Unstuffily, democratically, this book tries to help us derive good from things near at hand, everywhere, and it succeeds." *Spectator*

"Ultimately, like all polemical texts, *How to Be a Bad Birdwatcher* seeks to convert the reader to a cause. It does so with considerable success, and reveals that Barnes is neither a 'good' nor a 'bad' birdwatcher – simply a fulfilled and very lucky man." Stephen Moss, *Evening Standard*

"An amiable mix of memoir, the merits of binoculars, Charles Darwin, laughing gulls and how watching birds compares with his day job of watching England footballers." *Observer*

The Meaning of Sport by Simon Barnes is a celebration of sport and life by one of the finest sportswriters of his generation – wise, perceptive and unfailingly joyful, this is Barnes at the peak of his form." Patrick Collins, *Mail on Sunday*

"Free-flowing in its structure, thought-provoking in its content, wonderfully humorous and readable in its style, this is a sports book like no other." Leo McKinstry, *Sunday Telegraph*

In case of difficulty in purchasing any Short Books
title through normal channels, please contact
BOOKPOST Tel: 01624 836000
Fax: 01624 837033
email: bookshop@enterprise.net
www.bookpost.co.uk
Please quote ref. 'Short Books'